"*Mind Your Business* is an essential book for anyone who is facing challenges in setting up and managing a business. Knipping puts traditional management tools in a new perspective. He offers insight on how to write business plans and corporate mission, vision and value statements. *Mind Your Business* focuses on motivation, teamwork, marketing, risks and failures, transparency, corporate governance, strategies, happiness, religion and many more interesting topics in the business field. It is highly instructive and should be read by anyone in business."

Henri Th.M. Burgers, Curaçao
Attorney and author of legal essays and books

"Toine Knipping is one of those strange people who amaze you with what he has done and makes you believe at the same time that *you* can do it! A brilliant entrepreneur who makes the risks we all fear sound fun and enriching. No lecturing or arrogance in this most accessible book; just plain sound advice delivered with Toine's unique humour and style."

Kevin Grace
Board of TESCO PLC

"Without meeting Toine at the kibbutz in Israel in 1978, I would never have been a journalist. He guided me to Gaza. I had never heard of Gaza and I had no knowledge of the Palestininan-Israeli issue. I was so shocked the people and the situation in Gaza. It was the turning point of my life. After I went back to Japan, I decided to be a journalist and cover this issue. Toine is my benefactor."

Toshikuni Doi
Well known Japanese maker of film documentaries and political activist

When you meet Toine, he looks like a normal business man, but he isn't; he speaks like an entrepreneur, but he's more. Where many no-nonsense managers have a tendency to disregard spiritual values and principles, Toine shows with great clarity in his life and in this book how leaders should love what they create, live their dreams and leave behind a better planet for people to live in. Besides being a great leader, in *Mind Your Business* Toine turns out to be a writer of great sensibility and wisdom. How I wish there would be more leaders like him!"

Daniel Ofman
Founder of Core Quality Ltd. and inventor of the 'Core Quadrant'

"What I love about Toine's book is that it is not a theoretical concept. It rather is the journey of a self-made man, sharing his personal life and business experiences, combining it with the ideas of some great thinkers of this planet. This book makes absolutely clear what business is—or what it should be about while living a wonderful life."

Reinder Schonewille
International business consultant

"I read *Mind Your Business* book twice not because I didn't understand it, but because it was that good! I love anything that brings us to our basic nature, and that is exactly what Toine shows us in this book."

Jorge Carneiro
Portuguese entrepreneur and managing director of Sage Inc. in Portugal and Brazil

MIND YOUR
BUSINESS

Thoughts for Entrepreneurs

BALBOA.
PRESS
A DIVISION OF HAY HOUSE

Toine Knipping

ISBN: 978-1-4525-5494-5 (sc)
ISBN: 978-1-4525-5495-2 (e)
ISBN: 978-1-4525-5496-9 (hc)

Library of Congress Control Number: 2012911852

Balboa Press books may be ordered through booksellers or by contacting:

Balboa Press
A Division of Hay House
1663 Liberty Drive
Bloomington, IN 47403
www.balboapress.com
1-(877) 407-4847

Cover Image Provided by: Florence Knipping

Printed in the United States of America

Balboa Press rev. date: 10/01/12

For Kevin Grace, one of my co-students at INSEAD, as
he challenged me to actually finally write this book.

For Frank Aldrich, the greatest networker I ever met, as he taught
me most of the basic principles of doing and living business.

For my wife, Paula, as she not always agrees
with me but always supports me.

And for my children, Quinten and Florence, as I hope they
will read it and maybe even think about some of its ideas.

Contents

"It is not the critic who counts; not the man who points out how the strong man stumbles, or where the doer of deeds could have done them better. The credit belongs to the man who is actually in the arena, whose face is marred by dust and sweat and blood. Who strives valiantly; who errs and comes short again and again, because there is not effort without error and shortcomings; but who does actually strive to do the deed; who knows the great enthusiasm, the great devotion, who spends himself in a worthy cause, who at the best in the end knows the great triumph of high achievement and who at the worst, if he fails, at least he fails while daring greatly, so that his place will never be with those cold and timid souls who know neither victory nor defeat."

—Theodore Roosevelt

Disclaimer

My life is my story, as your life is yours. This book is designed to share with you my ideas about how to mind your business and how our minds can build meaningful businesses and help to give some meaning to our lives in the process. It is sold with the understanding that the author is not engaged in rendering legal, tax, accounting, management, psychological, spiritual, or other professional advice. If legal or other expert assistance is required, the services of a competent professional should be sought.

It is not the purpose of this book to reprint information that is otherwise available to the readers, but to complement other texts and thoughts. For more information, see the "Reference" section. It is available also in electronic form, so as to have minimal contribution to the depletion of scarce resources (printing a book requires the use of trees, ink, and thousands of liters of water). You may also wish to share your copy with others who may benefit from it. The net proceeds of the sale of this book will go to a project to help young entrepreneurs in India get off the ground.

This is not just another how-to book. There are enough of those. This is also not intended to be an autobiography, although by definition every book has autobiographical aspects.

I would like to make you, the reader, think about business in a more holistic fashion. It is not separate from life. The person that goes to work as a professional is the same person who makes love in the morning and goes jogging in the evening, and hopefully that person does all three with equal passion. I would like to illustrate that our minds are on earth to do much bigger things than just making money, or selling cookies, and that we all have a chance to improve our lives and the world.

I wish to challenge the readers to stretch their minds, to take new risks, to free themselves from the conventions that have been creeping up in their minds over the years, and to think fresh and do something new. This shouldn't be based on "how great I am" or the fact that I have all the answers, because I don't. I just hope to help you see how great *everyone* potentially is and that we all can make much more out of our lives than we ever imagined. Not one of us, luckily, has reached his full potential yet.

Following the advice in this book will demonstrate to you that literally everyone can be successful as an entrepreneur, but it will not necessarily make you rich overnight, nor will it solve your life questions. Anyone who wants to be successful in life can be so; there is really no magic to it, but you must expect to invest a lot of thought, passion, love, energy, time, and effort without a guarantee of quick economic successes. Being successful in business will not make you happy. It is the other way around; you will need to be happy with yourself first in order to become successful in business. Businesses do not flourish by themselves. It is people —like you and me—who build them, give them life, and make them prosper.

Every effort has been made to make the information in this book as complete and as accurate as possible. However, there will be mistakes, both typographical and in content. Therefore, this book should only be seen as a general guide and not as the ultimate source of achieving your life goals.

The purpose of this book is to educate and entertain. The author and the publisher shall have neither liability nor responsibility to any person or entity with respect to any loss or damage caused or alleged to be caused directly or indirectly by the information contained in this book.

If you do not wish to be bound by the above, you may return this book to the author for a full refund.

I grew up on a small mixed-fruit and cattle farm in the Netherlands. Both my father and my mother came from large families, and I had lots of uncles, aunts, and cousins. On Sundays, after church, some or a lot of them would gather at our farm to enjoy themselves and play cards. After having done that for so many years, their patterns of interaction had become kind of ritualized, and the same types of jokes were repeated week after week. Most of my uncles living in the same area were struggling farmers or had other small businesses. They were constantly facing the varied challenges any small business faces, but they were extremely proud of what they were doing and would not have wanted to change their lives for anything.

Just one uncle was not an "entrepreneur" (although that word did not yet exist at the time) but rather was the headmaster of a school (and probably had the most stable income of all of them), and at any of the family meetings he was the butt of jokes. It became pretty clear to me that if I wanted to earn the respect of my parents and other family members, I would need to become an entrepreneur and not a salary man.

My chance came when I wanted to join a weeklong scouting camp, but my parents decided it was too expensive. I started to grow parsley and other herbs and sold them door to door in our village until I raised enough money to go and pay my own way. Since that time I have never again been without a job or a business, as I learned that taking the initiative leads to many things. Of course you earn money that you can use to buy whatever you want, but, more importantly, every endeavor leads to new opportunities. Every business leads to new chances that, if you take them, will take you from one level to the next until you reach the sky.

As a student I learned that instead of doing everything myself, outsourcing was a way to leverage my time and efforts. I began renting out two very old vans to students who needed them for road trips, holidays, or to move apartments. After setting up the system, I let someone else run the business for a fee while I moved on to something new.

For me that something new was traveling around the world. I was lucky enough to travel for almost a year overland from Europe to Indonesia, spending months in Iran, Pakistan, India, Nepal, Myanmar, Thailand, and Indonesia. I also spent a considerable amount of time traveling throughout the Middle East, working in a *kibbutz* in Israel, and visiting Egypt at the time of the murder of President Sadat. Additionally, I made another memorable one-year overland trip from New York to Tierra del Fuego and back up to Brazil, visiting almost all the countries in the Americas.

At the kibbutz in 1978, I shared rooms with a Japanese student, Toshikuni Doi, a driven and disciplined person who aspired to become a journalist and had already spent a year in Israel without ever visiting the occupied territories. I took him on a tour of the West Bank and the Gaza Strip, where we visited several refugee camps and came to learn about the other side of Israel's economic and diplomatic success. Toshikuni, like me, was shocked by what he saw in the refugee camps, and for quite a number of years he returned to Israel to report for Japanese newspapers on the situation in the occupied territories. For a while we kept in contact, but after a few years the letters petered out. He first inspired me to look into Eastern philosophies, which laid the basis for my later love of Asia. My Japanese friend went on to become a famous author and filmmaker in Japan, so when thirty years later my family and I planned a holiday to Japan, his name resurfaced. It took less than five seconds to find him on Google. It turned out that the day I contacted him he was giving a television interview in connection with his latest movie on war atrocities in Fallujah, Iraq. The presenter asked him what had inspired him to choose the path he had followed and make political documentaries. His answer was that thirty years before he had made those trips with me in Israel. What a tremendous coincidence! And it was great fun to meet up again. We reminisced about old conversations we had in our younger, more idealistic days. We talked of how you were an accomplice of exploitation and suppression if you did not speak out against the malice in the world. He had chosen to expose mischief through the journalistic approach, while I had chosen to create employment, thus fighting poverty as the basis of all misery in emerging markets.

I finished my law studies with a thesis on breaking up financially unsound companies into parts that were still healthy and parts that were too inefficient or low quality to save—a subject that has come back time and again during my professional career and that has remained timely in every downturn of the market.

When I landed my first real job as a lawyer working in a bank, I soon became anxious about using only a small part of my talents in a job description that basically asked me to leave my brain at home and just do what I was told. In essence I was to sell selected investment and insurance products of the bank to innocent investors. This is also known as "private banking." Luckily, after a while, I was transferred into the high-potential class and, thereafter, became an instructor in the bank's credit and risk training department. That brought me back to New York. I remember one evening, after quite a few drinks, I was standing in Times Square with a couple of colleagues, and we looked at the ticker tapes and agreed that our measure for success would be to one day see our own company's name reflected there in bright neon.

The section of the bank where I worked changed hands, and I found myself one day back in the Netherlands in the "criticized loans" department. "Criticized loans" is bank-speak for loans that are at risk of not being repaid. The department is supposed to either help the corporate clients restructure so they can repay or initiate liquidation of their companies so the bank can recover as much as possible from the sale of the assets of those companies.

One of my clients was an elderly gentleman who had an outdated little factory. He was steadily losing money, as the business had not made timely adjustments to newer technologies and could no longer compete with bigger, newer producers and importers. One day I was supposed to meet the client to tell him that we were finally terminating our credit facility and that, as a result, his company would go bankrupt. The gentleman had always been punctual to our meetings, and it was a surprise to me when he did not show up. We contacted his secretary, who confirmed that the man had left the office in time for our meeting. It turned out the man had a car accident on his way to the bank's office and drowned in one of the thousands of Dutch canals. A few months later his life insurance policy provided enough money to cover the amounts outstanding to the bank, and my boss complimented me on another file that had been successfully solved.

That is when I decided to switch careers, and I ended up in a trust company in the Caribbean. I worked there for almost four years and thereafter, together with a colleague, started a "real" business; we called it Amicorp. *Ami* is Papiamentu for 'my' and sounds Spanish enough to create the connotation of being an *amigo*. "Friends you can trust" was our first pay-line.

The trust business proved to be a great business, as it built on the two main certainties in life: death and taxes. People need to plan for both, and successful, wealthy people more than others. When the economy is good, people make investment plans and need to structure new businesses; when the economy is not that great, taxes go up, and people need to be cost-conscious and plan carefully.

Taxes are a necessity, as they are the price we pay for civilization. Most tax systems are inefficient and wasteful, driving business and investments to places that provide the best possible services for the tax money paid.

Death is equally a necessity, as without death there is no renewal. Old ideas and power structures need to make space for new ones on a regular basis, so that mind-sets, society, and the economy can continue to grow. The paralysis we currently see at both the economic and political level in Western Europe, Japan, and the United States is the result of old power structures not dying quickly enough. Many of the current political and economic structures of Western society, mostly put together at the end of the Second World War with major modifications in the sixties, have clearly reached their "sell by" date. Additional shocks to our economic and financial systems will be needed in order to create the political and moral platform for rethinking the often unwarranted levels of consumption by individuals and governments, as well as the daunting levels of debt created by people and governments. There will have to be consensual and serious restructurings of the pension systems, the social benefits systems, and the roles, responsibilities, and benefits of financial institutions. Since many people will have to give up some of their entitlements and perks, this will not happen without a struggle and significant suffering.

New people are needed to clear out what was created by the previous generation. A pan-Eurozone tax system as per the German model will only emerge once the Europeans who remember the 1940s version of it have died. Steve Jobs worded it in his famous 2005 Harvard commencement address (which you can find on YouTube) as follows, "Death is very likely the single best invention of Life. It is Life's change agent. It clears out the old to make way for the new. Right now the new is you, but someday not too long from now, you will gradually become the old and be cleared away." When the baby boomer generation dies off, we will see a major shift in the direction of investments, just as the rise of the emerging markets has led to a huge shift in economic and cultural focus.

Working on transfers of wealth from one generation to the next as well as directing significant international investments is fun. There is a direct result of your work when good plans become productive investments.

Out of the woodwork, friends showed up to make the first introductions, to lend money, to give advice, to send clients, etc. And after a few years a stable and healthy business emerged. The first ten clients were not the ones I would have expected as our first clients, but most of them (or their children) are still with us.

One of our earliest and best supporters was Frank Aldrich. A retired banker who started his working life as a bomber pilot in World War II, Frank became a private banker in Cuba under Batista, serving clients such as Ernest Hemingway. He went on to become a corporate banker in Brazil, well known to the rich and powerful of Latin America. He co-owned a bank in Curaçao and another one in Haiti, and he always taught me to "be nice to people on your way up, as you will meet them again on your way down." At eighty-five he was still hand-writing over a thousand Christmas cards a year, each with a personalized message. His personal files include thousands of people he has met over the span of his life, dating back six decades. He is clearly the ultimate networker, and he introduced us to many of our early clients, most of whom are still our clients today. I learned that one should never make enemies, as everyone you meet remains connected to you, and somehow, somewhere, you will run into them again. Small favors you do for people today will pay back many-fold in the future. The more you give, the more you will receive in return.

Then there was Hans Crooij. Hans was an insurance salesperson who retired to the Caribbean and became kind of a guru to the employees in our company. Not understanding our business but having plenty of entrepreneurial experience, his insights and common-sense approach always either made people laugh or think. His unwavering support provided courage to some of our more ambitious projects.

And we will not forget the asset manager who one day walked off a cruise ship and into our offices. We set up a few hedge funds for him, and within a few years the funds became very successful, and he became seriously rich, inviting us to a ski holiday in Colorado. One day we wanted to make a rather large investment, and it was this guy who loaned us the money from his "petty cash." A while later, during the dot.com boom, his business tanked, and he needed the money back on very short notice, creating major cash constraints for our company and, needless to say, no more ski holidays.

There were, of course, lots of bigger and smaller regrets and setbacks, but in spite of them we managed to embark on an international expansion plan. The holiday trips I had made as a student to Latin America, the Far East, and India became the blueprint for our corporate expansion. Our company became almost by default an emerging-markets expert, structuring international direct investments. Having lived among Indians for half a year made it many times easier to step over the cultural divide and celebrate the differences rather than get frustrated by them. Having had parties in Rio and São Paulo made it less of a problem to establish an office there and start searching for clients. The "old stories" helped in breaking the ice and set us apart from the fly-in, fly-out competitors who neither spoke the language, nor appreciated the food on the street or enjoyed the local customs. Having been in Colombia, Russia, Pakistan, and Myanmar made those places a lot less scary than the news would make one want to believe.

A few years ago, I decided to participate in a management course at INSEAD, one of the better decisions I made in my life. The Challenge of Leadership (COL) course, as it was called, presented by Manfred Kets de Vries and Sudhir Kakar, provided me with some great reflections on myself, a few good ideas for business, and a number of wonderful new friends. Manfred Kets de Vries later explained the content of this course as follows, "Sudhir and I continue our 'struggle' to create a better world by facilitating COL. Your observations of 'a terrible childhood,' nasty 'suits' to fight, a depressed marriage, hidden dreams, crouching bosses, failed promotions and a messed up sexual life, very much sum up the human condition—how to deal with 'tragic human.'" Toward the end of the course I was sitting together with some of the participants, reflecting on how great an experience it had been. We were looking for a way to continue that feeling and maintain our contact by creating a joint project. After a long and noisy evening we came up with the most obvious of projects and a common fantasy among us wine lovers.

Would it not be great to own a winery? Having so much talent in our class, we thought we should be able to make a great wine as well. It's always tempting to look at someone else's business and conclude that you know more and better than they do. With that acknowledged, we agreed on the starting points of what we wanted to do with our winery.

First of all, we wanted to make a good and honest wine. Make the label say exactly how it is made, and explain in detail what parts of the processes and the wine are organic and what parts are not.

Secondly, create an image that would make our wine stand out from others in the crowd. The name we picked, *Alpasion*, could easily be conceptualized into a range of our fingerprints and signatures onto a bottle. In Spanish *Alpasion* is a combination of *alma* (soul) and *pasion* (suffering, or passion), and in English "alive" and "passion." The sales pitch would focus on pure nature, organic products, friendship in production, enjoyment of the wine, and honesty in product and price.

None of us knew anything about wine (other than picking nice bottles from a restaurant's wine list), so we decided to bring in the best young and innovative experts we could find. We hired a great wine maker, Karim Mussi, and a great agronomist, Guillermo Cacciaguerra, and visited many wineries, including all of our neighbor great winemakers in the valley (not an unpleasant task) and took advice wherever we could find it.

We decided to apply as many best agricultural and production practices as possible that would lay the foundation for a great wine. We sought the best location, focused on densely planted vines, pruned for low yield, carefully irrigated so that the exactly right quantity of nutrients and water would reach each vine individually, and prudently harvested all by hand. Constant self-improvement would do the rest. As Helen Keller said, "No pessimist ever discovered the secrets of the stars, or sailed to an uncharted land, or opened a new heaven to the human spirit." Once the vineyard becomes more mature we will also apply the methods of Masaru Emoto, to harmonize the crystals of wine with specific types of music. We were convinced the project would become a success because we had *decided* it to become a success. And to a large extent it already is a success, as we experience so much satisfaction and fun doing it.

At this current stage in my life, I look back with a smile and can see that *all* the events in my life, the big ones and the small ones, the good ones and the bad ones, the carefully planned ones and the random ones, have brought me to exactly where I am now. They have created a perfect set of circumstances for me, for my family, and for my business. Had even a minor item been different, a single event gone differently, I would have ended up in a totally different place, and that totally different place would have been as good and as perfect as the place I have currently ended up. But it took the whole universe to align to bring me exactly where I am today.

I am now writing down some of my experiences and little bits of advice, as I believe they can help others, maybe even you, in bridging the gap between thoughts about business and how to be an entrepreneur with thoughts about how to give meaning to your life and be satisfied, but not content, with your life. Everyone who wants to become a successful entrepreneur can. And being a successful entrepreneur is a nice building block onto which you can construct a meaningful life.

"When I was a boy of 14, my father was so ignorant I could hardly stand to have the old man around. But when I got to be 21, I was astonished at how much the old man had learned in seven years."

—Mark Twain

Acknowledgments

According to Nassim Nicholas Taled, the Lebanese author of *The Black Swan,* "Business books are invented, as a category, by bookstores for writings that have no depth, no style, no empirical rigor, and no linguistic sophistication." With that in mind I have tried to straddle more categories than just the "business" one and put my personal approach to being an entrepreneur in a slightly more holistic light.

There are a lot of people I want to thank for helping me organize and produce these ninety thousand words. The basic ideas had been floating around somewhere in my mind already for years, but it was my colleagues at INSEAD who helped me combine those ideas in a more coherent way, reshuffle my priorities in life, and understand the importance of taking action now.

Special thanks in that respect go to Bill Fisher, Jorge Carneiro, Kevin Grace, Are Kjensli, Jesper Nellemann, Henk de Jong, and Kathy Byrne. Luckily we also share a great wine project that we will enjoy for years to come.

Manfred Kets de Vries and Sudhir Kakar sat down with me, in the same hotel in Barbizon where the wine project started, and tried to impress upon me how difficult and time-consuming the process would be, and how few original books are being written, so as to test and strengthen my resolve. Katha Kakar and Sheila Loxham explained the steps and discipline it would take to complete this project.

Doing the research, and discussing bits and pieces of it with different people, connected or reconnected me to many great books on a variety of subjects (some of them in the 'reference' list). It made me think through my own paradigms and shift a few of them.

Jeannette Keizer critically read through each and every chapter of the book and came up with many valuable comments and questions that helped me formulate certain thoughts more clearly.

My friends and colleagues Mik Breek, Eric Boes, Henry Burgers, Mimi Chong, Yogesh Kumar, Binu Jose, Ganesh Babu Subramanian, Claudio Lema Pose, Maria Gabriela Soto, and Mignon Wortelboer all read bits and pieces and each added value from his or her perspective and area of expertise. Mimi is the person who planted many of the thoughts in my mind in the first place.

Kate Ribeiro did most of the editing and organized the publishing. Once the writing process became more serious, she was the one who kept me on track.

Jon Sheeser corrected a lot of the Dunglish in my writing, almost a lifelong task.

My daughter Florence designed the cover of the book and took my featured picture.

My wife, Paula, has been very patient. She let me do my thing all these months while I was working on getting this book on paper. One could not wish for a more understanding partner.

Chapter 1

What Makes Your Heart Sing?

The recipe for living life to the fullest—if such a recipe exists—is to laugh heartily and often, play with abandon, appreciate beautiful things, build and maintain deep friendships, take pleasure in family, and enjoy the task at hand. It is the journey of life that counts, not the destination. How we cope with the obstacles that we inevitably encounter on that journey determines the richness of our life. By extensive self-exploration we can all learn the lesson that most of our obstacles are self-made. If we want to, we can remove or restructure them. We can learn from experience.

—Manfred Kets de Vries

I purposefully decided to begin this business book with a chapter on the purpose of life. This may not seem to be the most logical starting point, but I believe that before establishing or taking over a business, it is very important to be conscious of what we are doing, why we do what we do, and why we want to be responsible for an enterprise and the many people who depend on it for their livelihoods. Once a business is born, it is like your baby. You have to take care of it, and you cannot help but love it. And whether you are a capable parent or not, you are responsible for it until it matures, leaves the house, or dies. I have stood at the cradle of a few businesses, and I assure you there are many parallels between setting up and running a business and bringing up your kids. And whether they become instant successes or limp along, I love them equally. Once you decide to become an entrepreneur, I am convinced the same will happen to you.

1

So you will have to contemplate what "makes you tick," what drives you to do the things that you do. Those may be totally different things from what you learned in school or at university, heard at the dinner table from your parents, shared with your friends on social occasions, or see as part of normal conventions. You will need to go deep inside yourself to discover what really drives you, what really makes your heart sing, and what really produces happiness and fulfillment for *you*. One of my favorite German writers, Rainer Maria Rilke, crystallized it as follows: "There is only one journey. Going inside yourself." If you think or meditate long and hard enough, you will discover that at the subconscious level there are a number of beliefs, ideas, and values that drive your life, maybe unbeknown to you, in a certain direction. It is what Sudhir Kakar, who is sometimes described as the psychoanalyst of the world, calls "the elephant" inside you. It is who and what you are, what your purpose for being on earth is, what your *dharma* is. You can nudge the elephant somewhat in one direction or another, you can reason with it, or you can ignore it, but it always remains an elephant and always does what that elephant is supposed to do.

Do not confuse this with determinism. The idea that your thoughts, character, or behavior cannot be changed, as they are prewired by your genetics or the way your early childhood evolved, has been studied in detail and proven to be false. In fact, the latest studies confirm that although, yes, all that information is in your DNA, and, yes, all the early childhood memories remain in your amygdala and reptile brain, they are only part of who you are. Less than 10 percent of how your life and health develop can be attributed to genetics and environment, according to stem-cell biologist Bruce Lipton in *The Biology of Belief.* You need not develop a heart condition just because your father had one. You need not be a bad businessperson just because your mother was one. You need not remain poor and ill-educated just because you grew up in a neighborhood of poor and ill-educated people. It is amazing the number of people who let their lives be influenced and limited in creativity and opportunity by thoughts about determinism. There are, however, millions of stories of people who did not develop the way their parents did or who did not remain ensconced in the mentality of the environment in which they grew up. Actually, I think believing in determinism is a poor excuse for not taking charge of your own life or taking responsibility for your own choices.

It has also been proven that all people have more or less the same amount of brain matter, and although some people are more naturally attracted to subjects like mathematics and science, and Asians usually are better at mathematics than Europeans (as masterly described by Malcolm Gladwell in his book *Outliers*), all people have the capacity to learn math if they really *want* to learn it. Some people have a higher IQ than others, so not all of us will learn to think like Einstein (whose brain has been investigated in detail), but all of us can think and have the ability to learn and master what we really put our mind—and our time—to. When scrutinized, most success stories at first reveal ordinary results by ordinary people. Then, on further study, they demonstrate persistent dedication by strong-minded individuals or teams. The underdogs become better and better to slowly but determinedly rise above the ordinary.

I think this is important to reflect on. To a large extent, we are completely free to develop our lives in the directions we choose—the directions that make our heart sing. If you feel a deep passion inside to become an artist or a baker, by all means you need to pursue that dream and become a really good artist or a really great baker. Ignore your father's advice about going to university and studying law as he did, for this will neither make you happy nor make you a good lawyer. It is a bit like if you were born gay; you can try whatever you want, but sooner or later it is best to come out of the closet and be who you are.

Coming from a family of farmers, entrepreneurialism was in my blood. From the moment I left university, I was basically just looking for the right idea, time, and moment to take the first step. Only later did I realize the many forms of satisfaction being an entrepreneur provided. Now I can hardly imagine living my life in another way.

Stephen Covey identified some of life's great motivating factors as to live, to learn, to love, and to leave a legacy. This is what they mean to me in my life.

- *To live* means that any business we are in should at least provide us with an income: a means of living and sustaining ourselves and our families. It should also give us job satisfaction, pleasure in what we are trying to do, and a sense of accomplishment. It should provide us with goals, dreams, and vision so as to give direction to our lives.

- *To learn* means that the business we are in should give us an intellectual challenge. It should keep us challenged and engaged and provide a sense of purpose. Whether it is cooking great meals, building beautiful furniture, devising great tax-planning solutions, or taking good care of customers, there should always be a challenge, a possibility of improvement, a perfection of a skill, and a growth in knowledge and experience. If we get the feeling we are reliving the previous day—day after day—it is time to change what we are doing. I have been in the trust business for almost twenty-five years, and I still thoroughly enjoy doing what I am doing. But I have organized my business and my life in a way that fits my dreams, ideas, feelings, and desires.

- *To love* means that we need to love whatever we are doing and share it with the people around us. As social beings, we enjoy, develop, and fulfill ourselves mostly through interaction with others; we all need close relationships, partners, friends, and colleagues. Sharing our accomplishments and acquisitions provides a great source of satisfaction. I consider many of the people I work with every day my personal friends. Our relationship goes beyond the work relationship. We share more worries and more happiness than we have to, but it enriches all of our lives.

- *To leave a legacy* refers to the need people have of doing something meaningful. To create something that will live or extend beyond ourselves adds value to society at large. For many, if not most people, the beneficiaries of their legacy are their children; for others it is contributing something new to society: an invention, a service, a thought, and so on. I would like to leave the business I was involved in building behind in such a way that it is enjoyed by our clients and employees and is an example to others in the same industry.

Depending on your character, you may find yourself gravitating toward one over another, but all four driving forces play a major role in our lives, and if one is off balance, you will feel it as emptiness in your life. When selecting the business that fits you best, you need to think through those motivators. If, for instance, leaving behind a legacy is really important to you, you might be better off writing cookbooks than starting a restaurant. If your need for love, companionship, and satisfying interaction is great, you might not want to seek a solitary activity that shuts you off from people, like scientific research or writing a book. If, however, you choose a business that requires many hours (as do most entrepreneurial businesses), you need to make sure the social aspects, intellectual challenges, and possibilities for growth are all present in sufficient quantities within your business. If you have to satisfy those basic needs outside your work, you will overburden yourself and create a very stressful life for you, your family, and your friends.

Manfred Kets de Vries, a famous Dutch psychoanalyst and deemed one of the fifty greatest thinkers of this age, describes the central driving forces in life as sex, money/power, happiness, and death.

- *Sexual desire* is the key driving force of humankind. Obviously we exist in order to continue our kind. The desire for sex determines to a large extent what we do, to whom we are attracted, how we attach ourselves, why we strive for distant goals, and why we can move mountains if we are sufficiently motivated.

- *Money and power,* as they are being earned, create the possibility to acquire material wealth, impress the people around us, and build independence, control, self-esteem, and even love.

- *Happiness,* the state of subjective well-being, is what we pursue most of our lives. We must remember to enjoy the journey while rushing toward our goals. And appreciate that we are in paradise already.

- *Death* is what gives finality to our live; it creates a sense of urgency as well as futility.

In Buddhism, life is all about making others happy in order to be happy ourselves. Buddhists are less goal-oriented than many others; they accept that things are what they are. Our role in life is embodied in what we are, just like leaves on the tree of life. We bud, we grow, we whither and decompose, and life continues. Our children take our place, the tree continues to live, and its leaves get recycled.

In Zen, life itself is the only thing worth living for. As a famous Zen *kōan* goes: before enlightenment you fetch water and chop wood, and after enlightenment you fetch water and chop wood. Nothing changes other than the intensity of your awareness and your consciousness of the present moment. The purpose of life will reveal itself as you go along: *move and the road will open.*

Hindus get to a similar state by practicing *Vipassana* or, in full, *Anapanavipassana: full awareness of breathing* by observing the Witness within you. The very act of evaluating each moment of your life will disconnect it from the past and the future, breaking the continuum, and making you aware of what is real and what is not.

In the Hindu philosophy, the four aims (*artha*) of a man's life (*purusha*) are called the four *Purushartas.* And life is not complete until all four have been achieved. If any one of the four is ignored, accomplishment is not possible, and life is not complete or satisfying. The results of your actions, whatever you did (*karma*), in the past and in previous lives define what you are confronted with today. Just as your actions today build up *karma*, you will be confronted with it later on in this life as well as in future lives. Moving your actions in the right direction and building good karma will gradually improve your life.

The four aims are as follow:

- *Dharma* is duty, virtue, and man's drive to be perfect in what he is. It is *being the "elephant" that is inside you*, and developing whatever you are capable of being. It is about self-realization on the moral level, which includes courage, honesty, reliability, tolerance, and charity.

- *Artha* is wealth, success, means, family, and the acquisition of material goods. This is self-realization on the social and active level.

- *Kama* is pleasure, sexuality, and enjoyment in all forms. This is self-realization at the sensual and bodily level. Read the Kama Sutra to get some three-thousand-year-old inspiration in this area.

- *Moksha* is the final and complete liberation from the material and emotional side of existence. This is self-realization at the spiritual level.

There are clear overlaps between Western and Eastern purpose in life. There are also clear differences. Asians are less self-centered and more community-centered and have less of a need to leave a legacy. After all, they believe that many will be back in a next life to work on other aspects of their souls on their way to enlightenment. That is great, but it will not work for everyone. I try not to take any chances, and so I try to accomplish what I can in this life. But I always try to figure out, when I meet someone, what cultural background that person comes from, as it influences so much of how he will think, feel, and react. When you want to do business, you will not get far without getting into the skin of the people you deal with.

I think it is important that you know yourself well and understand what drives you. If you want a comfortable life and do not want to spend too much effort on achieving financial security, entrepreneurship may not be your calling. You may not want to do "whatever it takes" to be successful. If you are a nervous person who readily panics or worries about the future, you may be lured more by the false security of working in a multinational corporation or a government department where others make the big decisions, and the continuity of your existence seems forever assured. If you are really shy or prefer to work by yourself, you also should not become an entrepreneur. As an entrepreneur you will need to be a social person. You cannot achieve much without communicating constantly with others around you. There is no such thing as a part-time entrepreneur.

When we started our Amicorp business, we were three partners: two in Curaçao and a third in Aruba. We discussed that what we wanted was to provide perfect service to a limited group of clients, in the countries nearby, with whom we could build close relationships and have time left over to enjoy life outside of work. As the years passed, two of us got caught up in the fun and satisfaction of building something larger than ourselves. We hired bright young colleagues with good ideas and more knowledge and drive than we were used to. We grew our revenues, increased the spectrum of our service offerings, conquered new markets, and reached bigger and more interesting clients and intermediaries. Our third partner stuck to the original concept, and so after a couple of years we went our separate ways. He continued with his office in Aruba as it was until he died, with limited business ambition and plenty of time for entertainment and enjoyment. That was his choice and the fulfillment of his goals in life.

We, the remaining partners, changed our priorities and goals several times over the course of the years and also whenever more partners or shareholders were added to the company. We spent many fun evenings deciding which new location we would add to our network. Is it more challenging to set up business in Moscow or in Beijing? Can we find more clients in São Paulo or in Jakarta or Mumbai? Can we use the solutions for the Mexican market in the Venezuelan or Peruvian markets? How will we deal with changing legislation in country A, and can we find the right people in country B? As we grow older and the more basic needs have been covered, goals pop up that are less focused on survival and more focused on development (product development, education, and social and environmental awareness), thus leaving a legacy and creating a structure that will survive and flourish long after we are no longer involved. We created a child-care center to celebrate the fifteenth anniversary of our Curaçao office and developed a number of fun, recurring fund-raising activities to help finance it. We created activities to support an orphanage in Bangalore. And we really enjoy stimulating our employees to spend time on socially responsible activities.

Then there is also the struggle to relinquish control over specific aspects of the business, whole departments, and, ultimately the entire company. This is not an easy process. I tend to compare this process to a man walking his daughter down the aisle when she is getting married. As her father, you know that you need to let go and that she will be happy with the path she has chosen, but it hurts to lose control, and it even hurts to see her happy without you being the source of her happiness.

One of the fundamental characteristics of entrepreneurs is that they are eternally optimistic and focus their attention on the positive side of life and business—the glass is always half full, and in bad times at least still a quarter full. It is never half empty or almost empty. Entrepreneurs are seldom fearful; they do not see themselves as victims of society but rather they help create it. The focus is always on what they want to achieve and not on the problems that constantly seem to be present in their lives. These problems never really bother them or make them depressed. And they don't fear the situations that lead to fight, flee, or freeze reactions either.

Entrepreneurs place their focus on what they want and not on what they fear. Doing this, they still face and solve problems in the course of creating the outcomes they want, but their focus remains fixed on their ultimate vision.

The way you talk about yourself and your life—your story—has a great deal to do with what shows up in your day-to-day experience. Your thoughts create filters through which you view your life. If you think of yourself as a victim of life, you filter all that happens to you through the self-pity lens, and you find plenty of evidence to support that viewpoint. That's why the orientation you adopt is so important—it exerts a powerful influence on your life direction.

Consider an eagle's point of view, and look at your life, your environment, your goals, and what occupies you. We tend to waste a lot of our time on nitty-gritty stuff that if looked at objectively is neither relevant nor important but takes up a lot of time and creates a lot of worries. If you soar with the eagles, you cannot even hear what the chickens say while they are scratching around way below you. And why would you, an eagle, even care? I was thinking about this when we recently made a wonderful *cabalgata*, trip on horseback, into the high parts of the Andes. We dressed up as gauchos, mounted the small but very sturdy horses from the Mendoza region, and slowly ascended up the slopes of the Aconcagua to above four thousand meters. Fortunately, the horses were very sure-footed and never missed a step up the steep and dizzying heights. We came to terms with concepts like climbing higher than where the eagles soar, and realized there is no limit to the sky. At night we would set up camp near a creek, use our smelly saddles as mattresses, and lay silently on our backs watching the stars. We had all at times been in five star hotels but now, for once, we were staying in a ten-thousand-star hotel. It is amazing how many more stars are visible when the light pollution of the city sky is eliminated.

Do not lose your focus by wasting too much time on the small day-to-day irritations, problems, and interpersonal frictions. Keep yourself firmly focused on the mission and the vision while guarding the values; move boldly forward and create momentum. The perspective will change, and you and your team will quickly rise, as on thermal streams, high above the mundane time-wasters, and achieve much more interesting things. Whatever gets attention grows in importance; whatever gets neglected shrivels in importance. *Use it or lose it* can also be applied to day-to-day irritations and minor problems.

As long as you think that the cause of your challenges is "out there," or as long as you think that *anyone* or *anything* is responsible for *your* problems or suffering, or for *your* success, your situation remains hopeless. It means that you are stuck in seeing yourself in the role of victim, that you are making yourself suffer in our paradise. You can stop your suffering the moment you realize it is completely of your own making. It takes only a second, flipping one simple switch in your mind, and you are free. Sit back for a moment and contemplate this. If you pick up only one thought from this book, this is it. How you lead and give shape to *your* life is *your* choice; how you look at and interpret the things that happen to you is also *your* choice! You can, of course, choose to spend a fortune on therapy to reach the same conclusion.

Vladimir Putin reflected on his purpose in life when he said, "Our task now is not to fix the blame for the past, but fix the course for the future ... to become what we are capable of becoming is the only end of life! So, my wishes (for the New Year) are that we should not have: Wealth without Work, Pleasure without Conscience, Knowledge without Character, Commerce without Morality, Science without Humanity, Religion without Sacrifice and Politics without Principle!"

For me (and not necessarily for you) it is important to feel as though I am building something useful and am contributing positively to the lives of at least some of the people around me. I don't want to contribute just to the lives of our clients, suppliers, and employees, but also to those in my social environment. I would never want my purpose in life to be just a warning to others, to add no value at all, to just vegetate, sit on a couch and consume. Once I learned that I am completely free to choose how I look at my environment (and that it does not really matter how others look at it), to choose my own goals in life, to judge my own progress, and to enjoy my own choice of successes, my effectiveness grew tremendously. I began to feel in control of my life—I began to feel challenged and fulfilled.

I am not privileged, because I chose my own path instead of someone else's. I am not lucky, because I created my own luck. I am not different, because anyone can do what I am doing. I am not an exception, because you too can do anything I have done. And for you it is the same. You do not need to be privileged, lucky, different, or exceptional in order to become successful. It is your choice, nobody else's. I chose my own destiny, and you can do the same. Create fulfillment and find meaning in your life. Entrepreneurship can be one way to achieve this.

> *"Ultimately, man should not ask what the meaning of his life is, but rather he must recognize that it is he who is asked."*
>
> **—Viktor Frankl**

Chapter 2

Am I Capable of Starting and Running a Business?

"Our deepest fear is not that we are inadequate. Our deepest fear is that we are powerful beyond measure. It is our light, not our darkness, that most frightens us. We ask ourselves, who am I to be brilliant, gorgeous, talented, fabulous? Actually who are you not to be? You are a child of God: your playing small doesn't serve the world. There is nothing enlightened about shrinking so that other people won't feel insecure around you. We were born to make manifest the glory of God that is within us. It's not just in some of us; it's in everyone. And as we let our light shine, we unconsciously give other people permission to do the same. As we are liberated from our own fear, our presence automatically liberates others."

—Nelson Mandela

When contemplating whether to start your own business, one of the first questions that comes to mind is, *Am I able to pull this off?* Of course that is a valid question. It is also a question that is difficult to answer.

It is easy to get lost in a myriad of practical issues such as: Do I have the right skill set? Is there enough money available to invest and make it through the start-up period? Is my product or service good enough? Will people like to buy from me? Will I be able to inspire my employees? These are all important questions to ask. Many of these questions cannot adequately be answered, other than by making it work. It isn't about thinking about it; it is about doing it. Remember, you are totally free to decide how you look at any aspect of your life. You will need some self-confidence to take forward steps, just as small children are prepared to fall a thousand times in order to learn to walk. If they sat back and reflected on whether they would be able to walk or not, many might never even try. Maharishi Mahesh Yogi, the Indian guru who in the late sixties inspired, amongst many others, the Beatles to change the world with their love songs and ballads, expressed it as follows, "When we think of failure; failure will be ours. If we remain undecided; nothing will ever change. All we need to do is want to achieve something great and then simply do it. Never think of failure, for what we think, will come about." More recently Sir Richard Branson summarized a similar idea in six words, *Screw it. Let's do it.* Oftentimes you need to just take a leap of faith; forget about the reasoning and just do it.

When I was growing up, I had the idea that I was on my own in a cruel world. I felt as though there were billions of competitors, and all vying for the same thing. I would need to compete with all of them in order to get my piece of the pie. And there was not enough pie to go around.

My parents, although very caring, were not necessarily very loving. Sure, they provided my siblings and me with life's necessities, but they never created an intimate environment where we felt loved, safe, and protected. They had lived through the Depression of the 1930s as well as the ensuing war. But these events left them, and many of their generation, constantly worrying about outside threats and sufficient supplies. We were perpetually conserving electricity and heat, saving bottle caps for the "mission," praying for food, preparing for the "Russian invasion," and waiting for disaster to happen. Over the years I have learned to look at the world from a different perspective, and that has made my life a lot simpler.

Years ago I alighted upon the abundance mentality. Mohandas Gandhi described it as, "There is enough of everything in the world to satisfy everyone's needs, but not enough to satisfy everyone's greed." The abundance mentality assumes that there is always enough for you, and that whatever you give away (knowledge, advice, love, gratitude, appreciation, etc.) will multiply, resulting in you getting back many times what you put in.

Once I could let go of the notion that there was not enough "pie" in the world, the second realization, that "It is better to give than to receive," was cemented. This notion from the Christian tradition is one that I had often heard about in church, but never fully understood until I decided to experiment with it. At first it seemed somewhat counterintuitive to search for a win-win in each relationship. To leave money on the table for clients and suppliers or to give away advice for free in the hope that prospects would become clients seemed a great effort to make in trying to prove a theory. Then, somewhere in 1993, I was asked to teach credit analysis to some of the management of the Central Bank in Havana, Cuba. At the time, our company was really small and struggling. I was teaching in a room dedicated to Ernesto Guevara, explaining the concepts of "American" credit analysis and how to analyze financial statements to an audience of rather skeptical people. After all, they had become bankers based on the political correctness of their ideas, rather than their financial skills. It took me several days to overcome their resistance against the unknown, their disgust of a foreign approach, and their fear of knowledge. But, by humbly spending countless hours going over the same concepts and listening intently to all counterarguments, we slowly built mutual trust. I ended up making great friends, got to know all the wonderful things about Cuba, and am still in touch with some business contacts there. In the end it is really simple; you have to believe in the power of purpose, the importance of action, and the ability to overcome all obstacles: The more you give, the more you will receive.

I grew up with Christian values, and, of course, they had their impact on how I think and what I believe in. I do not believe one's wisdom tradition by itself impacts who will or will not be successful as an entrepreneur. A recent study indicates that the greatest number of entrepreneurs, per capita, live in India; a lot of them are Hindu, some Sikh, some Jain, and others are Christian. There appear to be fewer businesses started by Buddhists/Taoists. (Steve Jobs was not yet a Buddhist when he started Apple.) There are lots of successful Muslim entrepreneurs in the Middle

East, North Africa, and in Indonesia and Malaysia; Jewish ones in Israel and the United States; and Taoist ones in Japan. I believe it is the value set and moral compass one has that determines his likelihood to establish a successful business.

At the soul level there is no scarcity. The more you serve others and share your knowledge, experience, and contacts, the more you get in return. There is no "my" business or "your" business, there is just "our" business. Working together, we add more value than we can ever add alone. Clients, suppliers, and employees who feel valued and treated well will make your company more successful and your life more fulfilling. Win-win will invariably produce better results than "squeezing the last drop out of the lemon."

Just as the bread and fish multiplied when shared nearly two thousand years ago (John 6:1–14), an abundance mentality, described in Covey's *Seven Habits of Highly Effective People*, will cause you to grow. Understanding this, there is but a small step to the realization that you can create your own success by helping others succeed. Steven R. Covey calls this looking for a win-win. This concept applies to any and all situations. If you find in any situation a solution that makes both parties win, you make a friend, create an ally, and obtain a loyal employee or a satisfied customer. Getting the maximum out of every deal is not creating loyal employees, satisfied customers, etc., and therefore does not lead to success in business.

Not everyone agrees with this notion.

Albert J. Dunlap (also known as Chainsaw Al) believes that business is primarily, if not solely, for the purpose of making money for its shareholders. He believes, "Business is about winning. Who comes in second is the first loser. If you want friendship, buy a dog. I take no risks, I got two dogs." Of course this approach is as valid as any and will help in creating a successful small business (out of a large unsuccessful business), but may not necessarily contribute much to your peace of mind and job satisfaction.

Once I mastered the abundance mentality and the win-win theory, my next great epiphany came when I realized that I am the master of my own destiny. I am not a powerless being who is to be managed or controlled by a third party or a God. On the contrary, I am in charge of my future.

Having grown up a Catholic, in the Christian tradition, this took me a while to understand. I was taught that the universe was created, owned, controlled, and managed by God (in a rather autocratic management style). He made the big decisions, and we, as people, were expected to carry out his will. If we would do that conscientiously, toil hard, follow a set of values or commandments and subscribe to an operating manual, the Bible, we would eventually end up in heaven, where we would spend eternity in joyful bliss. For me, this was not exactly an appealing plan for life.

The Judaic and Muslim traditions are very similar in concept; Jahweh and Mohammed call the shots while humans are to follow the paths set out for them. The values in the Torah, Bible, and Koran vary somewhat, as do the rewards in the afterlife.

In Hinduism the individual has more say. By carefully building up Karma, one can, at the end of this life, create a springboard toward the next turn of the wheel of Samsara and reincarnate in the next round as a better-prepared being, facing new challenges set by a whole pantheon of Gods. This, of course, will continue until, at the end of countless reincarnations, we have understood all questions, relinquished all possible temptations, and have readied ourselves for enlightenment. Only then, Hindus believe, will we enter a state where no further reincarnations are needed.

In Buddhism there is no God. And, therefore, there is no religion. Everything takes place in your own mind. *Tat Tvam Asi*, meaning "You are that," is one of the Mahāvākyas (Grand Pronouncements) in *Vedantic Sanatana Dharma*. The meaning of this three-thousand-year-old saying is that the self, in its original, pure, primordial state, is wholly or partially identifiable or identical with the ultimate reality that is the ground and origin of all phenomena. From there it is only a small step to the notion of the United Field, which states, "To think is to affect."

Lynn McTaggart, an American author known for conducting the largest mind over matter experiments, said, "The United Field theory assumes that the communication of the world does not occur in the visible realm of Newton, but in the subatomic world of Werner Heisenberg." Werner Heisenberg (Nobel laureate in physics) in turn said, "The smallest units of matter are, in fact not physical objects in the ordinary sense of the word; they are—in Plato's sense—Ideas. Reality is as delicate as a thought, existence is closer to being an association of ideas than a conglomerations of atoms." George Wald (Nobel laureate in biology) added, "The stuff of which physical reality is composed is mind-stuff. It is mind that has composed a physical universe."

You may not be looking for a discourse on science in a business book, but I think this piece of theory is important. Our cells and DNA communicate through frequencies. The brain perceives and makes its own record of the world in pulsating waves. A substructure underpins the universe that is essentially a recording medium of everything. It provides a means for everything to communicate with everything else. People are indivisible from their environment. Living consciousness is not an isolated entity. It increases order in the rest of the world. The consciousness of human beings has incredible powers to heal ourselves and heal the world. In a sense, to make it as we wish it to be.

Most scientific theory is based on the concepts of Newtonian physics, which are three-hundred-plus years old. Newton describes a very well-organized universe of separate objects operating according to fixed laws in time and space. While Newtonian physics works very well on one level, it doesn't cover everything.

Carl Jung, Albert Einstein, and Wolfgang Pauli reasoned that there were parallels between synchronicity and aspects of the relative theory and quantum mechanics. Carl Jung was convinced that life is not a series of random events but rather an expression of a deeper order. This deeper order led to the insights that a person was both embedded in an orderly framework and was the focus of that orderly framework and that the realization of this was not just an intellectual exercise but also a spiritual experience.

More recent discoveries in quantum physics are indicating that everything is connected. We now understand that there is one physics, that the laws of the quantum world are applicable to the world of visible matter. Those laws suggest that the observer has an effect on reality. And there is ample evidence that our thoughts have the capacity to change physical matter. That being the case, we have to rethink almost everything, because for hundreds of years we've perceived a world based on separation, but the world that scientists are discovering now is a world of unity, where all things are fundamentally connected at the subatomic level. A focused mind can effectively change intentions. There are people who are able to manifest things with only their thoughts because they are able to use the power of intention in a very sophisticated way. There are also those that train to be masters of intention, such as qigong masters, master healers, and Buddhist monks. All big thinkers, all great strategists, and all developers of ideas do exactly the same. Everything we see in the physical world around us was first just a thought before it became an invention. That concept also applies to the world of business.

The world was changed by Facebook, just as it was changed before that by the Internet, the invention of the phone, the train, beer and bread, going all the way back to the earliest inventions of mankind. All of those inventors had a great impact on society. They changed society and our world forever with what initially was only a thought. Also, the nature that surrounds us, the birds and the bees, the flowers and the trees, the moon and the stars, must once have been a concept, a thought, a design before they were a reality. This design, however, does not come from a third-party separate God. It comes from a universal consciousness, of which we are both an integral part and at the same time the total.

Interpretation happens at the level of the mind, but it is our individual souls that are conditioned by experience, and through that memory of past experience the soul influences our choices and interpretations in life. Deepak Chopra has described it as follows, "People who understand the true nature of reality, those whom some traditions call enlightened, lose all sense of fear or concern. All worry disappears. Once you understand the way life really works—the flow of energy, information, and intelligence that directs every moment—then you begin to see the amazing potential in that moment. Mundane things just don't bother you anymore. You become lighthearted and full of joy. You also begin to encounter more and more coincidences in your life. When you live your life with an appreciation of coincidences and their meanings, you connect with the underlying field of infinite possibilities. This is when the magic begins. This is a state I call synchrodestiny, in which it becomes possible to achieve the spontaneous fulfillment of our every desire. Synchrodestiny requires gaining access to a place deep within yourself, while at the same time awakening to the intricate dance of coincidences out in the physical world."

Once you think through the likelihood of everything being related and you realize that you are directly connected to all of the possibilities and power of the universe, it becomes conceivable that you can directly influence everything around you, because you are both part of it and you are all of it.

When you wake up in the morning, you are completely free to choose whether you get out of bed in a good mood or in a bad mood. The decision to look at the weather as gloomy or glorious, or greet your partner with joy or disdain, lies entirely with you. When you reach work you can see your colleagues as competitors or as allies. Your clients as suckers who should be parted from their money or as valued associates. Your work as inspiring or as dull. And, when you start your own business, you can see it as a gamble or as a challenge.

Victor Frankl, a famous Austrian psychoanalyst who survived three years in a Nazi concentration camp, wrote in his book *Man's Search for Meaning*, "Our attitude toward what has happened to us in life is the important thing to recognize. Once hopeless, my life is now hope-full, but it did not happen overnight. The last of human freedoms, to choose one's attitude in any given set of circumstances, is to choose one's own way."

He also concluded that by focusing on his spiritual life, he could maintain mental sanity and retreat to a place where the SS could not touch him. He concluded that a man who has nothing left in this world still may know bliss, be it only for a brief moment, in the contemplation of his beloved. In a position of complete desolation, when a man cannot express himself positively, when his only achievement is enduring his sufferings in an honorable way, in such a position man can, through loving contemplation of the image he carries of his beloved, achieve fulfillment.

In the end we are all souls, all ultimately and intrinsically connected. We are at the same time part of the whole as well as the whole. For me it is essential to understand this, as it is underlying most if not all of the relevant theory and approaches in this book. In India the thinking mind is *manas*. The intuitive intellect and the faculty of discrimination is *buddhi*. Individual awareness, the pure sense of I-ness, is *ahamkara*, which is the heart-mind and the witness, the little voice or thought constantly somewhere in your mind. All of these levels emanate from the individual soul of *jivatman*, which is our connection to the all-pervading, universal soul, the *atman*.

We are fully responsible for how we conduct our own lives. We can change the course it is taking. You may compare it to the track you are leaving in fresh snow when you are skiing. You can look back and try to draw conclusions from the shape and the general direction of the track. But, the track is not what moves you forward, nor does it give a guarantee of where you will be going from now on. It is the skier, you, who leaves the track, and you can decide to change your course at any moment in time. In the same way, your history does not determine where you go; it only shows where you come from. Your actions and your mind determine where you go, independent of both the past and the environment.

Deepak Chopra states, "Whatever else we are, no matter how much of a mess we have made of our lives, it is always possible to tap into the part of the soul that is universal, the infinite field of pure potential, and change the course of our destiny." You are one with the universe, yet at the same time, you are your own universe. And this makes us also realize that love is the only relevant emotion, the only emotion that stems from the mind and links us to all other parts of our universe. We can let go of the emotions at the (lower) ego level, where we used to see ourselves as separate from the universe. Anger, fear, jealousy, arrogance, and greed are all based on a scarcity and on an *I win, so you lose* mentality. Through this we see ourselves as an individual separate from the rest of the universe. We *must* understand this in order to become a successful entrepreneur.

Once we accept the idea that we choose our attitude, then we can also choose our power level. We are free to choose whether to have no influence on the things that happen around us or absolute influence. We can choose to make everything happen.

I constantly remind myself that I am both part of the universe and the creator of my universe. I have the power to look at everything as having been caused by myself, and, whatever that happens to be, it is both my responsibility and my accomplishment.

Deepak Chopra also noted, "The universal, nonlocal part of the soul is not touched by our actions, but is connected to a spirit that is pure and unchanging. In fact, the definition of enlightenment is "the recognition that I am an infinite being seeing and seen from, observing and observed from, a particular and localized point of view.

"Whatever else we are, no matter how much of a mess we may have made of our lives, it is always possible to tap into the part of the soul that is universal, the infinite field of pure potential, and change the course of our destiny."

When you accept the notion that everything you realize happens ultimately in your own mind, that the only person seeing things the way you see them is you, and that you are the one person who controls what is important and what is not, then you will create change in this world. You are the only person who determines what is a problem and what is not, just as you are the only one who can engender your success.

I consistently remind myself that I am both part of the universe and the creator of my universe, and that I have both the power and the obligation to look at everything as caused by myself. Whatever that happens to be, it is my responsibility, my fault, or my obligation to deal with.

Once I accepted the notion that everything I realize happens ultimately in my own mind, and that the only person seeing things the way I see them is me, our business took off. But before it took off, I also had to see that I am the person who controls what is important and what is not, what is a problem and what is not, and what is successful and what is not. It was only after all of that did the business grow.

And for you it is exactly the same; *you* are responsible for your life, and *you* are the one who will make *everything* happen in your life.

Shakespeare penned, "All the world is a stage, And all the men and women merely players; They have their exits and their entrances, And one man in his time plays many parts."

And when you realize that you are connected to and can influence the whole universe, you become powerful beyond belief. The world is at your fingertips. Mold it. Make of it what you will. Picture yourself swimming in the sea. Notice its endless and immense power. Feel the waves carry you, and sense how buoyant you are in its midst. Its waves will undulate this way and that, but it is you who will know how to swim, where to fish, or in which direction to sail.

Once you see yourself in the sea, you may try to see yourself as the sea. You have the capacity to become the waves, the motion, the vastness, the wetness, and the eternity thereof. Stretch your mind. Stretch your imagination. Like a muscle, it will only grow when stretched.

The same is true for any other aspect of the universe. A mountain may seem eternal and powerful, but if you take your time and have the right earthmoving equipment, you can move it anyway and anywhere you want, even if it has been in its place for hundreds of thousands or millions of years. It will disappear as a mountain, but it will remain as matter, as energy, just in a different shape and form, and with a different use. Moving mountains is not impossible; if you put your mind to it, you will achieve it. In fact, if you put your mind to anything, you can achieve almost anything. The triumph of the will was masterly filmed in 1935 by Leni Riefenstahl (in *Triumpf des Willens*). This film will teach you that the power of your will must at all times be harnessed by your moral compass, so as not to result in a criminal struggle against all and at the demise of all but those most fit.

Bill Gates changed the way the world operates by inventing a computer operating system. Steve Jobs comes up with the iPod, iPhone, and iPad, each a revolutionary change in the way millions of people work, play, and enjoy life. There is no reason why you cannot do the same; you have the same power they have and had to change the universe for the better and make a positive impact on the lives of many people.

Do you have to be exceptionally talented or gifted to do that? I do not think so. What it does take is a solid and novel idea, focus, a lot of practice and perseverance, and belief in yourself.

When we started Amicorp, we had $36,000 in capital, one shared PC, a sixteen-square-meter office, no clients, very few prospects, and only the vaguest of ideas of how and where to make money. I had a brand new mortgage, my wife had just had a baby, and a second one was on its way. My colleague Margaret Sankatsing had a baby in a *Maxi Cosy* under her desk. We did not have much to start with, but you better believe we were motivated, focused, and willing to work hard. We knew we had to find great solutions and clients before the money ran out, and with confidence in ourselves, we did just that.

Bill Gates changed the way the world operates by inventing a novel computer operating system. Steve Jobs came up with the *iPod*, *iPhone* and the *iPad*, each a revolutionary change in the way millions of people work, play, and enjoy life. There is no reason you cannot do something similar; you have the exact same power they have to change the universe for the better and make your impact on the lives of many people. Do you have to be exceptionally talented, have a garage, or be a college drop-out?

I do not think so. What it does take is a solid, and preferably novel, idea, and then focus, practice, and perseverance, attention to detail and clients, and the willpower to never give up.

> *"You don't have to be a fantastic hero to do certain things, to compete. You can be just an ordinary chap, sufficiently motivated to reach challenging goals."*

> **—Sir Edmund Hillary**

Chapter 3

Where Do You Find the Bright and the Right Idea?

"Opportunity is missed by most people, because it is dressed in overalls and looks like work."

—Thomas Jefferson

Any successful business starts with the right idea. This idea has to do more than just generate income and work. The idea has to stimulate the mind and fulfill a need in a way that it has never before been fulfilled. A business that just imitates the successful business idea of someone else will never be as successful and never have the same feel as a novel business idea. The many copies of Starbucks will never be as successful as Starbucks unless the people behind those businesses are able to add a new dimension or take the idea to the next level. Developing a similar coffee shop may create income and work, but it will not add anything unique and therefore will not *move* people the same way.

If you want to start a new trust company, you must be able to provide faster or cheaper services, be more personal in approach, or have novel solutions, better employees, or go where no others have gone before. Preferably you should do all of the above at the same time. In Amicorp we have always tried to steer clear from what our competitors have done. We have gone to new places, emerging markets, and we have offered different solutions. We have always tried to figure out where the markets or the regulatory environment would move toward, and act as if these developments were already in place. The few times we were tempted to take a me-too approach and copy the herd, setting up offices in overgrazed markets such as New York, Zürich, and London, we struggled to become successful or did not even make it at all.

In our aloe vera business we do not produce the standard skin-care products only, but we also produce health drinks for people with autoimmune diseases such as AIDS and diabetes. And we do not just cater to the wealthy and well-cared-for segments in the market of middle-class whites and "black-diamonds," but we distribute our products to the parts of the country where roads don't even exist, or if they do, they certainly don't appear on the GPS. Millions of South Africans live in these areas.

A great business idea has to move you; it must make you feel different. Therefore, any idea you may have for a business must be tested against, *How does it make me feel?* Or perhaps more importantly, *How do I want to feel?* Very simply, think of a business that will make you feel that way.

Most entrepreneurs want to feel:

- Security from creating a sound business.

- Strength in the social network created by establishing a business.

- Pride in adding something to society that was not there before.

- Achievement.

- Success (be it wealth, recognition, or status).

Amazingly, that turns out to be exactly how your clients, suppliers, and employees want to feel as well. So, when I begin a new venture, I think about how I want a specific business or project to make me feel, and then I design the venture around those feelings.

Now, where do you find the great idea? What has been the best idea ever? Creating your own life right—How did that start? According to Deepak Chopra, "Your 'soul' resting somewhere in the Universe, carefully selected a womb here on Earth. Two lovers, your biological parents, touched each other in love or in lust and conceived the conditions and the body your soul was waiting for." Great ideas are the same. They are floating around in the universe and need the right combinations of love, lust, and physical conditions to be born again.

If the idea behind your business is simply about work and income, then your business will be about work and income, and both you and your business will suffer. Your business will create stress; it will get ugly and tired and cynical. It will become a victim of all the customer abuses you experience, and it will lack imagination and become fearful and exhausted. There must be a bigger idea behind your business in order for it to become a great business. The bigger idea is what makes you see the obstacles as challenges to overcome and what will give you the strength to actually overcome them.

Many studies have shown that successful entrepreneurs are not more intelligent or more hard-working than other people, but what differentiates them is how they look at and deal with problems and obstacles. It is not that they underestimate them or ignore them, but that they see them as challenges needing to be dealt with, inherent to the goals to be reached. They treat them as obstacles to overcome and not as something life-threatening. In the same way, entrepreneurs care more about the people around them than the average person. Michael E. Gerber, a US management guru, wrote, "If you care to you will dare to. And nothing else will be required of you, other than the will."

I believe that some of the reasons why we at Amicorp were able to motivate our employees to provide good quality service, was because we made it clear from the beginning that we were *not* in any way interested in helping our clients evade taxes but rather plan investments clearly within the limits of the law. At the same time we explained that our company was not just about making as much money as we could but also about learning from the process, enjoying the ride, creating good jobs in emerging markets, and adding something useful to society. We shared those thoughts and feelings with the people around us, and as a result several of our suppliers and clients participate in our child project in Curaçao.

We tried to do the same with our aloe vera business, African Caribbean Aloe Products. We made it clear to all the people around us that the project was not just about making money but also about demonstrating to South Africans that white and black people can together create a new business that makes sense, adds value to the community, and brings useful, healthy, organic products to the market. Slowly but surely people began to see the truth in this. Last Christmas one of our clients in the Netherlands organized a community project in his own company and sent a container full of brand-new toys, clothes, soccer materials, learning materials, and furniture to the new compound we constructed for our nearly sixty farm and factory workers. Other farmers around us started planting aloe vera as well and now are upgrading their compounds and creating additional opportunities for more people in the *Afrikaner* heartland of the *Old Transvaal*.

In our wine business, COL Wines, we were able to raise capital when nobody was investing or lending money by focusing on the ecological aspects, the organic methods, the passion, and the friendship in the project. Our suppliers and consultants contributed more to the project than they were contractually obliged to. The project is becoming a success, not only because *we* want to make it a success, but because *everyone* involved in the project has been inspired to give it his best.

If you are not moved by your business, your business will suffer, your people will suffer, and your life will suffer. They will all suffer because you did not reach high enough or far enough. This is not because you did not know *how* to, but because you did not *dare* to or did not *care* to; your external circumstances are, if you try long and hard enough, you are bound to overcome them if you create enough positive feeling. Your whole environment will align itself to make your business a success.

Why is this so important to understand? It is important because it touches upon the very core of this book.

Albert Einstein, one of the brightest thinkers of his age, discovered that there is no fundamental difference between matter and energy, as matter in the end is energy, and that, therefore, everything in the universe is energy. Building on this discovery George Wald, a Nobel laureate and organic chemistry professor of biology at Harvard University, envisioned that mind (your mind) is the source of matter.

Matter is built from energy, and energy is built from information. Matter rises from consciousness. Mind, as information, is present in every atom. Mind is ubiquitous in our universe, just as wisdom is the basis of all existence. In the words of Walt Disney, "If you can dream it, you can make it." It goes even beyond that. If you can dream it, your mind will make it. This is not a novel concept. Does not the Bible already say, "The word became flesh and made his dwelling among us" (John, 1:14).

Your mind creates not only the idea but also creates the energy needed to generate the matter. Your mind makes dreams come true because it converts mind into matter. You are not only part of the creation; you are also, at the same time, the creator. You are the one who makes ideas come to life, as you are the one who *minds*. You are the one who converts the idea or dream into energy and, thus, energy into matter.

You are the one who will make hundreds or thousands of little things in the universe coincide to make the dream come true, to make the business you have in your mind become reality. Michael Gerber also stated, "A business without a dream is like a life without a purpose."

You can compare this the following way. When you create and send an e-mail, you convert your thoughts and emotions into energy waves that are changed in your laptop into small energy pulses that travel through space and time (the Internet). They end up on the Blackberry of someone on the other side of the world. By reading the words, the receiver reconverts the energy waves into emotions and thoughts. The Blackberry and the laptop are simply primitive electronic receivers, much more primitive than your body and mind. Many more thoughts and emotions are transmitted and received in nonelectronic ways, using the energy waves we consist of and that surround us. Our ideas and beliefs are like e-mails that are constantly sent by us in all directions and that are consistently received by all the people with whom we surround ourselves. You can change the character of your life by changing your beliefs. What you truly believe will become a reality, will come to pass successfully.

If, for instance, you open a coffee shop, it becomes a success because you believe in it, have a dream of how its atmosphere needs to be, and put life into it. There are lots of coffee shops around. Of course, location is important, as well as the types of coffee you serve, the quality of the seating, and the friendliness of the staff. Yet you will see that very similar-looking places can feel very different. Some places become very successful, and others remain very unsuccessful. The difference is in the spirit, the atmosphere and the feel you create. You very often can notice that coffee shops that are being sold, after having changed hands, become either much more or much less successful. You must also have noticed that when you are in a strange city, and you pick a place to drink coffee or go for dinner, you select on the basis of a feeling that has very little to do with the menu, the pricing, or the location. You pick the place that has a good *feel* to it. That *attracts* you, or that has a *soul*.

In my organization I see the same. We established over forty offices in many different countries. Some offices were an immediate success, while others took countless hours, and a great deal of effort, investment, and perseverance, and still struggled to become even a small success. After trying everything else, magic changes sometimes happen when the person in charge is himself being changed. The new person, doing the same things differently, can make all the difference in the world.

The same can be said when clients come in. Most new clients can choose between our business and the business of any of our many direct and indirect competitors. Whatever we do, in the end our service is not revolutionarily different from that of our direct competitors; our pricing is in the same range and the look and feel of the products and ideas is not that much different. Then why do clients choose our service over that of the next-door provider? Simple. Because they have *trust* in the person that attends to them, and because the documents and presentations *feel good* because the means of presenting the service inspires confidence. These are all intangible reasons, yet terribly important.

The successful entrepreneur can convert his personal dream into a product or service that resonates with the clients, the employees, and the environment. A wonderful, personal dream that does not make a connection with the perceived needs or the dreams of clients does not result in a successful business. The personal dream needs to be shared with the employees and the clients and then needs to become part of their lives as well. Your enthusiasm, confidence, and approach will have to resonate in such a way with the employees and clients that synergy arises, emotions strengthen each other, and a shared experience is born.

And lastly, do not ever let your ambition and enthusiasm be deterred by anyone.

> *"Keep away from people who try to belittle your ambitions. Small people always do that, but the really great make you feel that you too can become great."*
>
> **—Mark Twain**

Chapter 4

When Is the Best Time to Start a Business?

"We are now faced with the fact, my friends, that tomorrow is today. We are confronted with the fierce urgency of now. In this unfolding conundrum of life and history, there is such a thing as being too late. Procrastination is still the thief of time. Life often leaves us standing bare, naked, and dejected with a lost opportunity. The tide in the affairs of men does not remain at flood—it ebbs. We may cry out desperately for time to pause in her passage, but time is adamant to every plea and rushes on. Over the bleached bones and jumbled residues of numerous civilizations are written the pathetic words, 'Too late.'"

—Martin Luther King Jr.

There is really not a better time than right now to start a business. You could build a case to start a business once you have acquired enough education, knowledge, experience, a business network, money, paid off your mortgage, sent your children off to college, or whatever; but most likely by that time you will no longer have the energy, the drive, and the passion to start a business.

You may also argue that the best time to start a business was ten or twenty years ago, when you were younger, more energetic, and things were simpler—when certain inventions had not yet appeared and the world was not yet flat. None of that is relevant. Only one moment in your life is relevant. And that is the present moment. Dan Millmann, the writer of *The Way of the Peaceful Warrior*, wrote, "Right action at the wrong time serves no useful purpose. Stillness can be the most powerful action of all. Just as action can reflect courage, waiting can reflect wisdom. But if we wait until we have permission, until we feel more motivated, until it gets easier, until fear vanishes, until hell freezes over, we may miss the chance to act at all. If we wait for the perfect moment to come alive, we may discover we never lived at all." The past moments are past, and you can relive them and change your perception of them at will. Your memories are basically what you think of your past today. At once gone forever and at your fingertips whenever you need them. They will change over time as they suit your needs. You will adjust your memories to fit the way you look at your life today.

If you sit with people you have not seen for a long time, you will notice that you each recall the past in a way that fits your current situations and seemingly tiny events become larger than life. It is a normal human defense mechanism to adjust your thoughts and memories to the reality of today. That explains in part why you may think your life is sometimes inescapable, but it is not the present that is the logical result of your past, but rather the past that you adjust to fit your present reality, to create an explanation or even an excuse for why you are where you are. If your life is not a success, your failures will loom in your memories; if your life goes from good to better, you will remember the many little successes that seem to have inevitably led up to where you are now. My friends, who in their own eyes did not make it, recall the times when they were mocked or felt like failures; the friends who did make it remember heroic feats in joint experiences, and every time we meet, our stories become taller than they were before.

Your experiences may serve you well, as your prior experiences are very useful in avoiding problems. However, your experiences may also restrict you, as your memories limit your creativity. They provide a box with ever higher sides that limits your thinking. Your education, upbringing, and social conventions all help you to think within the box. Look around you; most children are very creative, and many young people are rebellious, thinking differently and not wanting to conform to society. But once you reach your thirties, your likes, dislikes, wants, needs, and goals somehow all begin to converge. We all seem to become more and more like one another. Because we feel safer in the crowd, being a conformist and doing what everyone else does becomes our safety net. As a result, creative abilities suffer.

The future will come one step at a time. There will never be a perfect moment in the future unless you make it perfect by starting today to make every step you take a step in the direction of your goals and dreams. And you will see that even if the journey is going to be a thousand miles long, the steps you take will make your goals come closer, as every step you take will influence everything else around you. Your efforts will shape the universe into bringing you closer to your goals. Paulo Coelho remarks, "The two worst strategic mistakes to make are acting prematurely and letting an opportunity slip; to avoid this, the warrior treats each situation as if it were unique and never resorts to formulae, recipes or other people's opinions."

Once you start formalizing your dreams, share your ideas with others, and start looking around for financing and clients and evaluating business needs. The solutions will present themselves magically when you need them because you will attract them, and they will feel attracted to you.

The path will open before you and become clear as you start walking it. You will encounter the right people when you need them; you will find the right solutions for your problems when they become acute. You will open a book and see the answers to your questions; you will meet a person, and that person will give you the connection or the introduction you need. You will have an idea, and soon someone will show up who needs that idea or the product you can make with it. There is no way you can plan or force this. Be confident, trust the universe, and be open for it to happen. You will need to have a certain self-confidence for the right things to happen at the right time. But as Paulo Coelho rightfully remarked, "And, when you want something, all the Universe conspires in helping you to achieve it."

Start your journey today because, in the words of Yamamoto Tsunemoto, "There is surely nothing other than the single purpose of the present moment. A man's whole life is a succession of moment after moment. There will be nothing else to do and nothing else to pursue."

In 1519, Hernan Cortez crossed the Atlantic Ocean from Spain with eleven ships and six hundred men. He set out to conquer Mexico City, referred to at that time as Tenōchtitlān, a city of about three hundred thousand people and the largest outside of China. When he left the harbor of Vera Cruz to go ashore with his tiny army and a small number of newly found local allies, he set his ships on fire as a clear sign to his men that he was in Mexico to stay and succeed or die there.

This was a great manifestation of singularity of purpose. Cortez knew his team would be much more focused on the task at hand if they knew there was no way back, no choice but to succeed, no life if they would fail. The resulting determination made them achieve incredible feats against huge odds. You cannot be successful if you do not focus on your mission and vision, if you have one eye in the rear-view mirror, or if you keep thinking about the meat pots of Egypt. You need to cross the Rubicon, cast the dice, make the waters part, and cross between them to face your new fate. Never look back lest you turn into a salt pillar, lose the race, or hit a brick wall. Once you make the decision to start your business, go for it with 100 percent absolute dedication.

And equally importantly, once you decide to start, get the show rolling, take immediate action. Do not spend a lot of time making plans, talking about the validity of your plans, or thinking about the certainty of potential success for your business. Just get going with the first step. Leave your day job, get some business cards, and make the first transaction—do something. The details will come later, for the direction will become clearer as you go. Start walking, and the path will open up before you.

"If I'd never picked up the first person, I'd never have picked up 42,000 in Calcutta."

—Mother Teresa

Chapter 5

Do We Really Need a Business Plan?

"You can map out a fight plan or a life plan, but when the action starts, it may not go the way you planned, and you're down to the reflexes you developed in training. That is where the roadwork shows, the training you did in the dark of the mornin' will show when you're under the bright lights."

—Joe Frazier

The old saying goes that a business that fails to plan is planning to fail. Of course those are wise words, but every plan is limited in what it can foresee. When I feel a bit down, I sometimes go back to some of the business plans that I have written over the past twenty years and have a good laugh. It is good to realize with the benefit of hindsight what the limitations of a business plan are. Few of us are able to accurately predict the future and much less to even foresee which ways the environment will develop. As John Lennon said, "Life is what happens to you while you're busy making other plans."

For thousands of years the world was thought to be flat until people like Nicolaus Copernicus and Cristobal Colon proved it was round. Thomas Friedman, in *The World is Flat*, barely five hundred years later became famous by proving it flat again, describing a brave new world with millions of new opportunities for rugged entrepreneurs.

The way you look at the world to a large degree determines the content of your business plan. Building a business plan forces you to focus on clearly describing your mission and visualizing your vision and the services you want to provide or the products you want to produce. It helps to prioritize your limited resources toward activities that will positively influence your cash flow. You cannot progress without a clear and quality business plan that attracts investors, convinces banks, and assists in securing certain permits. Most new businesses fail, not because the entrepreneurs are not working hard or the product or service is not good enough, but because the cash runs out, and the expenses mount faster than a steady, sufficient income stream builds up. Accurate and detailed cash flow statements and projections, updated once a quarter or even on a monthly basis, are the core of each and every business plan.

But never become a slave of your budget or your business plan. I agree with views of General George Patton when he said, "A good plan today is better than a perfect plan tomorrow." You will constantly need to update the plan or do things the plan never envisioned or budgeted for. When opportunities arise, you have to grab them whether they are in the plan or not.

In larger corporations it happens all the time that whenever an important business decision needs to be made, some party pooper distracts you from the essence of a creative discussion by asking, "Where is it mentioned in the business plan?" Or, when you come across a really great potential employee, "What is the amount available in the budget?"

If you let your business plan become a straightjacket and a restriction on your creativity, you will not be in business for long. The great opportunities, the life-changing events, and the intuitive decisions are not going to be planned a year or even months ahead and almost by definition will not appear in your business plan. And this, I would say, is a blessing.

At all times you need to remain alert, up-to-date, and aware of the opportunities that come up. Just as if you were sitting along a stream with a net, small fish swimming by all the time, but once in a while a big one passes by. That is the time to cast your net and secure the day's meal. In the words of Gautama Buddha, "Mindfulness is the path to immortality;

negligence is the path to death. The vigilant never die, whereas the negligent are the living dead. With this understanding, the wise, having developed a high degree of mindfulness, rejoice in mindfulness, paying heed to every step on the path."

A major part of your business success depends on how you engage with what presents itself from the entire field of all opportunities. Every challenge and every opportunity you need (and every problem you think you do not need) will present itself in its own time. A thought about creating a product, a service, or an event will present itself to you at the exact right moment. Or perhaps someone will call or send you an e-mail at a most opportune time. It does not matter whether the source is the internal or external self; the ideas are all coming from your own soul. Engage with what comes; your mind will choose among the indefinite number of possibilities those that at the moment are the ones you are most capable of handling.

Use your intuition. Stay alert, aware, and in the moment. Have all of your senses constantly open so as to realize what is happening around you. Take note of the opportunities and challenges as they present themselves. Engage with what comes. It may look like a thought coming from your head, an event coming from the world around you, or a coincidence in sequence of occurrences. Pick the ones that seem to create the most happiness for yourself and that make the most sense for your business. Most opportunities will pop up when you are enthusiastic, cheerful, sincere, and curious. You will close 57 percent more sales and become much more successful when you are happy. Stimulate yourself to be in that state of mind most of the time. Remember what Albert Einstein once said, "The intellect has little to do on the road to discovery. There comes a leap in consciousness, call it intuition or what you will, and the solution comes to you, and you don't know how or why."

With intuition, we know what we need to know, right when we need to know it. All information is available to us. You can even know the past and the future as if they were now. But you will have to trust your intuition, trust all the information you have available and not (consciously or subconsciously) discard the information that cannot be proven. A lot of knowing is not built on research, tests, linear reasoning, mathematical proof, spreadsheets or bullet-point presentations. Most knowing comes from the gut.

You *know* which person you interview is going to be a star employee. You *know* which client is going to be a great customer. You *know* which product is going to be a sales success, not just on the basis of objective information, but based on what you feel inside. Do not discount that gut feeling. Look back at and analyze your failures. In many if not most cases you can point out a previous warning signal, an event or a hunch that had already warned you things might go wrong. The person might not turn out to be who you thought, or the project or idea already had inherent weaknesses, etc. You ignore those warning signals at your own peril.

Also, if you analyze your greatest successes, in retrospect, you *knew* you were on to something from the beginning. There was something inside that told you to do exactly this, follow exactly this path, and deal with this person. While you are processing one or two things consciously (and women maybe a few more), your subconscious is processing millions or tens of millions of pieces of information simultaneously. By definition your subconscious has a *huge* advantage over your consciousness. Listen to it—all the time. And if you think you do not hear it, create time for it. Clear your mind from the constant clatter, the continuous humming of recurring thoughts. Take long walks in the forest, learn to enter into a state of meditation, go to church and pray, practice *Yoga* or *Vipassana*, or whatever brings you into contact with your subconscious. According to Sri Nisargadatta, "Most of our experiences are unconscious. The conscious ones are very few. You are unaware of the act because to you only the conscious ones count. Become aware of the unconscious."

The clutter in your life, those activities that fill your days but do not aid in any real progress, needs to be cleared out. Even though they may seem *important*, they need to be reduced in both importance and in consumption of time.

As an entrepreneur, why would you spend your days on the rituals of business that take up so much of your time? Supervising employees, having control over cash flow by writing all the checks yourself, sitting in meetings in which nothing is really decided, being copied in on everything your colleagues do, and getting involved in every little decision are not effective uses of your time. Trust your employees; organize the business in a way that everyone has enough challenges, tools, freedom, and authority. Let them do what they love to do and focus on selecting from the many opportunities those that make your business grow, to create something the world really needs or longs for, to make a leap forward in technology, to provide superior customer service, product design, sales approach, marketing acumen, or anything else creative that is most likely not described in the business plan but determines the difference between a merely average business and a very successful one.

The great success stories of our times are hardly ever the result of detailed strategic planning, but rather of knowing exactly what the world is ripe for at a certain moment. I myself could never have thought of Facebook as a concept; it needed a teenager to work that out. Our company once was offered some rights in the distribution of *Pokémon* in return for services rendered. We could not see the value in it and did not participate in its subsequent huge success. Similarly, we could have been part of the roll-out of *Casa del Habano,* a very successful Cuban cigar distribution chain. As nonsmokers we could not fathom the size of the opportunity, thinking only elderly gentlemen short of breath were still smoking cigars. Luckily there were other opportunities we *did* recognize, and we grasped them the moment they came by. Opportunities are like passing trains, either you jump on them when they pass by, or they are gone forever. If you need to ponder or look back into the business plan, they will have left you on the platform staring at the quickly disappearing lights in the night.

"You have to take risks. We will only understand the miracle of life fully when we allow the unexpected to happen."

—Paulo Coelho

Chapter 6

Where Can I Sign Up for Entrepreneur School?

"The fact that I was not a trained banker and in fact had never even taken a course on bank operations meant that I was free to think about the process of lending and borrowing without preconceptions."

—Muhammed Yunus

Of course many people who aspire to be entrepreneurs would like to go to entrepreneur school. This is a route that feels safe, fits into our culture of structured behavior, and limits the scope of skills required to make it work. If you pass, you are ready for it, and you will be successful. If not, you were never meant to be an entrepreneur. It is not your fault, right? You can learn to drive by going to driving school, to be a cook by going to cooking school, an architect by studying architecture. Similarly, can you become an entrepreneur by going to business school?

The answer to that question is not so simple. Many of the best cooks never went to cooking school but rather used their experience and intuition to make their best recipes. The best artists and designers often have limited formal education but boundless creativity and experience. Many of the most successful entrepreneurs are high school or university dropouts or suffer from dyslexia, attention disorders, or various other learning differences.

An MBA is very valuable; it looks great on any résumé, and it helps to open many doors that otherwise might remain closed. You usually get only one chance to make a good first impression, and a good education helps in making that solid first impression. The skills they teach you at a business school definitely have their value. These skills, however, are only a base. Success is something you have to create yourself once you leave business school. And many people who dropped out or never went to business school become equally successful in life. Do not fork over a small fortune for a great business education if you think it will guarantee you success. Doing so may be your greatest disappointment. You have to create your own success.

In addition, studies in economics, culture, history, law, psychology, quantum mechanics and physics, marketing, administration, fashion, art and advertising will also prove useful. But as Goethe's Faust rightfully exclaimed, "Now I have studied philosophy, medicine and the law, and unfortunately, theology, wearily sweating, yet I stand now, poor fool, no wiser than I was before; I am called Master, even Doctor, and for these last ten years have led my students by the nose, up, down, crosswise and crooked. Now I see that we know nothing finally."

It is the school of hard knocks, the school of life, that teaches you the most. If your eyes and your mind are open, you analyze well the situations you are exposed to. Teachers are many and everywhere; they will show up whenever you, the student, are ready. You may, however, not always recognize the teachers even when they are right in front of you. They are presented as your friends, your colleagues, your clients, your suppliers, people you meet on the street, or books you open randomly. You have to open your eyes and your mind to be able to learn. Study the people you meet—all of them; they will teach you more than all the books in the world can.

When I was teaching Chase Manhattan Bank's internal training course in New York, I had a few classes of new recruits for the bank as well as one class of "sons of." The latter was a mixed bunch of people who were admitted to the Chase training program, not on the basis of their intellectual achievements or promising skills but on the basis of their parents' relationship with the bank. One of my students turned out to be a son of a former president and clearly had come to New York to have fun and party. After he failed a couple of tests, I was made his tutor and thus carried the responsibility of teaching him until he passed. I spent many hours chasing him down, seeing a lot of attractive party spots in New York, but failed to pin him down. The bank was getting really nervous, including Bill Butcher, the president of the bank himself, and pressure was mounting on me to produce a miracle. As luck would have it, one day the guy packed up and returned to his home country, having decided he knew all there was to know about banking. This proved to me the old adage that you can lead a horse to water, but you cannot force it to drink. People will learn something only if they are receptive to it. Knowledge cannot be forced upon someone. Experience, yes, but even then the person involved needs to be open to extract the lessons from his experiences.

> *We are here to do.*
> *And through doing to learn;*
> *And through learning to know;*
> *And through knowing to experience wonder;*
> *And through wonder to attain wisdom;*
> *And through wisdom to find simplicity;*
> *And through simplicity to give attention;*
> *And through attention to see what needs to be done.*
> **—Ben Hei Hei**

You can, of course, start out by learning useful skills. As an entrepreneur it helps to have some accounting knowledge, to be able to read financial statements, especially to make your own cash flow statements and to know how a decision you contemplate influences your cash flow. It helps to have some legal knowledge—when to put an agreement on paper or when to call in a contract lawyer. It helps to be a subject expert in the business you are in, and it helps to read business magazines, be a member of industry pressure groups and focus groups, and to have a feel for what is going on in whatever business you have chosen.

It is very important to be in constant touch with your employees, have informal meetings, and regularly drink a Friday afternoon beer or two with them in order to know exactly what is going on in their minds, how they look at *your* business and the industry. Make sure you know exactly what they think about how they would solve the issues the company is facing.

It is also very important to be in touch with your clients and know exactly how they perceive your company. Do this not by creating some anonymous feedback form or impersonal telephone interview, but by going and visiting clients on a regular basis. Go to their place of business. Speak to the big clients and the small ones; speak to the decision makers at your clients' offices and to the receptionist, the messenger, and the person dealing with your company on a day-to-day basis. The people on the work floor will usually be much less diplomatic and much more outspoken about the quality of your work and how you stack up compared to your competition. I compare these meetings with the way a computer network operates. You can travel with your laptop, gather new experiences, send out new messages, and receive new impulses, but on a regular basis you need to plug into the network and synchronize all files, update the software and share the experiences so that everything runs from the same database again.

Remember, your employees and clients are by far your best sources of information and learning.

Also, your mistakes, your failures, the contracts lost, the prospects missed, and opportunities you failed to notice are great sources of learning. Analyze every client lost and every opportunity missed, as they give you valuable insight into your shortcomings and valuable information on how to improve your product or service. Be thankful and appreciative to clients who complain. Apparently they care enough about you and your business to do so. Listen intently and appreciate all feedback, however painful or nasty. These are rare opportunities to gain great insight. Clients who just leave you without complaining but do not ask for follow-up services, should be sought out and visited, as they can give you even more brutally honest advice. Sure, this may be advice you don't want to hear, but listen carefully, as you will gain an improved product, service, or organization. No organization is ever perfect. Accept that, and learn to listen to the messages in the feedback on the mistakes you have made. Then, act upon the information you have gathered. Your business will never be good enough; it will constantly need to be improved. As Paulo Coelho said in his manual *Warrior of the Light*, "A warrior accepts defeat. He does not treat it as a matter of indifference, nor does he attempt to transform it into a victory. The pain of defeat is bitter to him; he suffers at indifference and becomes desperate with loneliness. After all this has passed, he licks his wounds and begins everything anew. A warrior knows that war is made of many battles: he goes on."

Many mistakes and problems are of a procedural nature. Pricing is too high, delivery is too slow, service too lax, quality too mediocre. These problems are important but relatively easy to solve. Quality initiatives, system improvements, a focused approach, and discipline will go a long way. More complicated are client issues that relate to broken promises, dishonest behavior, rude treatment of individuals, and betrayal of trust. In those cases you will often have to go back to the drawing board, revisit your mission, vision, and values, reassess the personalities of the employees you have selected, your compensation schemes, and the targets you emphasize. Tough measures may be swiftly required in such cases. Paulo Coelho also wrote, "Every Warrior of the Light has felt afraid of going into battle. Every Warrior of the Light has, at some time in the past, lied or betrayed someone. Every Warrior of the Light has trodden a path that was not his. Every Warrior of the Light has suffered for the most trivial of reasons. Every Warrior of the Light has, at least once, believed he was not a Warrior of the Light. Every Warrior of the Light has failed in his spiritual duties. Every Warrior of the Light has said 'yes' when he wanted to say 'no.' Every Warrior of the Light has hurt someone he loved. That is why he is a Warrior of the Light, because he has been through all this and yet has never lost hope of being better than he is."

From your mistakes and failures you learn to become better and better. As long as you are receptive to learning and driven to be the best at whatever you are doing, your company will continue to grow and become better. Only the best companies in any region, any business, and any competitive sphere will ultimately be successful. And to stay successful that effort needs to be repeated every single day. Never be content with the quality level achieved. Never think you have reached the heights of your business. Never think your products need no further innovation. There are always higher quality levels to reach, better performances to achieve or to bring it back to the basics, "shower curtains to be tucked into bathtubs."

To be successful you need to have a mind-set focused on constantly becoming better and constantly being the best at whatever you do. With that mind-set you can be successful in basically anything. The former pro golfer Ken Venturi defined this effort perfectly, "I believe that any player who is a champion would be a champion in any era he lived in, because he would get himself to the level he has to attain to win."

So constant studying, constant quality improvement, and constant search for feedback are a few of the ways to learn and get ahead. But to really get ahead, to "boldly go where no man has gone before," you will need to be a lot more imaginative. Any study or research is about what is already there; any feedback is about what has already passed. Any evaluation or audit is like an autopsy, dissecting what is already dead. It cannot be brought back to life. However interesting, what has happened in the past is no more than the trail you have left skiing in fresh snow or the path you have hacked through the forest. They mean very little for the future and offer no indication as to where you are going You need to constantly decide to swerve your skis left or right around the big boulder, to create a path around or over the mountain, to create a new product or service, to make a new investment or not. To do research, to invest in a brave new idea or not, or to bet your future and the shop on something new or not demands imagination, perseverance, and courage. Albert Einstein said, "There are only two ways to live your life. One is as though nothing is a miracle. The other as though everything is a miracle."

Facebook did not exist ten years ago. Most of the gadgets created by companies like Apple and Samsung did not exist at that time either. Had not someone stuck out his neck and taken the decision to go forward and to push the limits, many of the successful products and services we see popping up all the time would never have been created. Of course, for every success there are ten failures. But that never deterred the real entrepreneurs from making the decisions, accepting the risks, and courageously moving forward.

The big successes are for the people who had the vision and the imagination to create something that was not there before and then the guts to convert their images into tangible products and services. According to Paulo Coelho, "There is only one thing that makes a dream impossible to achieve: the fear of failure."

Again, the direction in which the world is going, as well as the necessities your products or services will need, cannot be studied in books. You will get the ideas from your employees, clients, or even from analyzing how younger generations are living their lives in totally different ways than my generation does.

Surround yourself with great people whenever you can. Hire people that are better at some things (or all things) than you are. Hire them for their attitude, and train them for the skills they need. And, lastly, listen to all the comments and ideas that they generate over time.

You will see that the people around you, employees and clients, often will have ideas that are totally different from yours. It is easy to discount a lot of those ideas as off-the-wall, as not well thought out, as beside the point. But in the middle of a haystack of ideas you will find needles of genuinely good ideas that will be the seeds from which your future products or services are nurtured. Constantly have your magnets with you so you can detect those needles.

To get to these ideas, it is paramount to accept that everyone is different, thinks differently, and has different goals in life. And all of us can at any time do a lot better. Luckily so. Imagine how sobering an experience it would be if one day you could determine you are at that point living up to your full potential? Do not judge the people around you. Do not impose your own criteria upon the people around you. Accept and value people as they are and for what they are. Whoever you judge, positively or negatively, reflects on you. Again, according to Paulo Coelho, "We can never judge the lives of others, because each person knows only their own pain and renunciation. It's one thing to feel that you are on the right path, but it's another to think that yours is the only path."

Malcolm Gladwell, in *Outliers*, states that one needs at least ten thousand hours of practice to become exceptionally good at anything. It was ten thousand hours of playing together that made the Beatles play harmoniously and integrate sound and lyrics the way they did. It was lots of access to computers from a very young age that gave Bill Gates an edge when he started in the computer business.

We, in our business, became really good at compliant international tax solutions for people in emerging markets when we travelled year after year from city to city, visiting thousands of tax advisors, thousands of investment managers, and thousands of international law firms. Combining the experience gained from the many visits helped us in creating ever better solutions, building experience upon experience, and adjusting whenever a law changed, a regulation was adapted, or a train of thought reversed. Long after having serviced over ten thousand clients, we continue to create small study groups, discussing new solutions for familiar problems, or adjusting familiar solutions for new problems. Death and taxes will forever remain constant, so our business will continue to exist so long as we remain on the forefront of our field. In much the same way, the shoe shop needs to make sure to get the fashion for the next season in the store, while the restaurant needs to adjust to the latest tastes of the clientele, and the consumer goods producer needs to beat the competition with production of the latest gadgets.

None of this is a scientific process. As an entrepreneur, it is your task to distill your own ideas and those of you and your colleagues or employees into concrete action. You must sense the unspoken needs of your clients and prepare for the winds of change to blow.

This is not always so easy. Henry Ford, who was producing carriages before entering the automobile business, is credited with saying, "Had I asked my customers what they wanted, they would have asked for a faster horse". The automobile gave them a quantum leap to a new way of transporting themselves. You will need to find those quantum leaps. Build the innovations or create the improvements that make a real change. This will demand intuition and require a deeply felt love for serving others. And as with many of the learning processes in our lives, we will never reach perfection.

> *After a while you learn the subtle difference*
> *Between holding a hand and chaining a soul,*
> *And you begin to learn that kisses aren't contracts*
> *And presents aren't promises;*
> *And you begin to accept your defeats*
> *With your head up and your eyes open*
> *With the grace of a woman, not the grief of a child,*
> *After a while you learn ...*
> *That even sunshine burns if you get too much.*
> *And you learn that you really can endure ...*
> *And you learn and learn ...*
> *With every good-bye you learn.*
>
> **—Jorge Luis Borges**

Chapter 7

What Is the Importance of Top Quality?

"Good is the enemy of Great."

—Jim Collins

All management gurus agree that the need for top quality is absolutely paramount. Whatever business you are in, you will need to stand out from the crowd, excel in what you do, and make clients come back for more. Anything less than excellence is just not good enough. Compare it to a surgery that scores a 90 percent. That is simply not good enough for the patient. Scaling 95 percent of a mountain does not take you to the top, and a 99 percent safety record for an airline looks pretty bad to frequent fliers. You will, at all times, need to create a relentless drive for quality in your business.

What is excellence? What makes your product or service excellent depends on what the qualities are that attract the customers. If you run a restaurant, it is the combination of the quality, taste, originality, and pricing of the food, as well as the friendliness of the waiters, the atmosphere of the eatery, and the convenience of the location that drives its excellence. In a "good" restaurant, you wait longer for your food than in a fast-food place. So the speed of the service is less of a differentiator.

In our Amicorp business (implementation and maintenance of corporate vehicles used in international taxation), speed is the greatest differentiator, as usually investments and trade transactions are waiting for a structure to be put in place. It is also essential that the structure work perfectly from a legal, administrative, and regulatory perspective. It must continue to work, year after year, by being updated whenever external circumstances demand. For us, the "twenty-four-hour response time," "four-eyes principle" and "two-signature clause" are at the heart of our operations manuals, as those three rules capture most of the key qualities clients need from us (speedy service, brainpower, and security regarding a client's assets). As a result, we have clients who are the children of clients we had ten or fifteen years ago. We work with intermediaries over the course of their careers, staying in contact with them as they move from firm to firm and up the corporate ladders.

The differentiating factors vary widely from industry to industry. It is imperative to understand what can set you apart from your competitors, and what is important to your customers. Wal-Mart purposefully designed very modest meeting rooms, so as to communicate with suppliers the need for the lowest possible prices. Private bankers and investment bankers have very luxurious offices and opulent meeting rooms to impress clients with their success and create a "money is no object" atmosphere. In a business-to-business environment you may feel obliged to pitch to several layers of customers in one effort. The intermediary may be very concerned about price, while the end user places more emphasis on ease of use and personal service. Both need to be satisfied for the deal to close. Conrad Hilton, the founder of the Hilton hotel chain, was once asked to give the keynote address at a gala honoring him. Hundreds of people had gathered in the auditorium to pick up some of his *secrets to success*. He walked up to the podium, looked around the crowd gathered, and said, "Remember to tuck the shower curtain into the bathtub." Then he left the podium and returned to his seat. It may have been a puzzlingly short speech, but it emphasized exactly what it is all about—sweating the details, day in and day out.

For our five-year celebration, we took all of our employees to a behind-the-scenes tour of Disneyworld in Orlando, Florida. Among other things, we visited the studios where the Disney animated movies are produced. We were shown a few different versions of the big bad wolf chasing some piglets around a room, tossing all of the furniture around and banging the lamps. We had to comment on which version we considered had the best quality and why. We all chose the same scenes. Only after they explained it to us could we see that in the scenes we liked the most, the shadows of the piglets and the furniture moved in synch with the swinging of the lamps. *Banging the lamp* was a standard expression in the studio for making a cartoon look as realistic as possible. We converted that expression in our company to *keeping the clock coiled*, referring to the old-fashioned clock in our main meeting room that needed winding every few days. Without anybody being assigned the responsibility for keeping it ticking, everyone religiously looked at the clock upon entering the meeting room to assure it was properly wound.

What is important to customers changes over time. Great companies preserve their core values and mission, while their business strategies and operating practices constantly adapt to a changing world. They combine what their leaders are deeply passionate about with what they are capable of being best at and, at the same time, what makes economic sense. A great company is not necessarily a large company. A small restaurant or a small group of professionals can just as well be great, if greatness is what they aspire to be. A book like *From Good to Great*, by Jim Collins, describes perfectly those steps large companies have taken in order to become really great.

To make those steps work for your entrepreneurial company, start by using some creative imagination; visualize how greatness will be defined, and determine which elements of quality you will need in order to make your enterprise a success. Then imagine yourself as if you are already there. This will help you to believe in your ability to achieve those goals. Once Arnold Schwarzenegger became governor of California, he described it as follows, "I visualized myself being and having what it was I wanted … Before I won my first Mr. Universe title, I walked around the tournament like I owned it … I had won it so many times in my mind that there was no doubt I would win it. Then when I moved on to the movies, the same thing happened. I visualized myself being a famous actor and earning big money. I just knew it would happen."

My aspirations never included becoming Mr. Universe, as I understand one's goals need to be specific, measurable, attainable, realistic, and timely—the classic S.M.A.R.T. goals. If you meet with a prospective client and act as if you desperately need to close a sale, you will not close the sale. If you act confidently and radiate success, you will meet success. The way you think, the way you act, even the way you dress all contribute to your success. Rehearse the process multiple times, predict the questions that will be asked and prepare high-quality answers in return. Perfect practice makes perfect—doing something ten thousand times makes you a master, regardless of your initial talent.

One of our clients, a seasoned asset manager, secured a meeting with Bernie Madoff. Our client was trying to allocate a significant amount of money into his, at the time, highly successful hedge funds. Madoff told him that he had little time, his funds were closed, and he could not accept additional investments. That resulted in our client begging and pleading for the opportunity to invest money in the funds. In the end he was very pleased with Madoff's agreeing to "take only twenty million US dollars" from him. Madoff's humble and self-confident behavior, as well as the analysts' reports, never for a moment cast doubt on the extraordinary and unusual performance of his funds. Well ... not until the whole house of cards collapsed.

Once you have imagined yourself achieving your goals, visualizing the results, and practicing the moves, it becomes much easier to actually reach the results. And remembering how proud you felt when you achieved those goals, even if it is only in your mind at this stage, helps to keep you motivated for the long haul.

Learning to apply lucid dreaming (where you try to guide your subconscious toward your life goals while asleep) helps you to become vastly more efficient. Many books are written on the subject. The way I do it is simple. At the moment when I am ready to sleep, I organize my thoughts and select an issue that I would like to solve. I try and formulate it for myself as clearly as I can, and I try to look at it from all angles, clearly earmarking the possible solutions I see as just some of the possible solutions. With these thoughts as my last ones for the day, I turn the lights off and go to sleep. The hardest part comes when I wake up in the middle of the night or early in the morning. I then need to remember what I dreamt of before I become fully awake and rush to the bathroom. It helps me to write down the thoughts or the solutions reached during the night, but this requires a certain level of discipline. Through practice you improve, and after a while it becomes amazing what you can accomplish in the middle of the night.

Harvard University studies have shown that people with clearly defined, written personal goals make about ten times as much money in a ten-year time span as graduates without clearly defined goals in life. To dream purposefully of your challenges and goals helps dramatically in getting ahead.

When you are in a difficult situation, it helps to imagine that you will never give up. Be strong and refuse any setback preventing you from achieving your goals. A solution for the situation at hand is nearby, and you are going to find that solution. Believe you are then capable of implementing the solution, and don't be surprised when success meets you. If your position shoulders a tremendous amount of responsibility, visualize yourself making important decisions. Deem responsibility to be an opportunity rather than a burden. Picture yourself finding the right solution to a difficult problem, and enjoy leading your team to success. Lastly, share the praise and good feelings associated with the success.

Do not forget that Gautama Buddha said, "What we think is what we become." Those are words to be taken quite literally. Visualization and lucid dreaming help in becoming what we think, and by using the power of our imagination and energy, we are ready to influence and align the universe around us so as to realize our dreams and attain our goals. Practicing situations in our imagination will help us find solutions before the situations actually arise, and as a result we will deliver much higher quality results than without it. We will never be able to understand everything about *all* complexities of the universe. We have but one body, and it contains a brain of no more than three pounds of electrochemical jelly.

It may sound odd, but we know from neurobiology that the brain is always trying to push whatever is in our consciousness into the unconscious because unconscious processes are faster, more mechanical, and more automated. According to Sudhir Kakar, "One could even say that for the brain, consciousness is something to be avoided. We talk, see, hear, walk automatically, react automatically to most situations and make our emotional judgments from the heart (or the stomach, depending on the preferred metaphor) than from the head. This is not surprising, given the complexity of the brain, with its hundred billion neurons. Even something as simple as seeing color in a painting involves a huge and complex set of unconscious mental activities. Brain researchers estimate that our unconscious database outweighs the conscious one on an order exceeding ten, and in some calculations, hundred million to one."

I have lived in several countries over the course of my working life. I still go to the same tailor in Singapore and the same dentist in Curaçao. It is not only because I am a creature of habit (like everyone else) that I continue to go to them, but I like these people and believe they deliver quality. Last year I needed to have a molar extracted. The dentist, whom I have been seeing for years, brought me the news that the molar could not be saved—as if a dear family member were about to pass away—and he seemed to be much more moved by the loss than I was. The feeling he conveyed was that he actually *cared* about me and my dental issues, and that care incentivizes me to stay with him, much more than his technical skills or hourly billing rate. So *care* is what I connect with quality in these cases. If you think about it, *care* is what you wish for in most personal services.

In many businesses the clients are ultimately moved by the personal care they receive. Why does one good restaurant feel better than another? Why is one wine better than another? It is all very subjective. It all boils down to how the service or product makes you feel.

Consistency in delivering the feeling that the quality of your product or service exceeds the quality of all other products and services in your field can be enhanced by smart marketing and sales techniques as well as by implementing quality systems. Whether it is ISO quality standards and its many successors, or the Six Sigma with its green and black belts, or the very useful *kaizen* principle, which gets everyone in the organization involved in making small, immediate improvements and empowers people to stop processes that prove wasteful, you need to choose something that works for *you*. But remember, in the end it is your dreams, care, enthusiasm, and discipline that make your company truly great. ISO quality standards or Six Sigma will not move the whole universe to align with you, but you and your energy will.

Senator Ben Nighthorse Campbell, a Cheyenne of the Morning Star, has given us the following wise words, "The cost of excellence is discipline. The cost of mediocrity is disappointment. The cost of apathy is the greatest because the cost of apathy is failure."

Never accept mediocrity; never settle for good enough. Never be content. Nothing stops an organization faster than people who believe that the way you worked yesterday is the best way to work tomorrow. People who are satisfied with less than top quality will ultimately ruin your company; do not associate yourself with them. *But we have always done it that way* should be a legally recognized reason for immediate dismissal. The moment you are content is the moment you have reached the end of growth, the end of improvement, and the end of innovation. And very soon you will become history.

You will know intuitively where to find the excellence. To implement and produce excellence is merely hard work. It is why you became an entrepreneur in the first place. The best place to look for excellence is within yourself. Apply constantly and consistently the *abundance mentality*. Share everything you have, including your ideas, dreams, plans, and enthusiasm, and more and more of the people around you will follow you. Let fade away those who do not follow you in a daily drive for top quality. Do not settle for mediocre quality. Every day you will need to be able to look yourself in the eye and confidently say, "*This is the very best I can do.*" The rest is just doing it.

> "*There is not a moment when I do not feel the presence of a Witness whose eye misses nothing and with whom I strive to keep in tune. Truth is what the 'voice within' tells you.*"
>
> **—Mohandas Gandhi**

Chapter 8

How Does One Define the Corporate Mission, Vision, and Values?

"Let us be realistic, and do the impossible."

—Ernesto 'Che' Guevara

As an entrepreneur, you must have a compelling reason for why your business exists. This reason is what inspired you to go into business in the first place and what will inspire others to join your organization. It is not about creating a mission statement and simply putting it on paper but rather understanding and sharing with everyone the following: *Why does this business exist?* The organization's mission is similar to that of a lighthouse; it is a guide and reminder of why the organization exists. In essence, it is the purpose of the organization.

Although it is called the organization's mission statement, it is, of course, the mission statement of you the entrepreneur and of the rest of your team. An organization, however solid or long-lasting, remains just a legal entity; it is not a living being and does not by itself have a mission, heart, soul, spirit, ethics, or moral compass. Only the people who lead and manage it breathe life into it and give it meaning and purpose. The mission statement describes what gives meaning to your life, how you deal with and give form to your *Dharma* in life. And for the other team members, the mission statement should resonate with their missions in life and the paths they choose.

There are lots of examples of good mission statements: I guess Google's *Don't be evil* is most widely known. It is based on the twenty-five-hundred-year-old Buddhist tradition of the five moral precepts: do not kill, do not steal, do not commit violent acts, speak the truth, and abstain from taking substances that obscure the mind. It is important to do no evil because doing so will ultimately cause pain and suffering in ourselves. Suffering is what we are trying to avoid. Other mission statements refer to a corporate enemy. Honda, for example, at one time in the past stressed their desire to defeat Yamaha. This seems like a rather negative reason for a company to exist.

When we set out to formulate our mission statement, we spent a couple of rainy afternoons brainstorming about what we, as human beings, really stood for and what we really wanted to achieve with the company. Although they may sound like part of a democratic process, in the end mission, vision, and values cannot be compromised. They need to be clear choices, giving a clear direction to the company for years to come. People who join the company from then on have to subscribe to them or leave.

Basically, we are active in two distinct types of business: execution of cross-border tax planning and business-process outsourcing.

Cross-border tax planning is simply the structuring of international investments and income streams in such a way that the smallest amount of tax expenses is incurred in the process. The countries with more efficient double taxation agreements and/or tax systems will naturally attract more business and more foreign investments than those that are less efficient. Not surprisingly, open trading countries such as Great Britain, the United States, the Netherlands, Switzerland, Luxembourg, Hong Kong, Singapore, and Dubai have the main tax advantages and are used by residents of those countries as tax havens.

When my kids were little, they would ask me what my job was. I remember telling them I did roughly the same thing as Robin Hood—I took tax money from the Sheriff of Nottingham and gave it to the needy for more useful purposes.

Business-process outsourcing is seen by many people as stealing good-quality jobs from hard-working people in well-organized, high-income countries (Western Europe, Japan, and the United States of America) and moving them to far-flung places where underpaid and undernourished workers and child laborers in sweatshops produce goods and services that only lead to more profits for the producers. Somewhere along the way, people tend to forget that many of the goods and services they enjoy are affordable only because they are made in lower-cost countries. If the goods and services were produced at *local* production costs, people would not have the level of material wealth they have today. On a personal level, I take great satisfaction in knowing we have created challenging, high-quality, and well-paid jobs in a number of emerging markets.

So after a number of brainstorming sessions we came up with the following mission statement: *Amicorp delivers excellence that brings peace of mind to its clients, while saving them taxes, time and money.* The peace of mind for the clients, as well as the savings in both cost and time come from careful optimization of tax-planning solutions and delivering compliant, reliable, legal management and administrative services. Our statement may seem a bit boring, but then again we are not putting a *thousand songs in your pocket* or *sending a man to the moon.*

If you are doing anything as interesting as that, by all means make it part of your mission statement. Do not include in your mission statement those things that will not inspire or motivate you, your employees, or your clients. Statements such as *create shareholder wealth* or something negative like *beat the competition* lack positivism and passion. As an entrepreneur, you should have alignment and synergy between your corporate mission and your mission in life. As long as you are alive, your mission in life cannot be complete. The same can be said about your corporate mission; if it has been attained, it is not sufficiently ambitious. As race car driver Mario Andretti said, "If things seem under control, you are not going fast enough."

After the mission statement comes what George W. Bush, former president of the United States, called the "vision thing."

The vision basically explains how you will give shape to your mission. The mission should not change over the lifetime of the company. The vision is to be adjusted whenever your circumstances change materially. The vision should refer to what Jim Collins, the writer of *Built to Last*, refers to as "Big, Hairy, Audacious Goals." We chose as a vision, when we were still quite small (and it sounded a bit pretentious): *to become one of the top ten trust companies in the world and the best one in the emerging markets, while being soundly profitable, providing a safe and stable working environment for our employees, being environmentally conscious and contributing positively to the communities in which we are active.* We have come a long way to get there; it will soon become time to adjust the vision. Our mission and our values will stay the same, although the wording may be refreshed from time to time.

You have to paint your goals in broad brush strokes. They should be ambitious but not impossible to reach. They need to inspire you, your employees, and your customers. So a goal that emphasizes your desire to earn a lot of money for yourself, or simply create shareholder value, may inspire you, but not a lot of people around you.

Once you have formulated your mission statement and your vision for the next five years, the next step is to describe the key values that you want the company to have. These key values will set the boundaries within which you operate.

In our company we have selected the following sets of values:

- Integrity and honesty
- Loyalty and teamwork
- Quality and care
- Respect and equality

Why did we choose those values and not others?

We chose *integrity* as a value because in our business it is very important to do what we promise and to promise only that which we can actually deliver. We also want to make sure we stay clearly within the limits of the law and, more importantly, keep our clients within the limits of the law. Many people unfamiliar with our business believe that cross-border tax planning is about tax evasion, moving undeclared assets to disreputable tax havens and financing terrorists and drugs traffickers. The movie *The Firm* first painted this picture for our industry, and it was then strengthened by scandals involving companies such as Enron and Parmalat. Just as people who sell knives run the risk of their products being used to stab someone, the kind of corporate structures we establish for our clients can be used, and sometime are used, by people who evade taxes, hide taxable assets, and disguise ill-gotten gains, etc.

We chose *teamwork* as a value because in our business employees need to be able to rely on one another in order to deliver superior service. In our case, by definition clients use our services in a country other than the one they reside in, and most of the time two or three of our offices are involved with the same client service. This means that internal agreements must be made, and everyone must be able to count on those agreements. It is not an option to tell a client that you cannot deliver because a colleague failed to complete his part of the work on time. Therefore, everyone needs to work together to ensure delivery on time.

When something cannot be delivered in time, or when the quality turns out to be substandard, the client must be informed as soon as possible. This works best when you underpromise and overdeliver. If colleagues are *honest* with one another about their strengths and weaknesses, teams can work together with realistic expectations, and the organization can best benefit from what each individual member can accomplish.

We chose *loyalty* as a value because it is important to stand by our employees and clients in good times and bad. We want to be a service provider to a family or a business for many years. Our average client retention duration is fifteen years, and we have quite a few clients who are the children of some of our original clients. To date we have never had to lay off any employees because of difficult economic times. We constantly stay on top of everyone's motivation, attitude, and productivity. We understand that not everyone is 100 percent productive all of the time, and we realize that everyone's life has its difficult periods. In those times we want to support our employees. On the other hand, when employees demonstrate a perpetually poor attitude or cannot motivate themselves any longer, loyalty reaches its limit, and it is better for all involved to terminate the labor relationship.

Quality was another obvious value, as it is the only way for us to out-perform and out-compete our competitors. We have achieved above-average growth for almost twenty years and consistently gained market share by competing on the basis of the quality, depth, and sophistication of our services. Had we compromised or taken the competition as a benchmark, we would not have come this far. According to Leonardo da Vinci, "Simplicity is the ultimate sophistication."

Long-term relationships cannot be built with employees, clients, and other stakeholders without deeply *caring* for them. Giving employees the freedom to make mistakes, to go out and try new things, to create the next generation of solutions, and to find new ways to make us stand out from the crowd are all ways we demonstrate *care*. We try not to stifle our employees with excessive rules, and we are flexible when dealing with important personal issues.

Respect was chosen as a core value, as we work in a culturally diverse global environment. In our company our clients come from nearly one hundred different countries. Half of our employees live in Asia, and a quarter each in Europe and the Americas. We come from very different cultural and religious backgrounds, and we want every employee to understand and celebrate our differences. We want clients and suppliers to be treated with respect as well, for they are the reason we can continue to be in business. Respect will radiate positive energy that will create positive energy with our clients and suppliers and make for the long-lasting relationships we strive for.

Equality recognizes that we are all different and should be treated differently in accordance with the personality we have and the value we add to the company, but it acknowledges we all have the same value as human beings. Nobody is more important as a human being than any other, and nobody is so important that he needs to earn one hundred times more than someone else.

Once you have defined your mission, vision, and corporate values, you need to preach them, teach them, and live them every single day. This does not mean you should yearn for the day when you have fulfilled your mission and achieved your vision. As in all other aspects of life, it is the journey that is paramount; the work we create, the relationships we enjoy, and the happiness we create along the road are most important. Wherever we find ourselves that is where we are and where we need to enjoy ourselves. There is no destination, golf course, or retirement to look forward to. Living is your mission, and your business is just part of your vision on how to live it to the fullest. Your mission will never be completely attained while you are still alive because once all of your goals in life are realized, you are ready to leave this earthly existence.

Share the company's mission, vision, and values, and ensure that everyone in the company lives by them. It will make the rest of your work so much easier, as the mission and vision will become beacons to everyone, indicating which direction the company is going, while the shared values will set the boundaries within which everyone and everything will operate. Don't waste time writing a detailed handbook with endless internal rules that sit forgotten and get broken all the time. The alignment of the energy and the intentions and efforts of all people in the company toward your common goals will make you immeasurably stronger than any one individual can ever be alone, and the benefits will compound and accumulate.

"As far as we can discern, the sole purpose of human existence is to kindle a light in the darkness of mere being."

—Carl Jung

Chapter 9

Where Do You Stand?

"People are unreasonable, illogical and self-centered. Love them anyway. If you do good, people may accuse you of selfish motives. Do good anyway. If you are successful you may win false friends and true enemies. Succeed anyway. The good you do today may be forgotten tomorrow. Do good anyway. Honesty and transparency make you vulnerable. Be honest and transparent anyway. What you spend years building may be destroyed overnight. Build anyway. People who really want help may attack you if you help them. Help them anyway. Give the world the best you have and you may get hurt. Give the world your best anyway."

—Mother Teresa

Gautama Buddha said that we become what we think and that all we are is the result of our thoughts. Many recent scientific studies have proven that our genetics and our upbringing may have some impact on where we start out in life, but that our mind is strong enough to make us change into and achieve almost anything we want. There is nothing novel about this idea; in fact, it is at least some three thousand years old.

As a man acts, as he behaves, so he becomes.
He who performs good actions, becomes good.
He who commits crime, becomes a criminal.
By virtuous actions, a man becomes virtuous.
By evil actions, evil.
It is said that man becomes what he desires.

His will follows his desire, as his actions his will.

—(Brihadaranyaka Upanishad, 4.4.5)

For you as an entrepreneur this is good news. You can shape yourself into whoever you want to be. Apart from any restrictions that exist in your mind, there is only one general restriction, and that is what we call the *Golden Rule*. It comes back in virtually every culture in the world, and it is universally accepted as such: *Do unto others what you would have others do unto you.* It sounds simple and in fact is. That's what makes it such a good rule. It applies to any and all situations. Or, in a slightly different connotation by Oprah Winfrey, "Real integrity is doing the right thing, knowing that nobody's going to know whether you did it or not."

And a still less widely used version reminds us that whoever has the gold makes the rules. Two percent of the people in this world possess half of its wealth, while half of its people live on less than two dollars a day. Only 1 percent of the world's population makes more than $30,000 per year. This fundamental unfairness is the root cause of most crime, injustice, war, and misery in the world. Yet, if the whole world were lifted up to the average income level of the American citizen, we would need three earths to supply the necessary resources. It is one of our fundamental tasks while here on earth to right this injustice and inequality.

What is holding us back from doing what we instinctively know is the right thing to do? What prevents us from following the Golden Rule each step and every day? What stops us from living our dreams, from building something really great, or from being the best we can be? There are many things that hold us back; however, these restrictions are all just in our minds. They can be removed once we realize that we can break free from them. Sudhir Kakar compares them with the ropes that guide the elephant inside us. A baby elephant is tied to a certain place with a thick rope. Whatever it tries, it cannot break loose from the strong rope. Ultimately it resigns itself to its fate and no longer tries to break free. Over time the rope is replaced with a thinner rope, and the elephant continues to grow, but because of the memory of the strong rope from when it was a baby elephant it never again tries to test the strength of the rope and forgoes the freedom it could enjoy.

Similarly our self-consciousness, the thought of "what will other people think," is a hurdle preventing us from freeing our mind, from being creative, from thinking outside the box, and from wanting to realize our dreams. We don't even try to do many things in life because we are afraid of making fools of ourselves. We waste a lot of our energy in protecting ourselves and presenting a good, middle-of-the-road, image. As children we did not have such inhibitions, and we were therefore naturally creative. We let dreams and reality intermingle freely. Pablo Picasso once said that all children are born artists but that most are taught to let go of that skill. It is the unjustified fear of the unknown and what might happen that makes us self-conscious. It holds us back and hinders our creativity. When we walk into something in spite of this fear, it simply vanishes because by then the unknown turns into the known. The trick is not to think in terms of conquering fear but rather living with it and being with it. When we let go of our self-consciousness, we become more creative.

Many people think they do not have enough opportunities to showcase their creativity. They think the opportunities depend on other people or are created by other people, and as a direct result their creative abilities remain untapped. It makes no difference for these people because not being creative is not too inconvenient; it keeps them out of the limelight, helps them avoid attention and criticism, and allows them to continue life in quiet desperation. However, being free and creative is a refreshing alternative in a world where many think most solutions come ready-made. If you think everything has already been invented by people smarter than you are, and if you think you have little or nothing to add to the completed creation, (nowhere in the Bible does it say that God went back to work on Monday, after he rested on the seventh day; and had he insisted on a five-day workweek, we would not even have existed) you are wrong. If you believe that most of the things you do have already been researched and the "best" ways to do them have already been discovered, then put this book down right now and return to your day job. If, however, you are motivated by this free feeling, and are yearning to make improvements in our lives, society, and the world, consider being an entrepreneur. It is this mind-frame that sets entrepreneurs apart from the rest of the world. *Nobody is waiting for you to improve your life.* Well, luckily, most entrepreneurs do not think that way. They constantly feel free and are able to come up with improvements to our lives, our society, and our world.

Most of us follow the standard best ways without question. We perform a great number of tasks automatically. Many of these routine tasks are useful, and sticking with them allows us to accomplish many things without even thinking. They save time and space in our conscious mind while the unconscious mind performs the same routine over and over again. Mindfulness is needed to be aware of the automatic things we do, challenge our thoughts and habits, and, if need be, change them. Flickers of inspiration at such moments will help us invent new solutions, better ways, and novel ideas. If we are not very careful, over time we will develop attitudes and assumptions that will prevent us from thinking creatively, locking us into existing routines. We will become a prisoner of familiarity, and we will stop having great ideas. As a result, even when the need arises for us to think differently and generate new ideas, we will be unable to do so.

One of the greatest flaws in education systems today is the focus on the correct answer to a question or problem. When somebody asks a question, you generally give an automatic answer instead of a unique one, fearing it might be wrong. While this approach helps you to function smoothly in society, it hurts creative visualization and original thinking. Real-life issues are ambiguous. There is no one single answer to any problem. There can be several answers if you take the time to think about them. They may all be contradictory and yet all correct.

The fear of failure is something we are raised with and is something that is reinforced in school. It never just goes away. By the time we have finished school, the fear of failure has seeped into our system, and we avoid situations that could result in failure. We are careful about whatever we take on. The fear of failure does not let us try new things, crippling our creativity. Failure is too often seen as an absolute, an objective measure for how *good* one is. Nevertheless, some of the great inventions are the result of monumental mistakes or discarded trials and prototypes.

Creativity requires setting your mind free and finding the connections between things at a higher level. The diversity of your interests and experiences enhances your ability to find connections. If you read a lot, you will get more ideas; if you balance spirit, mind, and body, you will be pleasantly surprised to notice that there is great interrelatedness in almost everything. You start seeing new possibilities when you discover new connections. The great inventions of our times are somehow primitive reflections of what nature had already perfected. A plane, for example, has not yet reached the gracefulness and versatility of a bird; a computer is far from achieving the complexity and the creative thinking power of the brain, and the way the cells in the human body work together is endlessly more subtle and complex than the most efficient organization.

We tend to feel confused by the enormity and the complexity of the unified field of all possibilities, and we feel compelled to resolve any situation quickly, by making our world systematic and orderly again. We are likely to miss the key issues in our haste to do so, and we tend to oversimplify our universe. Albert Einstein said, "If you are not confused, you are not thinking clearly." The universe is infinitely more complex than we can comprehend and express, even though we are a part of it, and it is a part of us.

Something in the way we are being raised, or perhaps it is in our education system, makes us want to know things for sure in advance, rather than let them happen and find them out when the time comes. When it comes to creative thinking, not knowing is a good thing; not being held back by conventional thinking and ambiguity is a great thing. Certainty is the enemy of creative thinking and creative visualization. If we are certain about something, we do not have much leeway to generate new ideas, solve problems, or make our dreams come true.

The need for standard ways of doing things is perfectly legitimate, but then it gives rise to an ever-increasing number of rules that tend to govern our lives. While some of the rules are valid, some are totally unfounded. A former president of Egypt, Anwar Sadat, declared, "He who cannot change the very fabric of his thought will never be able to change reality, and will never, therefore, make any progress."

When we all think alike, none of us is thinking. However, our desire to belong is a powerful one. And in the end, all we want is to fit in. But fitting in is not going to set us free. We all want to be a member of the tribe and fit in, participate in the common tasks, and earn our own piece of the meat that is hunted and the berries that are gathered by the members of the tribe. In order to be free and creative it is important to have a mind of your own. To stand out you need to speak your own mind and to be your own person; you need to speak up. Time and again I am amazed how few people actually do so, even people who I often know are subject experts and have valuable ideas. Mohandas Gandhi taught us that, "A 'No' uttered from the deepest conviction is better than a 'Yes' merely uttered to please, or worse, to avoid trouble." I added this sentence to the "signature" of my e-mails in the hope to entice the people I work with to speak out.

As an entrepreneur, in order to be a creative, effective leader and, perhaps more importantly, a successful businessman, you need to be surrounded by people who dare to contradict you and who provoke you into thinking creatively by challenging your views and questioning your ideas. Many employees are, of course, careful not to have a difference of opinion with you when it comes to big issues, and, naturally for you, it is difficult to lose face or be proven wrong on these issues. Nevertheless it needs to happen.

People start off as unique beings. We are all very different from each other as children and young adults, with our very own likes and dislikes, yet as we enter our thirties, our preferences, needs, and goals somehow begin to converge. They seem to become more and more like one another. Many of us lose our creativity and become boring as well as bored. Many of us even pride ourselves for having firm stands, engrained habits, and inflexible attitudes. We have strong views and unshakable opinions. We become judgmental, blocking or ignoring other points of view. This results in reducing our options and leaving our minds with far fewer opportunities. As a result we generate fewer ideas and solutions. With an open mind, however, we have more choices, as our unconscious mind feeds more ideas into our conscious mind. Most Nobel prizes are won by elderly gentlemen, but the actual original thoughts underlying their life's work in most cases dates back to their twenties or even teens. How old were the inventors of Facebook, Macintosh, or Microsoft? The lesson to be learned: experience and creativity do not necessarily build upon each other.

Often we are in a hurry to find a solution, and we are satisfied with the first one that comes to mind. We stop thinking further, but if we hadn't stopped, our subsequent ideas would have become better and better. If we think we are creative and are convinced we will find the solutions and the ideas, then we will surely find them. Unfortunately, we do not always take the time for this. That is why I believe it is so important to take time out of each day to empty the mind and move away from our day-to-day work and worries. To reach a state of meditation, or *Vipassana*, practice yoga, exercise, or take a long walk and balance your spirit, mind, and body. Having distance helps in freeing and opening up the mind. It allows you to listen again to the voice deep within yourself, as well as the opinions of the people around you, without prejudice.

Once you have come up with your ideas and formulated your solutions, it is important to share them with the people around you. Similarly, you will need to share everything else you have: your experience, your dreams, and your doubts. The more you share and the more you give, the more you will receive in return. What you receive in return is not necessarily money. Money also is not necessarily what makes you rich or satisfies your senses and needs. As the Austrian psychoanalyst Carl Jung acknowledged, "Being unwanted, unloved, uncared for, forgotten by everybody, I think that is a much greater hunger, a much greater poverty than the person who has nothing to eat."

Your true worth is determined by how much more you give in value than you receive in compensation. How much more you will receive in compensation is determined by how many people you serve and by how well you serve them with your deeds. For this to happen you need to place yourself in the position of those others, understand their issues (whatever they may be), and place others' interests above your own. The better you do this, the more people will listen to you. The more they listen, the more they will support you. And the more they support you, the larger your influence will be.

For this, it is imperative to always think and speak well of others. Maharishi Mahesh Yogi, in his commentary to the Bhagavad Gita wrote, "When a man finds fault and speaks ill of others, he partakes of the sins of those of whom he speaks. What comes out indicates what's been inside. If someone never speaks ill of others, that means he has a pure heart, he doesn't have any wrong inside. And if wrong is stored, then the heart is not pure. Never think any wrong thoughts of others, nor speak them out. Never. It's not necessary to use our time and energy of thinking and speaking on something that does not improve our life, that does not help us to grow. It's not worth while. Spend your time and energy and get joy, happiness, evolution, more ability to enjoy, more ability to create."

The following story may illustrate better. There once lived a Brahmin whose wife was a devoted follower of Gautama Buddha. At first, he was indulgent toward her admiration. As her faith in the Buddha increased, the husband began to feel jealous. One day, he went to meet the Buddha with a plan to ask him a question that he thought the Buddha would be incapable of answering. That way, he thought, his wife's reverence for the Buddha would diminish. Face-to-face with the Buddha, he asked, "What is it that must be killed so that we may be able to live in happiness and peace?" The Buddha replied, "To live thus, we have to kill anger, for it is anger that destroys happiness and peace." The Buddha's words so inspired the husband that not only did his anger melt away, but he decided to join the order of monks. Eventually, he became an *arahant*, or enlightened being. His younger brother, on hearing about this transformation, became furious. He confronted the Buddha with a torrent of abuse. The Buddha sat quietly until he had finished. Then he asked the agitated man, "If you served food to a guest at your home, and the guest went away without eating anything, to whom would the food belong?" The Brahmin, caught unaware, replied, "To me, I suppose." Said the Buddha calmly, "Like the guest, I too do not accept your insults, so they belong to you." The Brahmin was left speechless. Like his brother, he realized his folly and joined the monkhood. The other monks who had witnessed this could not contain their admiration for the Buddha's ability to reveal the path of Dharma to even those who inflicted abuse upon him. The Buddha's simple reply to them was, "I do not return one wrong with another …"

Many years ago I visited the Louvre Museum in Paris and became intrigued with the frail statue of *Psyche ré-animeé par le baiser d'amour*, by Antonio Canova. The statue was based on an ancient Greek myth, and over the years I read and reread it a number of times. It is the story of Psyche and Eros or "soul and love." While the story involves various twists and turns, the moral is quite simple. Psyche's journey for her lost love results in terrible tales of suffering. The story tells us that for the soul to awaken and fulfill its potential, pain is necessary. Ultimately the two are united, and from them is born Pleasure.

This tale about Psyche and Eros tells us that the soul has two constants, it is beautiful and comes to its own through love. It tells us we become immortal, not through mystic flights of the transcending spirit, but by the downward path of destruction, pain, and death. We have to embrace the bitterness of our soul made flesh, our bodily mortality, before we attain immortality at the soul level. Contrary to popular belief of ascent through will and work, self-control, and self-denial, this story demonstrates that the one way to unite Soul and Love is through Pleasure.

Pain, suffering, challenge, death, disappointment: all are part of our reality. But if we remain authentic and give all that we have, especially in challenging times, we will prevail. According to Martin Luther King

Jr., "The ultimate measure of a man is not where he stands in moments of comfort and convenience, but where he stands at times of challenge and controversy."

By offering yourself, what you have and what you are, abundantly, to the people you deal with, you will receive manyfold in return. The miracle of the loaves and fishes (Matthew 15:36–37), goes beyond sharing one's lunch with a couple of thousand others. Jesus "took the seven loaves and the fishes, and after giving thanks He broke them and gave them to the disciples, who in turn gave them to the crowds. All ate until they were full." With the right mind-set you all can give abundantly. Move the energies in the universe, and you will be surprised at what happens in return to your modest entrepreneurial company.

> "The waters are in motion all the time, but the moon retains its serenity. The mind moves in response to ten thousand situations, but remains ever the same."
>
> **—Daisetz T. Suzuki**

Chapter 10

How Can You Be a Leader and Be Followed?

"The more you care about the powerless, the more power you have. The more you serve those with no influence, the more influence God gives you. The more you humble yourself, the more you are honored by others."

—Mother Teresa

Stacks of books and countless articles have been written on leadership. Some are really detailed guides on how the perfect leader thinks and operates; others include the description of heroic figures, while still others spell out leadership lessons from the lives of people who lived long before corporations (as we know them) were invented. Books such as Sun Tzu's *Art of War* or Machiavelli's *Il Principe* make for interesting and amusing reading and describe extraordinary feats by outstanding—at the least very eccentric—individuals. Do not become intimidated by the concept of leadership and lose sight of the fact that literally anyone can be a leader provided he has the followers. There is no need to be a superhuman or resort to extreme measures in order to be an effective leader. Leadership is a skill that can be acquired. Being a leader is a choice you can consciously make. Leadership is a responsibility, not a privilege, which makes you accountable to the group you choose to lead. Nobody can make you a leader but yourself. And luck has nothing to do with it. It is not luck that makes leaders, but leaders who make luck. Napoleon Bonaparte usually promoted his "luckiest" commanders, as he recognized that their "luck" would increase with their responsibilities. Thus the old adage, *the harder*

I work, the luckier I get. The opportunities you need to be successful are created, not found by accident.

According to Sudhir Kakar, recent neuroscience research using brain imaging has made scientifically clear what we, of course, have always known: the human brain is a social organ. Its physiological and neurological reactions are directly and profoundly shaped by social interaction. A human being is first and foremost a social animal. It has been demonstrated time and again that the daily activities most closely associated with happiness are social: working in a team, socializing after work, having dinner with friends, having sex, etc. Being part of a group that meets just once a month produces the same amount of happiness as the happiness that doubling your income produces. Many of the professions that correlate most closely with happiness are also the more social ones, such as corporate executive, personal trainer, and hairdresser.

But to come back to the social brain and its importance for organizational life, the brain experiences the workplace first and foremost as a social system. People who feel unrecognized or who have low self-esteem at work experience this as a neural impulse as powerful and painful as a blow to the head. The same neural region involved in the suffering of pain becomes active also in the experience of physical pain. The ability to intentionally address or target the social brain will be a critical leadership skill in the coming years.

I believe this cannot be achieved by creating a formal, hierarchical organization, where people have a place and a space determined by organizational charts, manuals, and procedures, but rather by creating a tribe-like culture where every member is valued and contributes according to his abilities. This is where employees feel appreciated for their contributions. The leaders of such organizations lead based on their ideas, their charisma, and the strength of their personalities, and not by the place they occupy in a formal hierarchy. A formal hierarchy may shed some clarity on what each person's role and responsibility are in an organization, but it must never become a limitation to people being creative, taking responsibility, helping each other, serving customers, making decisions, thinking for the company, and powering the company ahead. Too much structure, as well as too many rules, procedures, and formalities, kills all creativity in a company, and, as a result, its clients suffer. Even Jack Welch, a very successful propagator of well-structured big business, acknowledges, "In an organization where managers look up toward the CEO, they have their ass toward the customers."

So, what do you need to be an effective leader? The following is my list, which I do not claim to be exhaustive:

- **Authenticity.** Be yourself; do not try to copy the actions of someone you admire or whom you think is perfect. Do not act in ways that feel unnatural to you. You were created to be yourself—so be yourself! Don't act like someone you are not. Ultimately your true self will reveal itself. You can teach a tiger to jump through hoops and sit up, but sooner or later when you turn your back it will be a predator again.

- **Have a clear vision.** A company can have only one vision, and creating it is not a team sport; it has to come from the leader. It must be clearly formulated, and it should be revisited often. It needs to be reflected in and lived through your daily actions. It should be the measuring stick against which all actions of the organization are judged. Within the vision, creativity needs to be stimulated, and innovation and diversity in ideas encouraged.

- **Courage.** Someone has to take the risks, make the decisions, and keep the place humming. Even a turtle has to stick its neck out in order to move forward. The buck stops with you. People without considerable personal courage will never be good leaders. From time to time you will have to "boldly go where no man has ever gone before." Inevitably, mistakes should be recognized quickly and dealt with. On the larger, more meaningful issues, again, too much democracy will not work. Timid resolutions will not work, and neither will half-hearted plans. Small steps will get you nowhere, but bold steps may lead you to success.

- **Passion.** If you do not love what you do almost every day, you had better stop doing it. Passion is what spurs you over the many obstacles you come across on a daily basis. Passion is contagious; it is the oil that keeps the motor of the organization humming when things are not going smoothly. Without passion you will not be able to distinguish yourself positively from any competitor. Passion is the very foundation for success. Interestingly, it is derived from the Latin word for suffering. The two go hand in hand. If you have no deep passion for your business, everyone around it will sense that immediately and act accordingly. Without your passion there is nobody else's passion.

- **Initiative.** Action needs to be taken, while growth and evolution should be directed. The institution and its organization need to be designed and regularly adjusted. Ideas should be generated and decisions made. Do not worry about the decisions being correct 100 percent of the time— just make them. More companies go under because of inertia than because of wrong decisions. And remember, you have not failed to reach the finish line as long as you are still breathing. Pursue your ideas, and surpass your goals.

- **Motivation.** You will need to inspire others to share the vision, understand the mission, live by the values, and seek collaborative solutions to problems. However, remember that there is only one person to motivate you, and that is yourself. Your motivation needs to come from within. And the motivation of the others in your organization needs to come from within themselves. If it is not there, they had better look for something else to do—something else that lights their fire.

- **Compassion.** All of the people you work with, be they colleagues, employees, vendors, clients, or competitors, have their own personal goals in life. You will reach your goals when you can align your actions in such a way that you help them reach their goals. You will need to invest time and listen carefully to the hidden messages in what people tell you. Your success depends on the success of all the others around you. Mistakes will be made, in fact many, but be considerate for the mistakes that are made once, and tough on the ones that are made repeatedly.

- **Integrity.** You need to "walk your talk"; make sure you "say what you do and do what you say." If there is inconsistency between what you say and what you do, people will not follow you. If, for instance, you preach equality; don't have one group of employees fly business class while another flies coach. If you promote honesty, you have no choice but to fire people who steal from the company, even if it is only telephone time or stationery. Consistency in all your actions is vitally important.

- **Humility.** Even at the top of the corporate food chain, you cannot do it alone. Be humble, thankful, and appreciative of anyone who helps. Keep studying and learning as much as you can. Do not overcompensate yourself and others at the top at the expense of those further down. Everyone is important, and all need to share commensurately in the success of the company.

- **Moral Compass.** Most, if not all, of the above nine characteristics are also shared by the great dictators, the most successful criminals and the most unscrupulous of business tycoons. A sound moral compass is needed to make sure all the good characteristics also point toward following the right path to goals that benefit society as a whole, and not just toward the selfish, criminal, or greedy goals of a limited group, which is described later in the chapter on happiness.

Steven Covey, one of the most influential business thinkers, has defined the following Seven Habits of Highly Successful People:

- **Be Proactive.** You take responsibility for your own behavior. You choose how you feel under any given set of circumstances and how you react to the situation. You are not the victim of the circumstances. You create them and dictate them.

- **Begin with the end in mind.** You have a clear dream and vision of what you want to achieve. You live in accordance with deeply held beliefs and principles and understand you are connected to and responsible for everything else in the universe.

- **Put first things first.** You lead a disciplined life. You focus on what is important and has long-term impact, as opposed to what seems urgent but does not add value in the long run.

- **Think win-win.** You understand there is *enough* for everybody. You understand that for one person to succeed, it is not necessary for someone else to lose (abundance mentality). You look for solutions that are synergetic, are socially responsible, and have the least environmental impact.

- **Seek first to understand, then to be understood.** You listen with the intent to truly understand the other person's feelings, emotions, and thoughts. You do not draw conclusions before you are sure you understand.

- **Synergize.** You try and find solutions in which everyone wins. You choose alternatives that serve everyone's needs. You are creative.

- **Sharpen the saw.** You continue to learn and constantly use each experience as a way to improve your skills, feel deeper, and refine your thinking.

So what does this mean for your day-to-day activities as a leader of a team of people? There is no need to take the above list in the morning and decide which one of the skills as a leader you will be working on that day. You will need to work on all of them all the time, without becoming overworked and stressed out. As a leader you will need quiet time as well to reflect, to think, and to be creative. So if you add new tasks to your schedule, make sure to delegate old tasks to people who will feel empowered and motivated by the responsibilities and authority bestowed upon them.

Be yourself; be passionate about what you do; be the best you can be—again, every day. Deeply love all of the people you work with: your employees, your clients, your suppliers. Help them become successful. See yourself as their humble servant. If everyone around you becomes successful, you will be successful as well.

Joel Garfinkle said, "The task is to recognize that you are uniquely special, have something to give, some talent no one else shares in quite the same way. This gift needs to blossom so we can appreciate and enjoy the benefits of it and acknowledge you for it. You owe this to yourself and to all of us to honor your gifts, for only when you share your unique joy with the world does the entire world benefit. Every advance mankind has known has come because of someone's effort. Don't let shyness rob you and the world of the power and the passion that lies within you. No one can be all that you will be except you yourself. Follow your passion."

If you help the people around you become successful, you can gradually move from being the strategist to becoming the visionary. To draw once more on an old analogy with war, armies have served as models for large-scale organizations since long before big business was invented. The sergeants and the field commanders worry about tactics—how to take a particular hill or to effectively and efficiently reach a specific short-term goal. The generals worry more about strategy—how to conduct a major operation or a specific attack. The military's high command worries mostly about logistics—how to get the right men and materials in the right place at the right moment and how to outmaneuver the enemy by having the upper hand in both men and materials. Wars are usually won based on the relative strength of the underlying economies. How quickly and efficiently an economy can finance, organize, and produce a build-up in war materials and men is in direct relation to its success. The Cold War ended when the West could both outspend and outdevelop the Soviet Union in offensive capacity. It is the same in a company. You win if you are able to organize overwhelming force or are able to deploy the forces that you have so effectively and efficiently that you can outmaneuver the competition and gain market share and brand recognition. Your vision is key to aligning all the people who make the actual difference.

In 1988, my wife and I visited China. In Shanghai we took a trip on the Yangtze Kiang River past the swamps and rundown industrial areas of Pudong. Upon returning, at the dock we saw a small exhibition with a scale model of how the Pudong skyline was to look twenty years hence. It was a very futuristic skyline, straight from the *Jetsons* comics. People who passed by smiled at it or made sarcastic or disbelieving remarks. But twenty years later, it was all there and more. The Chinese government over the past thirty years has been extremely visionary and meticulous in converting its dreams and vision into reality. As a result, a large part of the Chinese population has been lifted from poverty in a relatively short period of time and can aspire to a much better life. Visionary leadership can, with time, hard work, and discipline, build incredible things. In spite of its obvious shortcomings, I have a lot of respect for what Chinese leadership has achieved during these last three decades.

The first time (long ago) that I told some of my close friends (in confidence) that a handful of us were building (in oversimplified words) a $100 million company, they laughed at the concept. Now that this is basically true, they are applauding the effort. The vision and the results are inseparable. If you do not start with a clear vision, and a "Big, Hairy, Audacious Goal," you cannot visualize what you need to do to achieve it. Once you have the vision, every step you take brings you a little closer to your goals. Ultimately you are bound to reach your goals, 100 percent success guaranteed.

To bring across the vision, you will at times need to be a strong commander. Sir Richard Branson, in his book *Screw It, Let's Do It*, tells us that you have to have guts in business. You will need to make the tough business and moral decisions that will put and keep the machine in motion. Do not become distracted by the people who complain or object. In Cervantes's *Don Quixote,* "The dogs continue barking, but the caravan just moves on."

As your team grows, you will be more and more often the storyteller rather than the commander, explaining the mission and the vision, and guarding the values of the company. Telling stories helps to create a picture in people's minds, leaving a much clearer imprint than any rules or handbooks. During hundreds of thousands of years of human existence, children were taught to hunt and gather by following their parents, who explained and demonstrated how to do it. Traditions and cultural habits and how the world and the universe work were explained in the evening around the campfires. Most people are still fascinated by the magic glow of campfires on a deserted beach or deep in a dark forest, and many people still feel a deep need to share unusual stories when quietly sitting around a campfire. Books were invented only a few thousand years ago, and most people learned to read only in the past century or so. But it is still more instructive to study people than books. Our mind picks up stories much easier and achieves a much deeper level of understanding than with instructions and printed materials. Take the time to build campfires and share your campfire stories.

When will you know you have become an effective leader? Look behind you and see who is following you. By definition, you are a leader only if other people are actually following you. You must lead from the front, always and courageously, and, therefore, you need to be ahead of your troops. But make sure you are not so far ahead that your followers can no longer hear you or see you.

Never allow your pace to be slowed down by the negative people around you. Ignore those for whom the glass is half-empty, who repeatedly complain, speak badly about others, and foretell disasters and obstacles. If you listen to them, you will never get anywhere. Just quietly ignore them and concentrate instead on the cheerful, optimistic people, who focus on the opportunities, for whom the glass is half-full, who see the good in other people, and who are optimistic and have their view resolutely on the bright horizon.

"We must, therefore, be confident that the general measures we have adopted will produce the results we expect. Most important in this connection is the trust which we must have in our lieutenants. Consequently, it is important to choose men on whom we can rely and to put aside all other considerations. If we have made appropriate preparations, taking into account all possible misfortunes, so that we shall not be lost immediately if they occur, we must boldly advance into the shadows of uncertainty."

—Karl von Clausewitz

Chapter 11

What Can You Manage and What Not?

"When making a decision of minor importance, I have always found it advantageous to consider all the pros and cons. In vital matters, however, such as the choice of a mate or a profession, the decision should come from the unconscious, from somewhere within ourselves. In the important decisions of personal life, we should be governed, I think, by the deep inner needs of our nature."

—Sigmund Freud

You can lead people, but you manage projects, issues, and departments. Even though people often confuse the two, leadership and management, there is a fundamental difference. The most important thing to manage and the core of any business process is cash flow. Whether you run a multinational company, a local restaurant, or a corner store, your cash flow is much more important than your net profits. You need to manage your business processes, keep your inventories low, collect your receivables, write off your bad debt, and depreciate your assets and also your old inventory. Many small businesses, although profitable, get into trouble by being too lenient on their business partners. Suppliers who do not deliver punctually need to be replaced swiftly. Customers who do not pay on time are no longer customers and should be eliminated. Investments also need to be made on time. Many investments need a long lead time to become productive. They need to be spread over time to have optimal effect on sales and minimal effect on cash outflows. If renovation and investments are postponed for too long, the quality and uniqueness of your products and services will diminish, and one day you will discover you are no longer as competitive as you once were. By then it is often too late to start investing, as, again, many investments need several years to mature to productivity.

You will need to constantly invest in new products and services. Whether this is in technology for the next generation of high-tech products, or by adjusting the menu in your neighborhood restaurant, your continued attention is required.

Your products and services need to be of top quality and need to permanently stay at top quality. There can be no concessions here. Whatever reaches the client in products and services needs to be right the first time. Your technology needs to be up-to-date, your packaging needs to be just right, your trade partners need to be treated with respect, and your service must be legendary. Being a highly ethical company with solid corporate responsibility helps to create the optimum brand image.

As mentioned before, it all starts and ends with top quality. The quality of whatever you produce or deliver needs to be consistently high. Having a reputation for excellent quality is your best sales tool. *Kaizen*, where literally everyone in the organization is encouraged to come up with regular small improvements, will lead to a spectacular increase in the number of useful suggestions for improvements and a marked increase in long-term quality. An open culture, where all involved are invited to speak their minds, is necessary as well. Focus needs to be on *processes* that can be improved, and not on *people* who do things incorrectly. Tough decisions and a lot of sacrifices may be needed to achieve top quality. Stop your production process as often as you need to, and forego as many sales as it takes in order to achieve and maintain top quality.

Creative thinking in an open corporate culture needs to be promoted; it is imperative when change is needed. As Boris Yeltsin advocated, "It is especially important to encourage unorthodox thinking when the situation is critical. At such moments every new word and fresh thought is more precious than gold. Indeed, people must not be deprived of the right to think their own thoughts."

To become a *number one* company, you need to make sure your employees are happy with themselves, so they are fully motivated to work for themselves. This is to be combined with a positive culture that is fully committed to quality and excellent client service, and where the evaluations focus on positive items, and the negative ones are dealt with appropriately. Good behavior needs to be rewarded. Bad behavior needs to be discussed and worked on, but not dealt with in overly negative ways. A negative approach never leads to a positive outcome. Criticism and harsh words take a lot of time to repair.

Empowerment and noninterference by letting everyone do his task will result in further improvements. Without far-reaching empowerment you cannot and will not cultivate an aggressive risk-taking culture, obtain quick decisions and quick actions, and achieve double-digit growth. Anyone, at any level, who makes decisions should be held accountable for those decisions.

The organization needs to stay lean. Waste needs to be eliminated at any level and regularly so that preventing it from occurring in the first place becomes second nature. Keeping the company's carbon footprint as low as possible as well as recycling or reusing as many materials as possible is smart. Luxury is not needed in most types of businesses, unless of course you are running a five-star hotel, restaurant, or spa.

You will need to standardize and centralize what is back-office or production, but customize what actually touches the clients and bring that as close to the clients as possible. All processes need to be focused on the client and need to work to the benefit of the clients and not just the organization. In any production organization there is tension between what the sales people want to sell (everything) and what the production people want to produce (one standard product). Just as a restaurant needs to offer choices, any company offering services and products needs to have choices as well as various price-points linked to the various service levels or product specifications.

Whether your company is a multinational or a neighborhood flower shop, your management issues are more or less the same. Even the flower shop needs to make sure the roses are fresh and the rent is paid. The receivables need to be under control, and the reputation in the community needs to be one of friendliness, superior quality, and dependability. Innovative ways to outperform other flower shops in the area must be on the forefront of the company's mind, in fact on the mind of everyone in the company.

Any process or procedure needs to strike a balance between being people-friendly and process friendly. Back-office people and organizational "experts" have the tendency to organize processes in strict flow charts, with limited decision points where thinking may take place. These approaches have their value in high-volume, standardized processes but should be handled with the utmost care in processes that are closer to the client. Nobody likes to be treated as a number or addressed through an automated voice machine. Never be tricked into converting your company into an impersonal organization where client requests are rerouted to anonymous help desks, and employees believe "big brother" is watching them.

Production and results information should be shared on a monthly basis with all of the people who are involved in the relevant figures. Solicit everyone's input so as to improve for the next month. Maintain a sense of urgency, or as my Korean friend K. R. Kim said, "Leaders should always create crisis, even during good times. When an organization feels comfortable with its success, its competitors are alert to prepare the next attack. Organizations must always prepare for the next battle. They have to always be innovative in terms of cost, productivity, and product planning. Business environment does not accept 'Happy Hour'."

The sense of urgency adds to the intensity of the process. Constantly delivering top quality requires concentration and a certain healthy level of tension. To feel challenged and stretched, a certain pressure on projects and results is needed. Goals always need to be stretch goals, targets always need to be realistic but stretch targets. Everyone should go home at the end of the day fulfilled and satisfied with the day's work, yet ready to come back the next day and further stretch the quality, goals, and production processes, until one day the company is perceived by the clients, the market, and society as a top-quality, number one company.

All these management skills have very little to do with your actual technical skills and your professional education. They are all based on your attitude, your value system, and the way you perceive the world and your role in it. A few years ago my wife and I decided to invest in the business of a South African friend of ours. He was a *Boer* and a farmer who left South Africa when *apartheid* ended but had always been desperate to get back. He had built a nice ostrich farm and an aloe vera plantation in Curaçao, and he now wanted to create a much larger aloe vera project in South Africa. We looked at the investment as a way to get to know the country and the culture, enjoy the wildlife, help out a friend, and be involved from the sidelines in a more back-to-basics and "earthly" business than the trust business. Together we bought a beautiful twelve-hundred-hectare farm with lots of game, including different types of antelopes, giraffes, zebras, etc.; we built a vacation home, and our friend began planting aloe vera as well as developing the plan to build a processing plant.

Then disaster struck, and our friend died in a car accident close to the farm. We were faced with the choice of abandoning the project, writing off at least most of our, for us significant, investment, and complaining about our bad luck. Or, we could continue with the project ourselves. We decided for the latter, and we bought out the widow of our friend. We picked up the pieces of the project (he being a farmer, of course, nothing was well organized or on paper), and we learned how to be aloe vera farmers. We also learned how to manage a game farm, how to build a factory, and how to deal with South African red tape and *confirmative action*, conservative and skeptical neighbors, a totally different culture, and the list goes on. We moved our daughter to boarding school in South Africa, and we somehow juggled our lives outside of South Africa while living 425 kilometers from the airport and one hundred kilometers from the nearest decent supermarket and restaurant.

A year and a half later we celebrated the official opening of our brand-new factory and, shortly thereafter, the launch of our first health drinks and body care products. At the opening ceremony we invited the farmers in the area, and I made a speech using the same words I quote from former president Nelson Mandela at the beginning of chapter 2. Although in that part of the Transvaal, Mandela is still seen by "bitter-enders" as a terrorist, farmers began working with us, as they respected our perseverance, commitment, and love for the land and the nature. I think it is when these types of decisions cross your path, the men are separated from the boys, and the entrepreneurs from the mere dreamers.

> *"This is the true joy in life, the being used for a purpose recognized by yourself as a mighty one; the being thoroughly worn out before you are thrown on the scrap heap; the being a force of Nature instead of a feverish selfish little clod of ailments and grievances complaining that the world will not devote itself to making you happy."*
>
> **—George Bernard Shaw**

Chapter 12

Do Teams Work?

"You may consider yourself an individual, but as a cell biologist, I can tell you that you are in truth a cooperative community of approximately fifty trillion single-celled citizens. Almost all of the cells that make up your body are amoeba-like individual organisms that have developed a cooperative strategy for their mutual survival. Reduced to basic terms, human beings are simply the consequence of 'collective amoebic consciousness.' As a nation reflects the traits of its citizens, our human-ness must reflect the basic nature of our cellular communities."

—Bruce H. Lipton

Teamwork is essential for success. What can be done by a group of people committed to common goals is many times more than what can be achieved by any one individual alone. Traditionally the success of a team was often measured on the basis of the strength of its leadership. But teams don't always need strong leaders. Many teams function best with limited involvement from the leader once the goals and the operating boundaries (mission, vision, and values) are clearly established.

One of the most successful and often studied (but never successfully copied) teams is that of the *dabbawallahs, a* lunch-box delivery system, in Mumbai, India. Mahadu Bacche, a native of Maval, came to Mumbai in 1890, looking for work. He worked at several odd jobs, including unloading cargo ships and hauling goods for traders, until he had the inspiration for the lunch-box delivery service. He began transporting hot food from homes to government offices in the Fort District on foot. His Maval compatriots, joining him shortly afterwards, began to be called *bhonawalas*—the meal men—by Parsi housewives.

They began spending their days walking from kitchen to office canteen as they connected middle-class south Mumbai with the imperial business district. The suburban railways in their present form were fashioned in part after their business. Women workers made gradual inroads into similar areas of industry, but the *dabbawallahs* remained a singularly male organization.

Their job was always about incredible physical stamina. Today, the *dabbawallah* might not walk from home to office, but carrying up to seventy-five kilograms of dead weight on a rush-hour morning train is considerably more challenging. As Mumbai stretched out and workers' commute times increased, so did the scope of the *dabbawallahs'* job.

Carrying a *dabba* (tiffin) from Parel to Fort may be a matter of comfort, allowing fresh food to arrive hot on a lunch table. But carrying one over the considerably longer distance from Borivali to Colaba and delivering it on time with Six Sigma precision is more about distributing labor. At such a distance, workers may start out from home well before lunch is made. The *dabbawallah* is a way to manage time for both the cook and the consumer.

In a city that developed haphazardly as a gigantic workhouse, organizations like the *dabbawallahs* are symbolic of how links between people can make up for, and sometimes overcome, the deficiencies of infrastructure. Like the markets around railway stations that stay open long into the night so returning commuters may shop for dinner, or small neighborhood stores that offer home delivery for even a single strip of paracetamol, the *dabbawallahs* are part of a vast unstructured labor force that exists primarily to make life in Mumbai easier: a service economy by any other name.

Despite faltering in the 1980s, thanks to internal administrative issues and radical changes to Mumbai's industries, the *dabbawallah* service survived, and by some reports continues to grow even today. Long after the demise of the large mills, the increasingly flexible work-hours in white-collar businesses, and the rapid rise of restaurants around work areas, approximately five thousand *dabbawallahs* still carry the colorfully coded lunch boxes to work every day, within two-minute time slots, for Rs.400–450 (Approximately 8-9 US dollars) a month. Their cooperative policies ensure that almost every *dabbawallah* earns Rs.6,000–8,000 a month.

The Gandhi cap covers the *dabbawallahs'* only computer—their head. Not wearing it makes a *dabbawallah* liable for an Rs.25 fine; the organization enforces this and other social rules rigorously. If it makes their work seem archaic, it also implies an unusually old network of trust. Today, young men from Maval still come to the city to stay with relatives, join the *dabbawallah* network and take over the running of the *tiffins* the way their compatriots did for generations. The efficiency, Six Sigma quality, and accuracy of the system have been qualities that myths are derived from. Countless organizations have studied what makes the system work. It has a minimal organization structure, it is an association rather than a corporation, and it works on the basis of color codes, combined with an unusual level of trust and camaraderie between the *dabbawallahs*. So far, nobody has really been able to copy the system.

There are other examples of companies run with minimal leadership. Morning Star is a tomato-processing company based in California, with annual revenues of $700 million and over four hundred employees. What makes the company remarkable is that it has no bosses, no titles, and no promotions. Anybody has the authority to spend the company's money; job responsibilities are negotiated among peers, and any compensation is peer-based. Morning Star is a company that has dispensed with management in the traditional sense of the word; that is, a group of chosen people in whom decision making is concentrated. Everyone takes part in the decision-making process, and decisions are made in the best interests of the company and its employees. The company is very successful. It has had double-digit growth in revenues and profits, while the industry's rate is 1 percent. It has funded its growth entirely through internal resources. It claims to be the most efficient tomato processor in the world. It became a *Harvard Business Review* cover story.

Studies at large manufacturing companies have proven time and again that, at a certain level and point in time, scale is no longer an advantage. It can even become a drag, as the ever-increasing complexity of the organization can reduce its creativity, nimbleness, and client focus. It has been proven that in units as small as seventy or eighty people, so many complex activities can be created as well as so much internal communication and so many internal responsibilities, that everyone can feel useful and busy without ever having a genuine client contact. This, of course, completely defies the original purpose of the organization. Some companies have subsequently cut up their organization into very small teams, and the result has been remarkable increases in efficiency and reduction in waste.

In your own organization, you will need to closely observe whenever you add a new layer of management, separate out a function, outsource a task, create more procedures, or add steps to the workflow. Decide whether those well-intended improvements actually lead to better and faster service. If not, you may want to consider making changes in a different way.

Open-source software is another rapidly developing area without a central command or a management team making all of the decisions. Many people enthusiastically contribute to the development of the system without wanting anything in return. As a result, it can be expected that open-source software will become the norm rather than the exception over the next ten years. Wikipedia is another example of a great service that has grown exponentially in spite of having a minimal formal organizational structure. Many people contribute their time and knowledge in order to build a knowledge base that benefits anyone with an Internet connection.

In the mid-1960s, Peter Drucker suggested the idea of the modern organization of knowledge workers (distinct from manual workers) in which it would be necessary to reduce the levels of hierarchy. Drucker argued that people with highly developed skills or expertise can give their best only through self-motivation and not through guidance from above. He predicted that with the rise of knowledge workers, firms would tend to become flatter. He was proven right. Since Thomas Friedman made the whole world flat by the inventions of the nineteen-nineties, things moved really fast.

Small-scale outsourcing to countries such as India started in the early 1990s when airline companies had their tickets processed there. Companies set up small-scale call centers and data-processing centers— pure back-office activities. When the Y2K problem was dreamed up (as you may remember, many computer systems were supposedly going to fail as legacy software had allegedly not been designed to deal with the change in the millennium), enormous numbers of IT experts were needed, and huge outsourcing centers sprang up in places like Hyderabad and Bangalore. After the Y2K problem was solved (or proven to be a hoax) those people needed to be kept gainfully employed, and other ways of outsourcing were devised. Very simple call centers helping with complaint settlements and advice on how to set your VCR, to very sophisticated knowledge-processing units were developed. As a result, useful skills in the outsourcing centers became scarcer, and salaries went up.

Not to be defeated, outsourcing companies now go "up-country," further from the big university towns, to secondary cities. Now, even the most traditional communities in Rajastan have been reached, where women, who are by religion prohibited from showing their faces and meeting strangers, work with a laptop and a satellite connection from their mud homes. They explain to people thousands of miles away how insurance claims will be settled or how tax returns must be filled. They earn a quarter or even less of what their counterparts in the big cities earn, and they do not need expensive office space.

In the meantime, competition is growing in the Philippines, and so the race for "value" continues. At Amicorp, we now routinely split outsourcing work into higher and lower value-added pieces, so the production of a standard set of financial statements may require the involvement of up to three different outsourcing centers. For example, we may use the Philippines for simple scanning and sorting work, India for actually making the booking entries and compiling the financial statements, and South Africa for the language skills to render the report in the mother tongues of the clients in Europe, who may not even realize their work is done in far-reaching parts of the globe. This is comparable to the food you eat and the clothes you wear. Much of it comes from an ever-increasing variety of countries.

Investment banks, which have a high concentration of knowledge workers, usually have very few levels of management. A large investment bank has hundreds of managing directors. A star trader could be a managing director without even having subordinates. However, while the number of levels has fallen steeply, few firms have been able to dispense with hierarchy entirely. The accomplishment of the tomato company, mentioned earlier, is that it has been able to abolish hierarchy altogether and that too in a manufacturing context. Everybody is involved in making decisions, setting targets, and reviewing performance.

A key element in Morning Star's model is what is called the "Colleague Letter of Understanding" (CLOU). Every employee negotiates his CLOU with all those affected by his work. This letter stipulates what each employee is to accomplish in a given year. Similarly, the company's twenty-three business units negotiate CLOUs with each other. Important decisions, such as staffing, are made entirely by colleagues working together. There are no promotions or demotions, as there is no formal hierarchy. People take on greater responsibilities after persuading their colleagues they can deliver. Disputes are settled via discussion, mediation, or decisions made by groups of six people. Performance is measured through feedback from colleagues on one's CLOU. Compensation is decided through elected compensation committees.

There are not many companies yet that consistently follow this model (although many larger organizations have introduced bits and pieces of it). Mom-and-pop shops have, of course, always worked like this all over the world, but this demonstrates it can also work in large companies.

Where is the lesson for your company? If you are not ready to abolish management completely, or even to eliminate some of it, you may still want to empower your employees to the maximum, by trusting them and by letting them make their own mistakes and take full responsibility for them. Teamwork needs to be achieved in some way. Interests need to be aligned.

Some internal competition may be useful. Teams who compete for the best performance in any given area, who deliver the best service, and who produce the most, can prove very useful. It can be very rewarding to have the best performers of a given month and year publicly awarded and recognized. It is also a good idea to incentivize this by creating bonuses, employee stock-option plans, and a certain level of performance-based compensation. Good salespeople are typically *Type A* individuals, who enjoy being in the limelight, who crave recognition and competition, and who need constant reassurance. Their needs should be met but kept in check.

Great care needs to be given in devising the system where rivalry is in the best interests of the customers. That rivalry should focus on creating better service or realizing more sales; and not on outperforming the others by making another team lose, infringing on sales teams' territories, or undercutting the pricing of another team. The larger team, the company, is always the more important one, and any form of internal competition that damages the overall team performance needs to be nipped in the bud. Do not spend too much time on devising complicated internal allocation systems. There is only one bottom line that really counts, and that is the "triple bottom line" of the overall company, not the results of the artificial internal subdivisions of the company. Employees need to be kept aware of that so as to avoid wasting resources in turf-wars.

The organization needs to be geared toward teamwork. It needs to help its people understand that they are not victims of society but the creators of it and can achieve anything they want to achieve, and much more if working as a team.

For this its members need to understand that, however much they see themselves as unique individuals, as separate souls, they are basically one with the universe, one with society, and one with their colleagues, and they will bring out the best in themselves if they work and live from that premise. A good read is Bruce Lipton's latest book, *Spontaneous Evolution*. He and coauthor Steve Bhaerman suggest that our cells are smarter than we are when it comes to creating successful cooperative communities. They explain how cells basically work as separate individuals but organize themselves to have a monetary system that pays other cells according to the importance of the work they do and stores excess profits in community banks. They have a research and development system that creates technology and biochemical equivalents of expansive computer networks. They have sophisticated environmental systems that provide air and water purification treatment that is more technologically advanced than humans have yet been able to develop. The same is true for heating and cooling systems. Just as in modern companies, the communication system within and amongst cells is like an Internet that sends zip-coded messages directly to individual cells. Unlike us, cells have organized full health-care coverage that makes sure each cell gets what it needs to stay healthy, as well as an immune system that protects the cells and the body like a dedicated police force. It makes for an intriguing analogy when you compare fifty trillion cells in the human body working together for the success of the individual with seven billion human beings working together for the success of the planet. Lipton points out that we haven't been doing nearly as good a job as cells.

Just as airplanes have not yet been able to copy the flight qualities of birds, and computers have not yet been able to copy the intuition of the brain, it will take a while before our society at large is able to copy the workings of a community of cells. Of course, there is also that small thing of a couple of billion years of development to consider.

Any company can and should provide mutual dependence and a shared identity, as well as supported diversity and mutual inspiration. This helps to grow self-awareness, to improve self-reliance, and to develop mutual respect for each member's strengths and weaknesses. It is important for all members to realize that the organization does not exist without its members, and that the members add new dimensions and challenges to their lives as a result of being part of the company. At the same time, the company provides safety, moral and financial support, and help in darker days. From the safety of the "tribe" that the company closely mimics, the person can work on his self-image, self-confidence, and self-sovereignty.

This strengthens the person to a level where he can be independent within the company. He can create original thoughts and ideas while being fully aligned with its vision and its goals. He can generate not only diversity within unity, but also unity within diversity.

Our company has set up forty offices in twenty-seven countries. Very often we would not know many people in the country when we first started up. We would begin hiring the very few we knew, or those who were recommended by the very few we knew. Many of the people we would hire would not come from our industry, but gradually would grow into our culture, adding to our diversity and adding more flavor and color to the mix of our company.

I love travelling to India. In the course of my life, I have been there at least fifty times. Whether I arrive at Amritsar, Bangalore, Mumbai, or Delhi, I always enjoy the moment I first step on the street. I am embraced by the busyness, the smells of food everywhere, the noise of the motor-rickshaws, the occasional cow crossing the street, and the impressive helpfulness and friendliness of the people. I, however, never really get used to their decision-making models. First of all, in India it is considered impolite to say *no*. People would rather promise you the moon and make you feel happy today than tell you the truth and know you will be disappointed tomorrow. My Indian colleagues are constantly trying to say what they think I want to hear, while I, as a straightforward

European, am always trying to get to the truth and figure out exactly what they think. When possible our Indian colleagues refer any and all decisions to a next higher level, leaving even the simplest decisions with the person in charge. There is an attempt to move everything to the all-knowing head office so nobody can get blamed for making a wrong decision. The problem is, the solutions are most obvious where the issues lie. Nevertheless, at any evaluation the exact same people will want to get higher up in the organization and capture a decision-making position. To break through a cultural pattern like this is, at least for me, really difficult. It is not enough to understand it, to discuss it with the people involved, and to make jokes about it. It also requires grit and perseverance to *change* behavioral patterns that are not constructive for the performance of the unit. This can be done gracefully but needs to be done forcefully. Predetermination and defeatism do not appear in the "thesaurus function" of an entrepreneur.

A company with a good and strong culture can influence the mind-set of the people who work there. Train people to think independently and quickly and to act decisively and effectively by showing them complete trust and allowing them to experiment with approaches that may or may not work. Empower them to have their own ideas and opinions, make their own decisions, and make their own mistakes (but not repeat them). And, alternately, the employee can make this work and become an effective leader himself by *accepting* the challenge, *embracing* the responsibility, and *wanting* full accountability for the tasks at hand.

The ones who will not make it and who you should not promote to be leaders, however successful they may be in their area of core competency, are the ones who are distrustful and who claim all honors for themselves and blame all failures on their team. They are the ones who are looking for internal competition, instead of cooperation within the company and with clients and suppliers; they are the ones who are impatient, expect miracles, have little self-confidence, and who are rude to people lower down in the organization.

Mutual trust is established by listening carefully to the opinions of everyone, by giving full empowerment and consistent sharing of all relevant information, and by making sure you maintain a culture of openness, in which information, including financial information, is freely shared. Trust is further enhanced by discipline and integrity. It is gained by not allowing infringements on the corporate culture and not permitting unethical behavior such as rudeness, greed, and dishonesty. All organizational behavior must be ethical. It must respect all related persons and institutions.

Every company needs to think about its social responsibility, environmental issues, safety of its employees, and the environment in which it operates. Good relationships with trade partners will also enhance the respect the company receives as a good corporate citizen. The employees will, in turn, gain respect from the larger society, and they will feel proud and work hard in the best interests of the company.

K. R. Kim built LG in India from scratch. It is now a $2 billion company. He said, "When we started our new operation in India, there was no recognition of our new company. But one day one manager told me he was getting recognition from his friends. Also good news was that they were saying it is becoming good advantage to get better partner in marriage. Number one company means the most ethical company."

"As long as his men full of good courage fight with zeal and spirit, it is seldom necessary for the Chief to show great energy of purpose. But as soon as difficulties arise then things no longer move on like a well-oiled machine, the machine itself begins to offer resistance, and the Commander must have a great force of will."

—Karl von Clausewitz

Chapter 13

What Is Essential in Marketing and Sales?

"Marketing is too important to be left to the marketing department."

David Packard

When we started out at Amicorp, we did not have any clients, so generating sales was a necessity. In those early days, I would just take a plane to cities that were not too far from Curaçao: Caracas, São Paulo, Miami, etc. I would visit their business district and look for the most prestigious office towers. I would go from law firm to law firm, tax advisor to tax advisor, and broker to broker, just knocking on doors without any formal introduction. There were, of course, many days where I became disheartened by the many rebuttals and rude reactions, but gradually we built our first little client base, and from there our network grew to become more and more fruitful.

Successful salespeople are born to be salespeople. They win people over by their knowledge of the product or service. The ability to break down the product to its bare essentials, direct their purchasers' thoughts toward closing the deal, and give the impression that *they* made a great deal are all trademarks of a savvy salesman. The best sales job I ever saw happened one hot afternoon in late 1979 on a bus somewhere in Baluchistan. Russia had just invaded Afghanistan, and several bands of tribal warriors were roaming the deserts of the border region. We were stopped by a mean-looking bunch of tribesmen, brandishing their *Kalashnikovs*. Their leader came onto the bus, looked around, made a short speech about the relevance of his cause, and then indicated an amount in rupees that the people on the bus would have to jointly contribute. All hell broke loose, and after some negotiations and gun-waving, a lesser sum was agreed upon. The tribesmen left the bus, sat down on the tracks, and drank tea. The bus driver took to the task of evenly dividing the pain over the passengers in the bus; most people on the bus were taxed on the volume of their possessions or the newness of their clothes, but as foreigners we had to contribute more to the cause, which we never really understood. After an hour the tribesmen came back, the amount was handed over, counted twice, and when deemed to be enough, the tension eased, laughter broke out, backs were slapped, and we parted like old friends. It seemed as though everyone was content with the deal he had made. The rest of the trip I kept thinking we had been *robbed*. The rest of the bus was in a festive mood, thinking we had *survived*.

You too will need to quickly resolve disputes. Conflicts and disputes drain energy. There are always a few notorious customers who never fail to complain, but, more often than not, the customer who takes the effort to complain is right. Solve issues quickly. Do not let problems linger. Satisfied clients speak positively about your products and services and refer new clients; dissatisfied customers speak badly about your service or product. Word of mouth has much more impact than any advertising campaign or marketing plan could ever have. Most of your new sales come from clients who give references to other prospects. Negative feedback spreads faster and further than positive feedback.

I always try to get a feel for the market, and whether or not I want to be in it. I would suggest you spend as much time as you can in as many of the market segments where your product is being sold as possible. Spend the largest part of your time with your clients. Listen to what they like and dislike about your products. Often with minor changes you can make your product much more attractive. Looks are very important in that respect. The packaging of your product, the presentation of your marketing and sales materials, and the look of your corporate image are very important. Uninspiring meeting rooms, ugly marketing materials, sloppy documentation, offering letters with mistakes in them, and clocks that have stopped do not bode well in the overall perception the client gets of your company. In the end, what you are selling is usually the perception of the quality of your product, rather than the product itself.

In many cases clients are not really in a position to judge the quality of the product. They may be able to taste the difference between a $10 bottle of wine and a $50 bottle, but not between a $50 bottle and a $500 bottle. It is all about perception. Perception is created by the way you present your products, as well as by what the customer hears from third parties about your product. The way you present yourself at industry fairs and seminars is important. This, of course, depends on what you want to sell. A restaurant that pretends to sell top-quality food cannot have plastic cutlery and do without at least a cotton tablecloth and crystal glasses. Good quality and great visibility are your best marketing tools. Make sure you have great salespeople who visit your clients regularly.

A good client is one who pays on time. Creating good payment habits requires some initial discipline, but it pays off very quickly. Providing good quality and having effective and efficient operations will result in good payment practices. After-sales service is also very important. The best way to increase sales is to sell more to existing clients. It takes five times as much effort to make a totally new sale than to make a follow-up sale to an existing customer. By creating novel ways of presenting your products, you will attract more customers. Novel does not mean expensive. Expensive marketing campaigns satisfy the ego of managers and marketing people but do not necessarily reach the end-user clients. Often the exact opposite occurs. If the advertising is too posh, clients sometimes shy away; if it looks too good, it must be super expensive, especially in emerging markets.

Your marketing and sales materials should emphasize your commitment to a clean environment—avoid waste of natural resources and show concern for society at large. We have chosen to convert our marketing materials to recycled paper products in order to emphasize our concern about minimizing our impact on the environment. Most marketing materials are viewed only a few times; many can be in electronic form only and do not require printing.

Loyalty programs are very helpful in retaining clients. They appeal to the need of people to connect. People will revisit a coffee shop or restaurant if they feel they are recognized, appreciated, and valued on a personal level. At Amicorp we created the "Red Carpet" program as our version of the loyalty program. In our business we do not need to woo clients with discounts, but the intermediaries we deal with, all well-to-do individuals, still are charmed by the sharing of new information, personal *info-tainment* events, and good meals.

Loyalty programs will work against you the moment you make them exclusive. Who has not experienced the embarrassment of wanting to make use of the executive lounge of an airline only to be refused because one has his six-year-old daughter with him or happens to be wearing slippers that day? It will take many, many positive experiences to compensate for that one negative one. Believe me, exclusivity is a very dangerous concept. Nobody wants to be excluded. Better to go for inclusivity. Extend your loyalty program, privileges, and special services to your friends and to colleagues of your loyal clients. Your clients will do the sales *for* you. Making your existing clients feel good will intensify the bond you and your brand have with them. Regularly present new ideas, create new services, and change something in the presentation. Create ongoing interaction, get excited about the clients' interests and needs, and ask for feedback. But always be personal. Never approach people in an impersonal way. Don't ask for feedback through a multiple-choice questionnaire or, God forbid, an electronic format. Rather, meet in person or over the phone, and be ready to bring to the table some new tips, useful ideas, or something that shows you actually care about the individual.

> *"Iron rusts from disuse; stagnant water loses its purity and in cold weather becomes frozen; even so does inaction sap the vigor of the mind."*
>
> **—Leonardo da Vinci**

Chapter 14

How Do You Deal with Risk and Failure?

"We have forty million reasons for failure, but not a single excuse."

Rudyard Kipling

I am proud of our team and our organization. We have come a long way, and still the adventure continues. In fact, I feel the best is yet to come. As our business grows larger and attracts more talent and more clients, we can bring more and more ideas to fruition.

Let us for a moment reflect on success and failure. The two are more closely related than one might think. There is no success without failure; however, there can be epic failure without success. We are certain to fail many times in what we do. The only way to avoid failure is to do nothing. Then you will not have failing projects but, rather, a life that has failed. When Thomas Edison had spent endless hours and money trying to perfect a commercial lightbulb, someone asked him whether he should not concede defeat and just give up. Edison is credited with having replied, "I have not failed 1,000 times. I have successfully discovered 1,000 ways to NOT make a light bulb." He pushed on and ultimately invented a workable lightbulb, laying the foundations for General Electric.

When we started Amicorp in 1992, the initial idea was to create services around the Curaçao Securities Exchange, which at that time was in the final planning stages and getting ready to be launched within months. The project failed and resulted in a serious delay—eighteen years! And by default we ended up in the trust business.

Many of our projects failed, many of our deals did not work out, and many of our ideas were just plain wrong. But each failure was a lesson in life. The more lessons we learned, the more successes we could achieve.

The time we live on earth is very short—seventy-five years or perhaps even one hundred if we are lucky. While we are here we must try to leave our mark, make an impact on our environment, and create our universe and master it.

Every morning we are faced with multiple choices. We choose to make the day a happy one or a sad one, a productive one or a fruitless one, an interesting one or a meaningless one. Are we going to share or be greedy—show arrogance or grace? The universe will adjust to our behavior without fail. After all, it is what we do that triggers all of the countless responses in the universe.

If we treat a colleague rudely, we will receive rude behavior in response. If we let a client wait because we hide behind a mindless rule or simply don't care enough to show proper etiquette, we will receive indifference or even hostility in return. If we behave arrogantly toward someone on the other side of the world, we will be let down and made to miss a deadline. If we kick our dog, it will growl and may even bite the hand that feeds it.

Similarly, if we help each other, everyone wins. If we treat every client as if he were the only one, he will be a pleasure to work with. If we build the best possible systems, products, methods, and services, the world will beat a path to our doors. If we treat our dog well, it will be a loyal friend for life.

In attempting to produce the best possible systems, to work out the best possible strategy, and to provide superb service, mistakes are inevitable. In fact, many will be made. They are an inevitable part of the process and cannot be avoided.

What is important is to learn from our mistakes and failures. For it is first of all necessary to own up to our mistakes and not ignore them, hide them under the carpet, or blame them on someone else. If we do that, we *cannot* learn from them. We need to learn from our mistakes, as mistakes and failures are the way the universe teaches us to progress, to get ahead in life, and to become better at our job and as a human being.

When a mistake is made, the relevant action is to analyze the mistake and see where you went wrong—go over what did not work and what needs to be done in order to rectify the mistake. More importantly, what you need to change is your procedures, ways of working and thinking, so that the same mistake never happens again. Do *not* blame your employees for making a mistake the first time. Making the same mistake twice, however, is a different thing. You want them to take risks, take initiative, do something, thereby making them susceptible for mistakes.

We had a nice little fund-administration department that was making some money and having great growth potential. At some stage, by looking at the behavior of our direct competitors, we reached the conclusion that the future of the fund-administration business would likely end up automated and would require very few people but lots of automation and high-tech infrastructure. As we did not have the money to make those investments, and we certainly could use the money a sale would bring to cover the expenses of some other investments, we decided to sell the business. This happened just at the ramp-up to a major growth spurt in the business, and we sold it for a modest sum of money, much to the regret of our long-term manager, Eric Andersen. By the time we realized that we missed most of the opportunities in the business and that the developments were not going as we had expected toward ever larger cookie-cutter funds but rather toward specialized tailor-made solutions, we had lost several years. Instead of crying over spilt milk, we decided to create a new fund-administration department, but this time with its complete back office in Bangalore. We learned from our mistakes and chose then and there to never be a lemming or go with the flow.

Every day we are confronted with different situations that give us an opportunity to either hide or to step up and lead—to either take the initiative and evoke change or to wonder what the hell happened. The only choice that is going to make you and others happy is the one where you *make things happen.*

You could come up with countless excuses for why you cannot do this, whether it is because you do not have the brains or the training, you are not a born leader, or you don't command authority. But the decision to move beyond rests within you. *Believe* you are the master of your own universe, and once you do, positive things will happen.

By doing what is good for the family, the team, the company, the environment, and the society around us, we fulfill our destiny, discover meaning in our lives, and feel happiness as we realize more of our inherent potential. Whatever wisdom tradition we adhere to, these feelings deep inside of us are the same. Why not listen to them, every day and in every circumstance?

If we realize we all have similar goals in life, and work together on making our team, our company, into a dazzling success, we will all benefit, and not just in salaries, bonuses, and job descriptions. The true benefit lies in the creation of friendships with colleagues across the globe and in the establishment of relationships with clients who depend and rely on us. By being an example in everything we do, we can make an impact on our entire environment.

Each failure presents an opportunity to learn, to rise to the occasion, and to make improvements. Each success is an opportunity to celebrate, to feel proud with our achievement, and to make plans for further mountains to climb, goals to reach, and meaning to be found. What we fail in today, we can learn from, improve upon, and do much better tomorrow.

> *"You grow older and wiser. In the early days you take every failure personally. But your skin thickens with age and you become more inclined to learn from your mistakes."*

> **—Cheong Choong Kong**

Chapter 15

What Is the Value of Time?

"Time is the substance from which I am made. Time is a river which carries me along, but I am the river; it is a tiger that devours me, but I am the tiger; it is a fire that consumes me, but I am the fire."

—Jorge Luis Borges

Hindu cosmological theory (as does quantum physics) teaches that matter is just appearance, and the universe is formed only of energy relations. At the root of everything there is a centripetal force that condenses and a centrifugal force that disperses, and the balance of the two gives rise to a circular motion that determines the movement of everything in the universe. Space and time are immeasurable. Nothing in and of itself is either too big or too small, and an instant is not less than a lifetime or a century. Time and space exist only in relation to living beings whose perceptions determine dimensions of space and whose body rhythms, such as heartbeats, measure time, thus making them completely relative.

Lawyers and auditors figured this out a long time ago.

The old joke tells of the recently deceased lawyer who arrives at the gates of heaven and runs into Saint Peter. He complains that he is too young to die and still has so many things to do. Saint Peter looks into his records and asks him how old he is. "Fifty-five," says the lawyer. "Strange," replies Saint Peter. "According to your overview of billable hours, you must be at least eighty-five."

Experience teaches us how to do in an hour what used to take us several hours to do. Current technologies allow us to do incredibly more work per hour than previous generations could do. Not two hundred years ago, it would take three to six months for a letter to make it from Europe to Asia and another three to six months to get an answer. Now you get a reminder on your Blackberry or iPhone if you have not answered a request within an hour. And yet seemingly you have less, rather than more, time to get done what you want to get done.

Applying your experience and education allows you to do in an hour what others need many hours to do. Do not bill this time saved as extra *hours*, for the time did not in fact speed up. The clock kept the same pace. Instead, bill the extra value (experience delivered) as extra *value* and not as *time.*

Waiting for an hour in the dentist's office or for a loved one at the airport may seem endless, while one hour spent *with* that same loved one or on a fun project flies by. Time is fungible. As the well-known Portuguese writer Fernando Pessoa said, "The value of things is not the time they last, but the intensity with which they occur. That is why there are unforgettable moments and unique people."

Many business activities are time sensitive. Airplanes need to depart on time, baguettes need to be fresh twice a day, and toys need to be in the toy shop in the run-up before Christmas. Everything has a deadline.

In service industries billing is often related to time spent on a project or a service. That time can be used only once.

Time is the only truly nonrenewable resource you possess, and it is one a leader, manager, or entrepreneur can never actually manage. You will need to manage instead the things that take up your limited time, realizing that time is precious and once gone will never come back. About 80 percent of our day is spent on those things or those people that bring us only 2 percent of the total result. Time is perishable; you can use it only once, and if you do not use it wisely, it is gone forever. It is like vegetables that rot if not eaten in time or empty seats on an airplane after takeoff. Do not waste your valuable time on meetings that last forever. In fact, do not attend meetings if there is nothing meaningful to discuss. Do not call meetings if you are not prepared to change your opinion on the issues at hand. Do not spend too much time on checks and controls; learn to trust your people, all your people, and let them do their things, so you can spend your time doing something different, something new. Do not spend your time on approving minor decisions or expenses; delegate as much as you can to the people around you. Let everyone make his or her own mistakes. Empower everyone, align everyone with the mission and vision of your company, and free up your time for creative activities, constructive meetings with clients, and development of new projects. Avoid any activities that are recurring. Your life is intended to be full of new experiences, not meant to repeat the same experiences, and the same day, over and over again.

We all have the same amount of time available, twenty-four hours a day, a lifetime worth. What we do with our time is what counts. When we grow old and look back on the amount of time we did not use to work on meaningful projects, spend with loved ones, or enjoy fun or relaxing activities, but rather wasted on internal struggle and competition, uncreative or unfulfilling activities, and useless or nonchallenging projects, we may feel sad and remorseful. We will have robbed our family, friends, colleagues, and clients of their precious time. The waste needs to be recognized at the very moment itself. There is nobody responsible for using your time wisely but you, yourself.

I know several people who have been spending years of their lives in jobs they do not like—others who are looking forward to retiring ten or more years into the future. That is a very wasteful way for them to use their time. With so many fun and rewarding things to do, they are held back by their own limitations. Jorge Luis Borges once said, "Any life is made up of a single moment, the moment in which a man finds out, once and for all, who he is."

We have enough time to do anything we want, as long as we put the things we really want to do high enough on our bucket list. We do not have time to do *everything*; that is why setting priorities is of such great importance. And the priorities to be considered are not often routine in nature.

The ancient Greeks had two words for time: *kairos* and *chromos*. *Kairos* means the right or opportune moment (the supreme moment) and refers to chronological or sequential time. It signifies a time in between—a moment of indeterminate time in which something special happens. What this special something is depends on who is using the word. While *chronos* is quantitative, *kairos* has a qualitative nature. What you do with your time and how you enjoy the successive moments of your life are what count, not the amount of time that is passing by. A long life can be very boring and a short life very fulfilling. How you make the moments of your life count is what is important. As Federico Fellini said, "You exist only in what you do."

A moment that has passed never comes back. An opportunity that is missed is gone forever. Carpe Diem—Live in the now; Carpe Noctem—seize the night, and let no meaningful moment pass by unnoticed. Jamsetji Tata, the founder of the Tata conglomerate, teaches to, "Be bold, be strong and take the whole responsibility upon your own shoulders, because you are the creator of your own destiny."

Start today, as, whatever your age, you have the same amount of time available today, and you are the same person you were meant to be, whether you are in the body of a teenage, a middle-aged, or an elderly person.

> *"Please allow me to wipe the slate clean. Age has no reality except in the physical world. The essence of a human being is resistant to the passage of time. Our inner lives are eternal, which is to say that our spirits remain as youthful and vigorous as when we were in full bloom. Think of love as a state of grace, not the means to anything, but the alpha and omega. An end in itself."*
>
> **—Gabriel García Márquez**

Chapter 16

What Use Do We Have for Gurus and Consultants?

"Management consultants: They waste time, cost money, demoralize and distract your best people, and do not solve problems. They are people who borrow your watch to tell you what time it is and then walk off with it."

—Robert Townsend

As you meet various people along your path, you will come to understand which people are your *teachers*, and which people are *teachings* for you. Some teachers are obviously still working on themselves, and they feed you by sharing their experiences. Others serve as living examples of the opportunities and pitfalls along the way, helping you to reflect on the direction of your own path. Whatever the intention when you first started out, they become teachings for you.

Choose your teachers carefully.

Being an entrepreneur is not easy; in fact, one could say you need all of the advice you can get. That said, you need to look very carefully at why, where, and from whom you seek advice. And then you need to always see advice for what it really is—just advice. It is not the gospel truth, nor is it an unbreakable rule. It is just someone else's opinion, shedding light on what remain *your* issues and *your* decisions.

People often seek advice on topics that are outside of their area of expertise. Often it concerns issues outside of their core competency. A baker, for example, will most likely need very little advice on baking bread and cakes. He may, however, need advice on selecting the most cost-effective oven or choosing an accountant, auditor, lawyer, or financial advisor.

When you start out, you will want to use as few advisors as possible, since professional advisors are invariably expensive, and their contributions are not always obvious from the beginning. In that case start out with seeking professional advice only in the areas that will have a lasting impact. In the example of the baker, selecting the oven and a good legal structure would be points on which to seek advice. You can always keep the books yourself while your enterprise is small. This will help you focus on your cash flow.

You will never find a shortage of free advice. There are many government institutions that offer free advice to start-up companies. A lot of it is a waste, as it is given by people who have never seen a start-up, but some can be very helpful. More practical and to-the-point advice can come from other businesspeople. You will be amazed how many people will gladly and without compensation help you when you simply ask for advice. Retired people love to stretch their brain in an effort to help solve some problems, and successful entrepreneurs revel in helping struggling start-ups, as it reminds them of their fledgling days. Do not forget family, neighbors, or members of your local service club as willing resources.

It is not always necessary to find people who are subject experts in your area of business. Entrepreneurial wisdom is easily transferable from one business vertically to another one. I was greatly helped by a man, Karel Franken, who never finished any formal education. He started out as a window cleaner and during his active life built a cleaning company with up to fifteen hundred employees before he had to sell it for health reasons. The window cleaner had no clue about international tax planning, but he gave me great insight on how to motivate employees, how to become more disciplined, and how to work within narrow margins, being efficient, and delegating when appropriate. In the end our drive for ISO certification and the beginnings of our Six Sigma project came from his advice.

Hans Crooij, a retired insurance salesman, helped us with the pension and insurance issues but also acted as a *consigliore* for many of the people in the company. He considered me too weak on people—always giving too many chances (probably true), and he helped me to think deeper about the added value of each individual in our company.

Retired banker Shon Max Henriquez made a few appearances in the very early days when I was struggling with issues of greed and moral values. He made it very clear to me that if you intend to stay in business for a long time, you can *never* take any shortcuts. He taught me to take life as it comes: *In dubio abstinae.*

Another retired banker, Frank Aldrich, took me all around Latin America and introduced me to hundreds of people. He taught me to *always* be nice to *everyone* and not just the ones who are important today. He stressed that everything is in constant flux, and all of the people you meet today will somehow be able to influence your business tomorrow. Until today Frank's contacts still help me tremendously.

Edgard Lotman proved to me that there are also bankers who do not fit the standard profile and who stand with you in difficult times.

Jon Sheeser, ex-international banker, taught me the importance of consistency and continuity. Just as money in a bank account accumulates with compounded interest, all of your other efforts compound as well. Small losses, be they people, products, or projects, are very important, as they tend to compound to big losses if you do not cut them quickly. Small profits on people, products, or projects are okay as long as these have the possibility of compounding year after year. Our company is built up of some fifteen thousand small positive cash flows. Each of them may not be very material, but all of them together create a stable, sound, and continuous cash flow that propels our business forward.

Camillo Bozzolo, yet another retired banker, taught me that acting with grace and magnanimity will help you win over a lot of people. This, in turn, will allow you to accomplish things you would never have been able to do.

Rudi Viljoen, organizer of the Warriors' Extreme Gap Year programs, took care of my son for a while, as well as organized trainings for our employees and taught all of us how important our chosen attitude and values are.

Nico Buren, a tax advisor, while working closely with many people in our company, became like a father to me in the process. He would call me at odd hours, including the middle of the night, and usually start with a very stern, "Young man." He would tell me what I was doing wrong, and not always in the most tactical way. He helped us greatly improve the quality of our solutions as well as our internal organization. When Nico died, the successor partner to the same tax-advisory firm, Cees-Frans Greeven, worked as an intern around the time we started Amicorp. Our lives continue to run in parallel, and we help each other out, although I still miss the old man sternly addressing me as "young man."

Notary Harry Burgers helped us a lot with the design of new solutions, providing intellectual challenge when the day-to-day work could make anyone complacent.

There are many others; in fact, the list goes on and on. Come to think of it, I was helped by so many people that I don't think I'll ever be able to reciprocate by helping that many people in return. None of them *ever* asked me for money for their advice, and *all* of them really enjoyed helping our then small company become more successful.

An outside perspective is valuable when evaluating issues within your company. Being deeply immersed in your own business, you often miss great opportunities or fail to notice blatant mistakes. Gaping holes in your organization and the problems that linger cannot be solved at the same level of thinking as the level at which you created them in the first place. As Swami Prajnanpad observed, "The state of mind is a vicious circle. It creates problems for itself and then tries to resolve them."

Those people were valuable to me, as each has his own experience, his own expertise, and his own mind. That is what you should be looking for in your advisors. A twenty-eight-year-old with two MBAs and experience at a consultancy firm can be great at creating spreadsheets or formulating the obvious, but more likely than not, he has no clue as to what your real issues are.

Only those who have been where you want to go can confidently show you the way. Think about that next time when you ask for tax advice, investment advice, or marketing advice. This one rule, over three thousand years old, is from the Bhagavad Gita (4:34). It is all about doing business while doing good. Pay attention; it can save you a lot of money. Send that money to your favorite charity instead. "Those who themselves have seen the Truth can be thy teachers of wisdom; ask from them, bow unto them, be thou a servant unto them."

In big companies money is always available for professional advisors. Not only are the issues that bother large companies more complex, with a larger impact, but also large corporations gather in lots of people who are not particularly entrepreneurial and who are looking to "cover their asses" by buying advice.

If your company is losing money because its business segment is declining, call in McKinsey, pay them a fortune, and surprise-surprise, they will tell you to downscale and eliminate departments, products, and markets. You can then hide behind a shiny report, complicated spreadsheets, and analyses full of Harvard jargon. You can then sheepishly explain to your workers that it was not your choice or preference, but that the "experts" told you to eliminate their position.

Also, when you want to do something while unconsciously certain you'll fail, you seek advice so you can blame someone else for the failure. Make sure to recognize these character weaknesses in yourself. Go to your trusted gurus, straighten your back, and work out something a bit more courageous, a bit more creative, a bit nobler.

While Nassim Nicholas Taleb reminds us, "Suckers think that you can cure greed with money, addiction with substances, expert problems with consultants, banking with bankers, economics with economists and debt crises with debt spending."

The truth is, there are always some professional advisors you do need. Shunryu Suzuki once said, "In the beginner's mind there are many possibilities, but in the expert's there are only a few." The list begins with your accountants and auditors. These are the people who, from the outside, look at the financial health of your company and can help you avoid making mistakes. Your auditors do not necessarily just need to be the people who come to the field after the battle to clobber the wounded, count the fallen bodies, and steal from the dead. They can bring objectivity and sound judgment, and, mixed with your enthusiasm, that can be a winning combination. You can learn from your auditors.

Legal advisors can help you protect your business from legal pitfalls. Good contracts and good general conditions are of great value, as they will prevent problems down the line; clarity prevents conflict. Technical experts in all areas help you to avoid set-ups that later turn out to be inefficient. They may help to improve efficiency, quality, and dependability.

Experts on corporate governance are increasingly important in balancing the different interests united in the company as it grows. Human resource experts are important to make sure you deal correctly with a myriad of legislative issues and keep track of training and development needs. Private bankers are generally mostly interested in their private interests but have the addresses of the best restaurants in town at their fingertips. You can use them to deal with excess cash in case you find casinos too uninspiring. Never be shy to ask for advice. You can always learn more.

There is no rule which says that as a leader or entrepreneur you are supposed to know everything. There are so many areas of knowledge, so many new developments in the world, and so much diversity that you need all the help you can get. But never forget that however much advice you collect, you are the decision maker—the responsibility remains yours and not that of your advisor. *Never* hide behind someone's advice; and keep using your own brain as well.

> *"Brothers, the cause of suffering is ignorance. Because of ignorance, men do not see the reality of life and allow themselves to be imprisoned in the flames of desire, anger, envy, anxiety, fear and despair."*

**—Suttapitaka, Samyutta-Nikaya,
Dhammacakkapavattana Sutta**

Chapter 17

Are Employees the Most Valuable Asset to Your Company?

"I don't believe in just ordering people to do things. You have to sort of grab an oar and row with them."

—Mohandas Gandhi

Sooner or later your growing company will be faced with hiring employees. Employees are coworkers, colleagues who are not owners of stock in the company they work for. It remains, however, very important that they become owners of the mission, vision, and values of the company. It is up to you, as the entrepreneur, to convince them that joining your company out of thousands of options around is the best choice they can make with their precious time on earth. Steve Jobs said in his commencement address at Stanford University in 2005, "Your time is limited, so don't waste it living someone else's life. Don't be trapped by dogma, which is living with the results of other people's thinking. Don't let the noise of others' opinions drown out your own inner voice. And most importantly, have the courage to follow your heart and intuition. They somehow already know what you truly want to become ... stay hungry, stay foolish."

There are plenty of books that explain the techniques of how to select the right employees, but I am not going to get into all that. The most important thing is to find people who will, at least to a certain degree, share the same passion for the business you are in or the service you are providing. A team that is not rallied behind a common goal will never be successful. Great work will be done only by a team of people who love what they are doing.

Like Steve Jobs, you would want people who cannot wait for the sun to come up in the morning so they can go back to work. That means that you need to be able to rally them behind what your company stands for. As Steve Jobs said to former PepsiCo executive John Sculley, whom he was trying to hire for Apple, "Do you want to spend the rest of your life selling sugared water, or do you want a chance to change the world?" Make sure you are able to clearly describe how *your* company is going to change the world. Nobody gets truly motivated by selling sugared water.

Of course, you need to find people with the skills your company requires, but more important than skills is the attitude and the approach individuals have toward the job.

If someone is willing to master the work you are doing and bring a level of passion to the company, then take a chance on him or her. Changing someone's character and/or attitude after the age of six is a difficult, if not impossible, task.

Titles, degrees, and diplomas all mean very little. They indicate that people have some degree of intelligence, have mastered some degree of practical skills, can sit still for hours and listen, and can easily feel motivated or pressured to do what you want them to do. But that should not be what you are looking for in potential employees. You want them to bring their full personality to the office—their passions, their interests, their ideas, their creativity, and their dreams. The ones who check their brain at the entrance, conserve their passion for their hobbies, regularly watch the clock to see how much time has already passed, or treat their job as a way to make a living give you only a small percentage of what they potentially have to offer. Do not accept that. You pay a salary to get a complete person and his complete personality; do not settle for half a person. Keep searching until you find the right employees. Never settle.

A significant number of entrepreneurs are high school or university dropouts. Many have dyslexia or other learning difficulties, and still more have been fired a number of times from a job. The more creative, productive, and out-of-the-box thinking the employee is, the less likely it is that he was a model student. In general it is not a good idea to try and find people via executive search firms and headhunters unless you are looking for very specialized skills. Referrals from existing employees, people who work with your clients or suppliers, or people you train from scratch right out of school or university are often a better bet. Résumés of people that are generated through search firms are often inflated. People who use those services are typically motivated by *having a job* or *making a career*, which they translate into high salaries, and after eighteen months they are often off to the next career step, unless, of course, you have already fired them. An entrepreneurial business is not about *making a career*. It is about having a life and living it to the fullest. The job or the career needs to become a *calling*.

Highly qualified people often interview very well. They are able to weave a very convincing story about who they are and what their past achievements have been. This, of course, is no guarantee for future results. Most, if not all, have studied your website, and many will have even checked you out on Google, LinkedIn, or Facebook to see what your personal interests are and what kind of people you like. They will, therefore, be well prepared for the more common questions. You will have to find the questions that will give insight into their souls, a bit like how Peter Falk as Inspector Columbo used to ask the tricky questions when he was already on his way out and the suspect had let his guard down.

The traits that make for outstanding achievement are not intelligence, academic performance, or which university one has attended. The traits that make for success cannot be taught in a normal classroom. Passion and focus and the ability to understand and inspire people, to read situations and discern underlying patterns, to build trusting relationships, and to correct one's shortcomings are innate qualities possessed by your great employees.

Most of these traits are formed in infancy. According to a recent study, an infant's brain is creating 1.8 million neural connections per second. The crucial element here is the relationship with the mother and the love that flows through this connection and into the baby's brain. People who were securely attached as infants tend to have more friends at school. They tend to be more truthful throughout life. As colleagues they are more trusting and forthcoming. They feel less of a need to show off or inflate themselves in others' eyes. Men who had unhappy childhoods are three times as likely to be solitary at age seventy. So finding out what kind of childhood people had, what they do in their spare time, and what kind of social life and hobbies and interests they have, might make a lot of sense.

Spend a lot of time on selecting the right people. The key rule is hire slowly and fire quickly. The candidates who focus on compensation and benefits can easily be passed over. You need the ones who are really interested in your product or service and who want to share the dream of your mission and the passion for its goals. If you see their eyes turn away when you get enthusiastic about your product, service, or future plans for the company, you should stop the conversation right there and then. If, on the other hand, you see a spark light up in their eyes and a growing enthusiasm when you describe what the company stands for and what it contributes to society, you may have a winner. Some of the best people I have hired over time were people who did not have the greatest résumés but who did share or develop a deep passion for the business, had a real interest in the customers, and had the curiosity to learn something every day. Some of the worst people I have hired include the ones who thought of themselves as being great, did not necessarily gel well with clients and colleagues, stopped learning because they knew it all, and did not produce because they could not muster the interest or the passion for the services we render or the well-being of colleagues and customers alike.

Once he or she is on board, it is important to make the new employee feel welcome. First impressions are the only ones that make an impact. Quickly familiarize him or her with the inner workings of the company. Don't just focus on the tasks, but stress the importance of the mission, vision, and values of the company. Introduce your new employee to the task at hand and help him or her develop a personalized set of targets or *key performance indicators*. Set these indicators for the first three months as well as for the first year. These targets should include financial goals of the company, goals related to the development of the organization, and goals related to the development of the individual. To get the best out of your new people, targets need to be formulated in such a way and conditions need to be formulated in such a way that together they instill in the new recruits a sense of purpose, a sense of impact, a sense of competence, and a sense of self-determination.

It is important to take good care of your employees. Of course, salary and benefits have to be largely in line with the market for the skill-set hired (and whenever you can afford it, slightly above the market), but compensation is a sort of hygiene factor. Like the place of work, it has to be there for people to be able to work properly, but it is not a real motivating factor. People get inspired by the purpose of the company, the teamwork, The interactions, by what they learn, and by needs to be achieved in order to improve the world or to delight a customer. In short, what motivates a person is a sense of belonging, a sense of meaning, and a sense of enjoyment.

That can be achieved by producing a great meal in a simple restaurant, by providing great service in a bookkeeping company, or by making life-changing inventions or improvements. In addition, people get inspired by the team they play on and the recognition and appreciation they receive from peers, colleagues, clients, and supervisors. People crave appreciation, and it is not given often enough.

The purpose of a company, as well as the purpose of the job, needs to be described in terms that people can relate to. Nobody can identify with "producing small music machines that have high performance and are made of superior metals and plastics." But lots of people can relate to "putting a thousand songs in your pocket." Making a lot of money can never be a target; it is the by-product of producing a superior product or delivering a superior service.

You will have to give the right example and share the work with the people on the floor. You must understand what goes on in the minds of both employees and customers. In many larger organizations this gets completely forgotten. Senior managers often create more and more distance between themselves and the people they are supposed to lead. They surround themselves with luxury and perks, start flying first class, and lose touch with reality. Sooner or later the company suffers from it. But the words of Eleanor Roosevelt are still true today: "It is not fair to ask of others what you are not willing to do yourself." You cannot really run a company if you do not understand in detail its inner workings and you do not feel its pulse on a daily basis. If you do not get your hands dirty, why would others feel inspired to do so?

A written job description may be useful, but it needs to be crafted very carefully. It should not become a limitation to the potential of the person involved and should always include "and all further activities that may be for the benefit of or in the interest of the client, the department, and the company." If your company is small enough, you may prefer to forgo the job description altogether. You don't *ever* want to hear in your organization something like, *that is not my job,* or *I was not hired for that,* or similar creativity- and flexibility-killing expressions. Great companies like Southwest Airlines make sure that pilots help load bags from time to time, and all employees help clean up and help guide passengers. This is to make sure no employee forgets who they actually work for, as well as for all to appreciate how hard the work of some of their colleagues actually is.

Going through internal training programs may also be very useful. A new employee may not get a lot out of the actual initial trainings and might not immediately absorb a lot of the background on the company itself, but it is a good way to get to know other employees—some experienced and maybe others less experienced. The details he will pick up over time. Understanding the general direction is indispensable. Share as much knowledge as you can, for knowledge needs to be like air; you take it in, process it, live off it for a while, and then you share it again, so others can use it as well.

I think it is less useful to study manuals or sit at a computer for days and read "the way we do things here." Manuals, internal memos, and guidelines are just pieces of paper if the new person is not properly and thoroughly aligned with the overall mission, vision, values, and goals.

Using the value set as a guideline and the mission and goals as the lighthouse by which to steer, a new employee will start to find his direction pretty soon. He can always look into manuals for specific data once he comes across a situation that requires specific guidance. Once an employee knows what his goals and targets are, he needs to be given *freedom* to figure out the details himself and reach his goals in any way he sees fit. This, of course, should always fall within the boundaries of the company's values.

Do not waste your time on telling people in detail *how* to perform their functions. A lot of creativity, job satisfaction, and progress is lost because we spend way too much time on telling people *how* to do their work. You hired them, so you have already ascertained that they know how to do the work. Focus instead on *what* needs to be done and *why* it needs to be done. Detailed instructions may work for a place like a McDonald's hamburger joint, where people get a handbook on how to flip a hamburger and exactly when to add the tomato, in order to ensure that the five billionth burger tastes exactly the same as the four billionth burger. Of course, methods like this result in close to a 100 percent annual turnover rate. But for most businesses, the personal touch, the personal attention to the customer, and the personal thought that goes into a product, service, or the process is too important to compress into strictly regimented rules and procedures.

Regular feedback is very important. This can best be given in an informal setting using situations in the workplace as coaching moments. Of course, you should always follow the all-important rule that criticism should be given wisely and behind closed doors, and praise should be given loudly and in the open. However, between people of more or less similar levels (not necessarily similar job descriptions), it is important to create an atmosphere in which everyone dares to speak his mind and criticize not only a product or a process, but also the way it is handled by coworkers or even superiors. For the work floor to function effectively, everyone needs to feel free to speak his mind and even be blunt or direct (not rude) in his comments. This is the only way everyone can feel part of *our* product or service and real ongoing improvements can be made. Whether you make a product, deliver a service, or just act as a link in a much larger chain of production, remember, good enough is never good enough—only excellence is acceptable.

When employees are several more steps removed on the corporate ladder, you need to be careful how to communicate, as such people are not always able to see the full picture, or at least not on the level that you see it or the other way around. They may feel constrained, challenged, or threatened by the difference in level. You should still solicit honest feedback, but you may need to balance the results you get with other sources of feedback.

People outside your team, and people who are purely in support functions that carry no *real* power, should always be treated with utmost respect. They have little or no way to improve whatever crisis situation you may find yourself in. These people include receptionists who do not give you access to a person you wish to visit, airline employees who try to book you on another flight after your original one has been cancelled, or taxi drivers who miss a turn when you're in a hurry. Colleagues and other associates who are rude in those types of situations reveal nasty streaks in their characters. They need serious coaching to prevent this habit from becoming part of their behavioral pattern and ultimately affecting other employees or even the company itself.

It is great when you can ask employees what they want or what they need in order to develop themselves, but in our organization this question ended up creating a lot of problems. Some employees started to study Italian or Papiamentu—totally useless for our business. You will need to steer the choices, make clear which skills will help the company, which are nice to have, and which are not of use to the organization. Many people still have the mistaken idea that making a career means moving up to management. Not only does that often go against a person's character, but it also fails to recognize that the needs of many companies can be better served by having more specialists, instead of advancing their most skilled people into general management positions. There are lots of ways to grow, in depth, for example, rather than in status. Our company needs more domain specialists and knowledgeable people than managers, for instance.

In my opinion it is very important to know exactly what skills and positions the *company* needs now, in six months, and in two years. That way we can *design* what positions we *need* as a company. We can position them one versus the other in order of *importance* (not just looking at how high they are on the organizational chart) and check people's interests and strengths on the basis of the company's needs.

Every workplace has a number of rules. The more rules there are, the more they are broken, so restrain yourself from introducing *more* rules; focus on values instead. Inevitably, and unfortunately, rules are sometimes broken. This happens in a variety of ways. One category is simple: people break the law by misappropriating company property. Stealing company assets, misusing the telephone or the Internet for personal use, and falsifying paperwork, including expense receipts, are a few examples. Usually there is no other remedy than letting the employee go and maybe even reporting the behavior to the police. The monetary value of the breach is really not of any importance. If people steal a dollar, they will also steal a million if the right opportunity presents itself. Another category is breaking ethical or moral codes. Crossing company guidelines and customs, acting on the edge of the law, hiding relevant information, regularly arriving late, teasing or insulting coworkers, or committing actions bordering on sexual harassment are a bit more difficult to deal with. And, unfortunately, almost all of us will at some stage break a rule, on purpose or unwittingly.

Whatever the seriousness of the breach, these are situations to be dealt with immediately. The relevant employee needs to be informed as to why certain behavior is not acceptable. The focus needs to be on the behavior and not on the employee. Where appropriate, agreements need to be put in place to avoid similar behavior from occurring again at some stage in the future.

Taking notes and confirming agreements to change behavior are fine. Once you get on the path of formal written warnings it is basically too late, and you are merely documenting an exit plan. In many countries, however, this is obligatory, but in reality it's a general waste of time; it creates bad blood and negative energy.

Firing employees is something we all would prefer to avoid. It is inevitable when someone clearly cannot cope with the requirements of the job at hand, and there are no other suitable positions within the company. This usually indicates a hiring mistake, as at the time of hiring it should be clear what an employee has as formal skills and what skills he can acquire by learning or training.

Having let go quite a few people in the course of my career, I dislike doing it and thus try very hard to avoid hiring the wrong people in the first place. To illustrate this, let me share with you the following anecdote. A couple of years ago, I went to Mexico to fire our office manager. That person was clearly colluding with employees of at least one of our intermediaries and siphoning off the company's money for his personal needs. Nevertheless, it pained me to have to eliminate him. I had gone to Mexico with a colleague, and after we solved the issue of the manager we set out to drink some *tequila con sangrita*. Long after midnight I went to my room at the Nikko Hotel. The door seemed stuck, so I applied my strength, which was fortified by the tequila, and I used my weight against the door. The complete door, including the frame, collapsed, and I fell very noisily into the room. A naked American jumped out of the bed, threw his hands in the air, and screamed for help ... or maybe mercy. After some consternation, it turned out that the same room had been issued twice. I was upgraded to the presidential suite. Nevertheless, I prefer not having to fire too many people.

From time to time you will encounter employees who may have the skills but lack the right attitude. This category is not a problem, if their performance is also low and their goals are not being met. These people do not fit into your organization and will be much better off elsewhere. You will often see that if you execute that process appropriately, you will later hear from them that being let go was one of the best things that ever happened to them. The hardest category of misfits to deal with is the category of the people who have the right skills, who perform well in the sense that they meet their targets, but who in the process repeatedly disrespect the company's values and/or insult, mistreat, or abuse their colleagues. Of course you would like to keep these employees, if only they would ... etc. But, unfortunately, that does not often happen. Do not *ever* be tempted to let someone get away with consistently disrespecting your values and breaking your internal rules just because he is a high performer. The negatives far outweigh the positives. You will create the impression that your values are not that important after all, and that others also have permission to break them; you will create the impression that you do not treat everyone equally and fairly.

I have at times broken this rule, and once I finally was willing to accept the truth and let go of the person concerned, there was a big sigh of relief in the organization, as well as within myself. Often as the leader you are the last person to realize that someone is not performing well. On the other hand, I cannot remember a single case where I let go of someone who was behaving unethically and later regretted it. When I was at INSEAD I committed in one of the training sessions to releasing a list of fifteen more or less senior people in our organization. It took me almost two years to let go of fourteen of them, and number fifteen seems to have made a real turnaround. I felt extremely relieved when the last one was finally gone, and so did the people around me. There should be no place in any company for people who regularly talk behind other people's back, people who constantly complain, promote negativity, and claim things are outside of their control. People who are greedy at the expense of their colleagues, and who promote destructive internal competition, are toxic to your environment. Negativity gets a lot of attention, and everything that gets attention grows. Rigorous measures must be taken the moment you can no longer ignore the problem.

Often this negativity slowly creeps in; it is the result of employees who are too comfortable in their positions, developing a sense of entitlement. The notion that "the rules are there for anyone but me," or "I have been here long enough to not have to produce anymore," or even, "I have earned my stripes and now others can do the work," is a dangerous one for employees to have. Very dangerous, and if you have not taken enough attention and nipped this behavior in the bud, then there is no other choice than to have those employees leave. Remember, someone's track record is irrelevant to his performance today. Performance is about what we all produce today and our plans and ambitions for tomorrow. Live in the *now*. If the performance is no longer there, and, more importantly, the ambition is gone, it is time to cut the ties.

In every organization it is key that all employees have the feeling they are treated equally and fairly. The organization will work only if the great majority of people feel that the company is "their company." The feeling needs to be of *us* rather than of *them*. High performing *assholes*, therefore, need to be forced out of the organization as soon as they are identified, no discussion.

Only then can the remaining people feel and act as one team. For a team to function well, all of the team members need to feel appreciated and have their rightful place on the team, more commonly referred to as a tribe. In African philosophy this principle is called *Ubuntu*. Nelson Mandela explained *Ubuntu* as, "A traveler through a country would stop at a village and he didn't have to ask for food or for water. Once he stops, the people give him food, and entertain him. That is one aspect of Ubuntu, but it will have various aspects. Ubuntu does not mean that people should not enrich themselves. The question therefore is: Are you going to do so in order to enable the community around you to be able to improve?" Archbishop Desmond Tutu, in his book *God is not a Christian*, offered the following definition, "A person with Ubuntu is open and available to others, affirming of others, does not feel threatened that others are able and good, based from a proper self-assurance that comes from knowing that he or she belongs in a greater whole and is diminished when others are humiliated or diminished, when others are tortured or oppressed". Ubuntu is the essence of being human. Ubuntu speaks particularly about the fact that you can't exist as a human being in isolation. It speaks about our interconnectedness. Desmond Tutu: "You can't be human all by yourself, and when you have this quality— Ubuntu—you are known for your generosity. We think of ourselves far too frequently as just individuals, separated from one another, whereas you are connected and what you do affects the whole World. When you do well, it spreads out; it is for the whole of humanity."

Working in a well-structured team helps to get the best out of each of its members. Combining complementary skills and sharing enthusiasm and common goals will create job satisfaction. A good team is like a tribe where members have a natural role that fits their level of development, their skills level, and their needs. Well-functioning tribes think that they are invincible and that the world is a great place. They can move mountains and enjoy the process.

Most people are familiar with the pyramid described by Abraham Maslow. Basic human needs, such as the need for food, shelter, and sex, need to be largely fulfilled before there is genuine interest in and sufficient attention to the fulfillment of higher-level needs. These higher levels include achievement, respect of others, creativity, and morality. These activities are not separated in time and space, but the stronger the foundation is, the more focus can be on higher levels and challenges.

As an entrepreneur you need to be there and assist your employees to climb the Maslow pyramid. Compensation needs to be competitive for your type of business. There is no use being skimpy, as paying peanuts will get you monkeys. And many of the other *hygiene* factors that dominate the lower levels of the pyramid are not expensive. Flexible work hours and flexibility in dealing with school kids, sickness, pregnancy, and family needs, don't have to cost that much and can create corporate loyalty.

Sensible stimulation of people to study and develop their skills and experience will earn back money for the company. Any person who actually reaches the fulfillment of everything he was intended to be when he was born into this world is a huge asset for any company. Recognizing the performances of teams as well as individuals can be a great motivating factor. Remember to keep the rewards inclusive and not exclusive. Rewards do not need to have a great monetary value. But they must come from the heart and be handed out wholeheartedly. And when they are issued, the reasons why they are issued need to be explained to all.

One of the more dreaded ritual events is the annual or semiannual evaluation, especially if those evaluations lead to surprises for the people who are being evaluated. Dale Carnegie described it as follows, "The resentment that criticism engenders can demoralize employees, family members and friends, and still not correct the situation that has been condemned." It is much better to deal with praise and areas of improvement during the year than to keep them all for a formal appraisal moment. If you ask people what their individual contribution is to a team effort, whether it be household chores in a family or work performed on a team, the totals of the members' individual contributions will always exceed 100 percent.

At the moment of a year-end evaluation, the team spirit disintegrates, the supervisor hides behind his status and the employee may go home humiliated, underappreciated, and bereaved by his feeling of being one of the team. In the least intelligent of cases, evaluations are combined with a requirement to promote or reward the top x percent performers and let go of the bottom x percent. This is a sure way to end up with people being promoted beyond their level of confidence and competence—the Peter Principle. People leave the organization just to avoid ending up in the bottom x percent, while all of the people in between focus and worry about how they will look in their evaluation rather than on their actual tasks. And "360-reviews" are even worse, especially when conducted with certain anonymity. They are plainly destructive for team spirit and should be avoided. Feedback instead should be continuous, mutual, ad hoc, open, and frank.

For the same reason, I believe anonymous employee surveys are also bad ideas. They invite people to complain and sow distrust without coming up with solutions. Open town hall meetings, where people are invited to speak their mind and where hard issues are openly discussed and suggestions heard, are oftentimes better. People who do not feel comfortable to speak their minds in public should be invited to use the open-door policy rather than hide behind suggestions on a piece of unsigned paper. A manager who is surprised by the anonymous feedback he obtains from a "360" or an employee survey has three choices. He can ponder whether he has lost contact with the base, or he can suspect someone of trying to undermine either his authority or the team spirit and cooperation on the work floor, or he can try and solve an issue that may or may not be real. In all cases it would have been a hundred times better if the issue had been out in the open.

Ranking employees is also not a good idea. In high school this may have been a favored way for intellectually challenged teachers to make artificial distinctions between students, thus limiting their potential by telling them they are not good at something, but it reduces the person's creativity and his desire to aspire to more challenging tasks. Having an entire department ranked fixes the pecking order and kills upward mobility. Is one human being more valuable than another? Is one task less essential than another? All members of the team must contribute something that is essential to the functioning of the team. For example, the receptionist is as essential as the salesman, the designer, the production assistant, or the leader; otherwise she should not be part of the team. In our company the teams of receptionists form an invaluable front line in the areas of customer contact and document flow. Yes, some skills are more scarce or unique than others, and those workers are compensated for those skills. But that compensation reflects on the skill and not the human being.

For the same reason, labeling people is also never a good idea. When we were born we all had unlimited possibilities and opportunities within us. From the moment we went to kindergarten, our parents, teachers, and everyone else around us have limited our mental and physical opportunities by pigeonholing us into ever narrower specializations. You are a boy, so you do not play with dolls; you enjoy alpha subjects, so you will not be good at beta subjects; you love rock and roll music, so you will not appreciate classical music. An asset manager drives a sports car, an auditor drives a Volvo, a vegetarian hugs trees, and a meat lover is more aggressive. And on goes the list until your interests, habits, and way of thinking are conditioned to fit into the pattern of expectations or, worse, until the people concerned start believing that they are good at or interested only in a very limited number of things. This is a pattern of behavior that makes you use an ever-smaller portion of your brain and limits your dreams. As a kid you could imagine yourself as a pilot one moment and as a farmer raising pigs the next. What happened to your childhood dreams? Who gets to choose what you are capable of? It is only you, yourself.

People should be trusted and appreciated for who and what they are. I think each individual is perfect, as he was created in his own way. You just need to find the right way to tap into the person's potential and deal with the person's challenges and life goals. Only if you are able to align the life goals of the individual employees in your company, will you be successful at leading a growing company. You will not achieve that by ranking them, boxing them in, or labeling them. You will have to give them your friendship and your trust. Nourish their dreams, afford them the freedom to make mistakes, and pursue challenges that will lead to both failure and success. You will need to be honest with them and tough on them. Present worthwhile challenges, so they can tap into their full potential and feel satisfied by the end of the day. Let them stretch their brains, be challenged, and grow in creativity and knowledge. Like muscles that are regularly stretched, this is one way for them to become stronger.

And, of course, the feeling needs to be mutual. This is how Steve Jobs formulated it when he addressed Stanford graduates, "You've got to find what you love. And that is as true for your work as it is for your lovers. Your work is going to fill a large part of your life, and the only way to be truly satisfied is to do what you believe is great work. And the only way to do great work is to love what you do. If you haven't found it yet, keep looking. Don't settle. As with all matters of the heart, you'll know when you find it. And, like any great relationship, it just gets better and better as the years roll on. So keep looking until you find it. Don't settle."

Everyone in your company needs to be equally important; everyone should be valuable, but nobody should be indispensable, and nobody should feel above the rules, beyond cooperation, or entitled to an easy life because he has been with the company for so long. Past performance is no reason for slacking today. Each person should add value to his workplace every day. That makes each person equally valuable. The workplace you create should be the preferred place for an employee to spend his days.

This implies that everyone will need to be inspired and empowered to live his or her own dreams *for* the company and *within* the company. You can delegate tasks, projects, and targets, but such delegation will work only if the employee commits to the task, project, or target. You can stimulate your employees to take the initiative, but in the end initiative can only be *taken*; it can never be *given*. Real authority is also not given; it is taken. Just as love can never be taken; it can only be given.

Along the road, successes need to be celebrated, failures need to be analyzed, and lessons need to be learned. Constant improvement needs to be made. The team will need to laugh and cry together, and its members will need to stimulate each other to become ever better at whatever they are doing. The trip along the road needs to be enjoyed by all, at least the majority of the time, as it does not only take up at least eight hours of your limited time on earth each day but is also a pathway to self-discovery. For every goal that is achieved, a new one will arise, for it is not the moment that is significant, but rather the journey. The goal will never be reached, as after each mountaintop that is conquered a new one will arise.

At Amicorp we depend a lot on close and trusted international cooperation, so we celebrate the differences in culture among our various offices. When it is *Diwali* in India or in Singapore, and *Sinterklaas* in the Netherlands, or when we light a *pagara* in Curaçao, we make an effort to explain the reasons for the celebration to the rest of the group. When it is *Ramadan* we explain to all that some people cannot eat or drink until sundown and may be less productive than normal. We wish each other merry Christmas, happy Eid, a good Year of the Dragon and Russian New Year later than European New Year. Employees speak on a daily basis to each other over the phone and via Skype, and slowly learn to appreciate their colleagues' cultures. We have an Amicorp cookbook with recipes from all over, and many offices are adorned with little flags from different countries they work with. Small statues of Ganesh protect work spaces all over the world. People go to international weddings and dress in garb from other parts of the world. Initial discussions about which food, approach, or culture is better have long been replaced by more and more interest in the lives of colleagues and appreciation for the richness in diversity.

> *"It wasn't the reward that mattered or the recognition you might harvest. It was your depth of commitment, your quality of service, the product of your devotion; these were the things that counted in a life. When you gave purely, the honor came in the giving, and that was honor enough."*
>
> **—Scott O'Grady**

Chapter 18

Who Pays the Salaries and Calls the Shots?

"A customer is the most important visitor on our premises. He is not dependent on us. We are dependent on him. He is not an interruption in our work. He is the purpose of it. He is not an outsider in our business. He is part of it. We are not doing him a favor by serving him. He is doing us a favor by giving us an opportunity to do so."

—Mohandas Gandhi

Whatever your ideas, however great your mission, or however delicious the cookies you bake, if there are no customers buying them, you have a problem. The ultimate test of any service and any product is: will clients buy them? Any business needs to create customers. No business can exist without clients. Management guru Peter Drucker said, "The single most important thing to remember about any enterprise is that there are no results inside its walls. The result of any business is a satisfied customer."

Your relationship with your clients walks a fine line. On the one extreme many people, including all of your salespeople, like to please the clients and give in to their every wish. This is often translated into the adage: "The customer is king." Tempting as that can be, the client needs to remain a client and not become an absolute despot. I strongly disagree with the approach of former US President Richard Nixon, who said, "Never say no when a client asks for something, even if it is the moon.

You can always try, and anyhow there is plenty of time afterwards to explain that it was not possible."

You will need to charge a fair amount of money for your services, and you may have to negotiate conditions like price and quality from time to time. Sometimes the demands of the client are just not reasonable, and you have every right in the world to demonstrate that to him. Good clients pay their bills on time Never accept delays in payment by clients with the excuse that they are *good* clients. People who do not pay you on time are no longer clients. Do not let them poison your organization; eliminate them as quickly as possible.

On the other extreme, there are people who see clients as disturbing their workday, as the people who are never satisfied, always complaining and never willing to pay enough. In your organization these are usually not the salespeople but the production and back-office people. Henry Ford's words, "Any customer can have a car painted any color that he wants so long as it is black," become a mantra of limitation for them. I understand where they come from, and every organization needs to strive for efficiency, but in day-to-day business reality, a business needs to produce what the market demands. For them I have these words of Albert Schweitzer, "I don't know what your destiny will be, but one thing I know: the ones among you who will be really happy are those who have sought and found how to serve."

Truth lies somewhere in the middle. The client needs to become your best friend and a partner in business. He needs you as much as you need him. If you start with acknowledging that, you are already halfway there. As supermarket owner Sam Walton put it bluntly but accurately, "There is only one boss. And that is the customer. And he can fire everybody in the company from the chairman on down, simply by spending his money somewhere else." You can run a business without employees. In fact, many businesses have no employees, but you can never have a business without clients. The employees are there to service the clients and work in their best interests. It is *never* the other way around.

Many companies, large and small, are wise enough to build very close relationships with their clients. For instance a car-part manufacturer or a supplier to the aircraft industry cannot plan without a very close and clear understanding with its clients: the car or aircraft manufacturer.

In a small business it is no different. If you have a coffee shop you will need to position yourself in a way that is attractive to your customers. You cannot have twice the pricing of your neighbor further down the street if your product or ambiance is not significantly better. Henry Ford repeatedly said, "It's not the employer who pays the wages. Employers only handle the money. It's the customer who pays the wages."

When we were relatively new as a trust company in Curaçao and started to have demanding, spoiled clients in Europe, we habitually made sure that the office would be manned from 6:00 AM, to partly bridge the time difference. On local national holidays, like the queen's birthday for example, we would always have, and still have, a skeleton staff to take care of urgent client needs. Clients who call from the other side of the world and get no one on the line may panic and wonder if someone made off with their money.

The last few days before the Hong Kong handover on July 1, 1997, we worked twenty-four hours a day, setting up companies for property owners who at the last moment concluded they might one day need the protection of the Dutch Investment Protection Treaty. This type of flexibility is very important in building your name as a customer-oriented business and will bring you great results.

Our best-timed investment ever was when Denmark drastically changed its corporate tax legislation in a surprise move just before the end of 1998, effectively converting it overnight into a tax haven for international investors. We visited Copenhagen the first week of January, 1999, to learn more about the consequences of this legislative change, and, from a freezing phone booth, we organized resources and flew in staff from the Caribbean in order to open our Copenhagen office the following week. We ended up making good money in Denmark, because we were the first international service provider offering the new opportunities to tax advisors everywhere within Denmark's network of double taxation agreements. More importantly, as a result, we became recognized as an innovative, proactive and enterprising service provider, which greatly helped us with some of our other active projects. A few years later, when the legislation was slowly but steadily repealed, we sold our operation in a management buyout. It continued as a successful local accounting firm, and Jesper Holm Nielsen, the buyer, continues to be a good friend of our company.

The better you know your clients, the tighter you can become with them and the more loyalty you can command. You have to regularly exceed their expectations by fully understanding their needs. And, of course, never disappoint them on the standard execution level. If you regularly speak to your clients you can draw conclusions from the feedback you get on how to improve your service or your product. Never just blindly do what your clients suggest. Steve Jobs once said, "You can't just ask customers what they want and then try to give that to them. By the time you get it built, they'll want something new."

We earlier saw that Henry Ford concluded that had he listened to his clients they would have just wanted a faster horse. You are the entrepreneur. You are the one who will need to make the big leaps in progress. You are the one who needs to come up with revolutionary ideas. You are the visionary expert.

In bigger companies there is a need to bring processes back to manageable size, and departments are shaped to be separate "profit centers" or "businesses." Initially this may start innocently enough, but if you do not watch carefully, before you know it, what started as a simple allocation of expenses and income to measure performance in smaller units becomes a tool for internal competition. Departments may start fighting for their bottom lines with other departments within the organization as fiercely, or even more fiercely, as they do with clients. There are no such things as *internal clients*; in the end *all* income comes from external clients only—there are no exceptions. There is a fundamental difference, and employees constantly need to be reminded that employees in other departments are their colleagues and that by definition their goals and targets *must* be aligned. Time and money spent internally on reallocation of clients, markets, income and expenses is like rearranging the deck chairs of the Titanic on the night it hit the iceberg. It is a waste of resources, and it needs to be treated as such.

Clients are, by definition, only people outside your company. Keep them very close and understand their every wish. To quote US President Lyndon Johnson, "It is better to have them inside the tent pissing out, than outside the tent pissing in." The quote may be slightly out of context, but it ultimately argues that any improvement to your organization should ultimately benefit your clients. A proposed adjustment that may make your procedures easier or your internal organization better but does not lead to better, cheaper, and/or faster service to your clients is, by definition, *not* an improvement.

Spend as much time with your clients as you can afford to, and listen to what they say. Do not draw conclusions from secondhand comments. Dutch hotel entrepreneur Gerrit van der Valk once told me, "You will not make money sitting in your office." We once made a short trip to look at a potential investment in a hotel in Venezuela. We ended up together buying containers full of potted plants, furniture, tiles, and more, but we decided within five minutes of arriving at the hotel that it was not suitable for the purpose of their group. The deals we did on our way there and back and the contacts we made during the trip, however, paid off over time.

The more personal your service to the clients, the better it is. German supermarket magnate Karl Albrecht said, "There is no such thing as internal clients. If you're not serving the customer, you'd better be serving someone who is." Make sure you and your people *never* forget this. I see that as our organization grows, it is easy for some to forget it exists only to service clients. People may be misled to think internal functions are equally important. They are, however, only in as far as they directly serve the ones that service the clients. You must be very careful not to develop a separate purpose, and you should never allow the creation of goals that are not directly aligned with client needs.

Internal services tend easily to grow out of control and need constant review and pruning, as the people working in them have little or no direct client contact. The moment I hear people in our organization even *suggest* that clients need to wait or cannot be serviced because we are budgeting, training, meeting, celebrating, or reporting, I know it is time to get my pruning tools out and get in front of our troops to remind them for whom they actually work.

> *"The true leaders serve. Serve people. Serve their best interests, and in doing so will not always be popular, may not always impress. But because true leaders are more motivated by loving concern than a desire for personal glory, they are willing to pay the price."*
>
> **—Eugene Habecker**

Chapter 19

Is It Important to Have Your Suppliers as Your Business Partners?

"Quality in a product or service is not what the supplier puts in. It is what the customer gets out and is willing to pay for. A product is not quality because it is hard to make and costs a lot of money, as manufacturers typically believe. This is incompetence. Customers pay only for what is of use to them and gives them value. Nothing else constitutes quality."

—Peter F. Drucker

Many management books dedicate at least one chapter to explaining which stakeholder is the most important to a company. In tallying the possibilities, most of the votes tend to go to the employees. Naturally, many management gurus vote for the employee as they cater to salarymen who one day aspire to become CEO and need the support of other salarymen to get there.

The unions, as well as many CEOs of large corporations, also vote for the employee. The employee needs to be happy in order to be able to make the customers happy, who in turn will use more of the services of the company. Herb Kelleher of South West Airlines said, "If the employees come first, then they're happy. A motivated employee treats the customer well. The customer is happy so they keep coming back, which pleases the shareholders. It's not one of the enduring Green mysteries of all time; it is just the way it works."

Other managers, most entrepreneurs, and the owners of mom-and-pop shops vote for the client as being most important. They, of course, recognize that the employee is part of the family and will be taken care of commensurately. Without clients there is simply no business. The employees are your leverage to reach more clients.

Bankers, asset managers, and investors usually vote for the shareholders as top dog. They provide the funds without which there would be no company in the first place. Whatever the company does, it must first and foremost look after the needs of the investors, the shareholders, and the financiers of the company.

Academics and sociologists vote for society at large as being the key stakeholder. The triple bottom line of companies like Tata, and more recently, European and American firms with corporate social responsibilities, reflects that. Moving forward we will see more and more companies take this approach. A few different experts have other key stakeholders in mind, such as Larry Julian, the writer of *God Is My CEO,* who has an obvious candidate for this position.

When the time for the farewell reception comes, another seldom mentioned contender comes up: family. Partners and children are typically ignored in the day-to-day practice of corporate business, but they loom large at times of promotions and on the last day of someone's career. Retirement speeches often include sentiments such as, "Without my partner defending the home front, it would not have been possible," or, "I'm finally going to spend more quality time with the family."

Many stakeholders receive few or no votes in this silly competition of who is most important. The suppliers, strangely enough, are part of that group. In certain countries, they usually get the short end of the stick if a corporate restructuring requires a company to go through a Chapter 11 reorganization (bankruptcy) in order to increase pay for employees or improve margins for shareholders. It keeps corporate misfits like American Airlines flying and second-rank car manufacturers producing, all while suppliers suffer.

When economic times are bad, the suppliers are the first to be asked to give up some or most of their margin in order to maintain the margins for the company they supply. Sometimes they have to pay for the wasteful habits of some big industries, the too-big-to-fail part of the banking industry, and the nonviable but politically protected businesses.

Too often companies fail to realize that suppliers are just as vital a part of the value chain of a company as every other stakeholder. By making one stakeholder more important than another, one embraces the scarcity mentality (Steven Covey) and puts too much focus on just one aspect of the company.

I would say all stakeholders are important. All interests in the company need to be served in order to provide the best possible service for its clients. Suppliers, clients, and employees all need to come out winning so that money can be earned for shareholders and society at large. We, at Amicorp, lean heavily on our suppliers in tough times, but we always make sure they are well cared for in good times. We always try to leave some money on the table for everyone we work with. For this, it is important to deal with only good people. You can never make a good deal with bad people. Do not do business with unreliable, greedy, immoral, or dishonest people—ever. Not as employees, not as clients, and not as suppliers. If you do, sooner or later you will be disappointed.

Once again, in setting the priorities in the big corporate balancing act, you will need to use your values and your moral compass. That is true for a small entrepreneurial company or for a big multinational, as well as for society at large. The values we choose determine the priorities we set. We have to forever stay faithful to our values and dare to live with the consequences of acting consistently. This means that from time to time we will need to choose joyfully to give up profit, to lose people, and to forego business in order to stay true to our values, to serve the environment, to be a valuable contributor to society, and to not make money from polluting, illegal, or immoral business opportunities.

> *"We cannot be both the world's leading champion of peace and the world's leading supplier of the weapons of war."*

—President Jimmy Carter

Chapter 20

With Whom Do You Compete?

"The first and most important rule to observe ... is to use our entire forces with the utmost energy. The second rule is to concentrate our power as much as possible against that section where the chief blows are to be delivered and to incur disadvantages elsewhere, so that our chances of success may increase at the decisive point. The third rule is never to waste time. Unless important advantages are to be gained from hesitation, it is necessary to set to work at once. By this speed a hundred enemy measures are nipped in the bud, and public opinion is won most rapidly. Finally, the fourth rule is to follow up our successes with the utmost energy. Only pursuit of the beaten enemy gives the fruits of victory."

—General Carl von Clausewitz

Business is not war. War is the oldest form of competition between human organizations; business is a relative newcomer. There were no large business organizations (with a few exceptions, such as the Dutch and British East India Companies) until a mere two hundred years ago. Humans have been fighting wars for millennia, and war has driven the evolution of techniques for organizing, supplying, leading, and motivating large numbers of people. To use the words of General Carl von Clausewitz again, "Rather than comparing war to art we could more accurately compare it to commerce, which is also a conflict of human interests and activities; and it is still closer to politics, which in turn may be considered as a kind of commerce on a larger scale."

Almost every business has competitors. If you make a great wine, you are competing not only with the other great wines of the region, but with all the great wines of both the Old World and the New World. In addition you are competing with lower-quality wines, which can compete on price but not on quality and taste, and basically any other drink in the world, including water. Your task is to set apart your wine in such a way that it seems to have as few competitors as possible. Tony Alessandra said, "Being on par in terms of price and quality only gets you into the game. Service wins the game."

A few years ago I was invited to an exclusive wine tasting in Shanghai. A somewhat snobbish French wine exporter did the honors of introducing ever better and more exclusive French wines. In true Chinese tradition, the retail price of each bottle opened was loudly pronounced, and as the prices rose, the hissings and other sounds of appreciation when the price was mentioned grew louder. By the end of the evening, we reached a very exclusive wine; I think it was a Château d'Yquem. Its retail price was outrageous. One of the guests next to me, a wealthy Chinese manufacturer, asked the wine exporter, who was pouring the wine as if it were liquid gold, to top off his glass with Seven Up. The Frenchman acted as if he had been stung by a hundred bees at once and was completely in shock. The neighbor next to the manufacturer came to his rescue and said, "No, you cannot drink that wine with Seven Up." The wine exporter came back to his senses and started to breathe again. Nevertheless, then the second Chinese connoisseur said, "It is much better with Diet Coke." That was the end of the evening for that Frenchman. He almost choked on the sacrilege. But the Chinese wine market is growing rapidly in size, and many Chinese have the money to purchase exclusive wines that are to their taste. Chinese wines are slowly but surely starting to win certain blind tastings, but it will be years before Chinese wines gain the international acclaim that French wines or New World wines possess. Reputation is a major component of setting yourself apart from the competition.

One company that has excelled in setting itself apart from the competition is Cirque du Soleil. It is beautifully described in the book *Blue Ocean*

Strategy, by W. Chan Kim and Renée Mauborgne. Basically Cirque du Soleil created an entirely new category of entertainment by taking attractive elements of both classical circus and theatre while leaving out the less desired elements of both. The result was a business that even today, twenty years later, has virtually no competition.

When South West Airlines began, they developed short-hop, no-frills, point-to-point flights at very low prices. By doing so, they competed with the full-service airlines on price as well as with car travel, creating a whole new category of frequent flier.

Blue Ocean Strategy as a concept is, of course, not new; Cristobal Colon sailed over the blue oceans westward instead of eastward using Chinese maps and navigational methods in order to find a shorter route to China. He was attempting to significantly reduce transportation costs on Chinese goods. Although the direct goal was not achieved, this later turned out to be one of the better private-equity investments ever. In the end, your goal is for your competition to become largely irrelevant. You ultimately want to be competing only with yourself. Do not get distracted by what others in your industry do; this may lead to imitating them. Competing makes you unhappy; it makes you believe that what someone else does or is, is equally or more important than what you are or what you do. Do not fall into this trap. Set your own standards and constantly try to surpass them, rendering the competition irrelevant. Constantly look for ways to set your business apart from that of the competitors. Do this by offering novel products, being in novel markets, or having a novel approach. Although *Blue Ocean Strategy* is easy to understand, the book does not really explain how or where to find such Blue Ocean. Finding the areas where the opportunity to significantly differentiate exists in your business is not always easy. But if you put your mind to it and realize all opportunities are within your reach, you will find previously unknown market segments and means of distribution; you will find a new pricing policy to make the market bigger; you will create the great innovation and develop a completely new product. As an expert in *your* business, you are ideally suited to find the "Blue Ocean" opportunities, provided you focus your mind on doing so.

Basically competition is irrelevant. We do what we do, and we try to do it the best we can based on knowledge, creativity, execution skills, and perfect service. The moment you start looking at the competition is the moment you are tempted to copy them. At that moment you are lost, just as sprinters and cyclists are overtaken if they start doubting and looking over their shoulder. As this is such an important principle, we included it in our key slogan: *Stand out from the crowd*. We tried to approach the market in a different way from our competitors. Trying to think a few years ahead, we focused from day one on countries that at that time were called underdeveloped, but which later became developing nations and now are emerging markets: BRICS, or Tigers. Not only have these countries shown significantly more growth in the past twenty years than more developed markets, but there has also been significantly less competition.

Competition with outside parties is essentially a waste of time and resources and takes focus away from the one who it is all about: the client. The client is the one setting the standards for your business. Competition internally is even worse. It leads to wasting resources on infighting instead of conquering the market. Internally you can have a certain level of friendly rivalry that may lead to good performance, but under no condition should such rivalry take attention, focus, and service away from clients.

> *"I do not try to dance better than anyone else. I only try to dance better than myself."*
>
> **—Mikhail Baryshnikov**

Chapter 21

How Does One Finance a Company?

"Nobody can make you feel inferior without your consent."

Eleanor Roosevelt

Sooner or later most companies will need outside financing in one form or another. If you are contemplating starting a business, you will need some money to live on while you are getting your business off the ground. If you start very small, you may be able to depend on your savings, run up some credit-card debt, or borrow some money from friends and family. But once your business has gotten off the ground, you may need to move to a larger space, create more professional products, invest in a marketing campaign, hire employees, and construct a factory or take over a competitor, a supplier, or a complementary business. You will be faced with financing questions along the way.

The first of these questions is: Do you really want outside financing?

Any form of outside financing entails a large responsibility for you as an entrepreneur, as any financier, any lender or investor, expects firstly to be repaid and secondly to make a return on the funds loaned. In addition to any financing becoming a huge responsibility, it means giving up a part of your freedom. You will need to agree on interest rates and payback periods that will restrict you in making other decisions. You will have to disclose information you might have wanted to keep confidential, such as how much cash you have, the details of your marital status or prenuptial agreement, the value of your house and other assets, or your health (for life insurance purposes), and so on.

Accepting financing also increases your risks. Very often, entering into a loan means providing collateral by pledging assets outside your business. It means guaranteeing obligations on behalf of your company, agreeing to covenants that, depending on the size of the loan in relation to the profitability of your company, can be very onerous. These can include conversion rights, warrants, and pledging of shares that may even lead to the loss of your business if you cannot meet the conditions of the loan.

The above is the good news. It means someone is willing and able to grant you a loan. Since the financial crisis of 2008, with many lenders deleveraging and cutting back on lending, it has been especially difficult for entrepreneurs to find financing on acceptable commercial terms.

The more common sources of financing include: friends and family, banks, leasing companies, angel capital, venture capital, private equity, and initial public offerings. When you are starting up, it is usually a waste of time trying to get financing from banks, so save yourself the frustration. Banks like to analyze the past in order to draw conclusions about the future; they look at the tracks you have left behind in the snow to determine where you are heading. So, as long as you have no past to analyze, they will be very hesitant to lend you any money, however tight your business plan looks and however promising your financial forecasts are. Exceptions are when you have a proven track record (as an entrepreneur, not as an employee), when you work within a proven framework (such as a franchise organization), when you have plenty of collateral (the family silver), or when you do not really need the money, as you then have a very strong balance sheet.

Friends and family are your best bet when you are starting up. On the positive side, friends and family may be flexible on the terms of the loan, may not demand hard collateral, may accept your word as your bond, and will probably be flexible when your proven venture is not off to the flashy start you anticipated. On the negative side, you will be mixing friendship or family with business, which may result in problems spilling over from the business side to the friends and family side, if things do not go as planned. And do you really want your uncle or your eighty-year-old grandma poking around your business affairs? Regardless, in most families there usually is a very limited amount of money you are able to raise this way.

So, once you have exhausted your own savings, borrowed the maximum you can from friends and family, and have been rejected by a lot of banks for additional financing, you may find yourself going hat in hand to angel investors, venture capitalists, and private equity financiers.

At this point in time you really need to think long and hard about why you want the money, why you need the growth, and why you are prepared to sell your soul to the devil. This is the moment to reread Johann Wolfgang von Goethe's *Faust*.

Venture capitalists may give you the money you need to expand when you need it most. They may take risk along with you when you see significant opportunity for growth. They may also provide experience in financial matters that exceeds your own experience, contacts you do not have, and a harder, much more commercial approach to business than you do. They may also think very short-term (their investment horizon typically does not extend beyond three to five years), impose short-term cost cutting and profit maximizing measures you may not like, and restrict your freedom in ways that make you question why the hell you became an entrepreneur in the first place. If you break one of the many covenants you agreed to when you obtained the investment, you may find yourself quickly in a situation where the once so friendly investors have all the bargaining chips in hand and threaten to take control of your company at bargain basement prices or enforce management decisions you would never have made yourself. If there ever was an area of business where the traditional *caveat emptor* (buyer beware) applies, this is it. If you go for private equity, make sure you find investors who are interested in the company for more than just the money.

Once your company has an established track record, a proven history of profit generation, and a stable cash flow, borrowing money becomes easier. To be accepted for bank financing you will need plenty of documentation.

Your mission, vision, and values need to be formulated into a business plan, where you need to demonstrate how you will generate enough cash to repay the loan, even if things go significantly less than planned. You will need past financial statements that show a proven track record as well as financial projections that predict the future to be bright enough to easily repay the loans requested.

Additionally, you will most likely need collateral. That will give the bank a backup source of cash in case your primary source of income, for whatever reason, stagnates. Many banks look for a second source of collateral (guarantees, personal assets) should the first one (receivables, inventory, business assets) not be sufficient in value to cover the loan. Basically, you will need to prove that you do not really need a loan in order to get one. And, *please*, always keep in the back of your mind that when the going gets tough the bankers will panic and ask for their money back. There is a lot of truth to the saying that banks lend you an umbrella when the sun shines and ask for it back when it begins to rain.

Never leverage yourself to the maximum; never trust everything your friendly bankers say. The people you speak with are never the decision makers; those will be an anonymous group of people you will never even meet. They will have no clue what your dreams are and what you are trying to achieve. And finally, never accept financing that depends on everything going well in order to be able to meet the loan conditions. Everything that can go wrong, sooner or later, will go wrong.

It does not necessarily have to be you who falls on hard times; it may also be your bank. In the past few years, many healthy companies have gotten into serious trouble just because their banks have failed. Investments in toxic "assets," country debt of overleveraged countries, credit-card debt, housing bubbles, and deleveraging and stricter central bank supervision have brought many lenders into trouble not of their own making. Do not think your bank is immune to that. No bank is too big to make stupid mistakes. After all, banks' decisions are made by people who, by definition, make mistakes.

When you need larger amounts in order to pursue significant acquisitions, to buy out major shareholders, to create a new product, to build significant production facilities, or to become a global player, you may wish to contemplate issuing listed bonds or becoming a public company.

Becoming a listed company involves getting naked in public, making everything you do fully transparent, documenting every business decision you ever make, giving up control, creating a lot of checks and balances, and putting yourself under the scrutiny of people who may or may not understand your business, mission, and vision.

On the other hand, becoming a listed company also means becoming very visible, benefitting from an enhanced image, setting yourself apart from privately owned companies, and creating an image of size, quality, transparency, and adherence to the rules. Your competitive situation may be greatly improved.

In our company at one stage or another, we have dealt with almost every form of financing. Our best experiences have been with friends and family, as well as with some angel investors, as informal, yet close, personal relationships work well in an environment of trust. We had a terrible experience with a private equity company, which brushed over the fine print when we were looking for money at a time when an attractive acquisition opportunity came along. The company turned out to have all kind of tricks hidden in the fine print; and when it got into trouble during the dot-com bust, the company came banging on our door, cashing in the investment.

The key lesson I have learned over the years is that money does strange things to people. Remember my personal experience in the introductory chapter of working at a bank. You had better stay very much on the safe side. Do not let yourself be lured into overly leveraging yourself or your company. Do not let greed drive you to the limits. Do not think that *return on equity* is more important than a safety net, and do not think your coshareholders will be happier if you get the maximum out of their investment this year while risking the life of the company. Make sure the providers of financing have an interest in your company that goes beyond making a return on investment. It is always easier to speak to people who are your friends and who share common interests than to speak to cold moneymaking machines.

As an entrepreneur, you first need to safeguard the continuity of your company. And often that means going slower than you would like. Most companies do not live long; in fact, only one in ten lives as long as five years. Most do not make it because their cash flow is insufficient to sustain operations. Business life is highly uncertain, and there is little or no mercy in the market for small companies that get into financial trouble. Be very conservative on the financial side, hire good financial experts, find yourself an experienced CFO (once you reach to that size), make sure you have at least monthly cash flow statements, make sure your administration is *always* up to date and reliable, and, as soon as you can afford it, have your books audited, whether it is a legal requirement in your country or not. This is one area where experts come in very handy and where your intuition may need to take a backseat to a conservative approach and a "better safe than sorry" mind-set.

> *"I wish that dear Karl could have spent more time acquiring capital instead of merely writing about it."*
>
> **—Jenny Marx**

Chapter 22

How Does One Combine Friends and Family with Business?

"It is not so much our friends' help that helps us as the confident knowledge that they will help us."

—Epicurus

Being an entrepreneur forces you to make difficult choices. One of the more difficult ones is how to balance the wants and needs of your business with the wants and needs of your family and friends.

In our business there is the opportunity, as well as the need, to travel a lot. For the last twenty years I have been spending almost one-third of my time on the road, visiting clients and intermediaries as well as our own international offices. During school holidays we always tried to combine business needs with family time. We enjoyed visiting the countries that during the rest of the year would be nothing more than a succession of anonymous offices, hotel rooms, and taxi rides. In the process we acquired a nice collection of international friends and got to know people and cultures we would never otherwise have encountered as mere tourists.

We lived for fifteen years in the Caribbean. There, we enjoyed the beach, island life, and sailing, among other things. My wife became a sailing champion, my son an expert skateboarder, and my daughter is still culturally more an Antillean than anything else. Later we lived for four years in Barcelona and enjoyed the architecture of the city, the *tapas* and the *cava*, the various wineries, and the mountains for skiing in the winter and hiking in the summer. Then we moved to Singapore, where we enjoyed all things modern, the beautiful cultures of the mysterious Asian countries in the vicinity, and the fact that everything worked perfectly. In between we got to participate in weddings and parties everywhere. At some point we spent a year and a half in South Africa working on the development of an aloe vera project and the construction of a factory. We organized many game drives and got to know African wildlife, game management, and seasonal patterns. We did this while learning to cope with the remnants of the *apartheid* culture, the overwhelming problems of poverty, AIDS, crime, and lack of education and opportunity in the search for a new, viable economic, social, and political framework for South Africa.

My kids grew up with all of this. They speak several languages and are less culturally biased than I will ever be. They have uttered phrases such as, "Do we have to go to Hong Kong again for spring break," or, "Can we pass by Singapore on our way from Johannesburg to Curaçao because I really need to go to *that* hairdresser." On the other hand, I also remember my son at age six or seven trying to stop me from going to the airport yet again, by spreading himself on the hood of the car, and my wife calling me back from business trips on more than one occasion for some family emergency. The pleasant aspects of this lifestyle are balanced by the less pleasant. They cannot be separated from one another.

Travelling a lot means missing school and family events—missing out on some of the *firsts* in your kids' lives. Sometimes birthdays are celebrated over the phone as, regrettably, you are not always home when you should be.

As an entrepreneur, and especially a travelling one, it is not always possible to balance family and business to the satisfaction of both sides. My wife has chosen to have limited involvement with my business and never to work in it—a choice that was not always convenient but all in all has worked well for us. As a result, she was neither involved in the significant ins and outs of the company nor with many of its people. She has often called Amicorp a clan or a sect that excludes anyone who is not a member. This is an important part of my emotional and social life, and it takes place outside of hers and our shared interests. Not being involved in the business side of it, her link with the company was hardly more than knowing many of the people involved, visiting some of the offices on special occasions, and painting the annual group calendar that we annually send to our business associates.

The hard choices always remain. In the words of Katz and Liu, "Many professions presume total dedication as a prerequisite for advancement. Out of this presumption has grown the myth of quality time, in which marital, social, and family relationships are pigeonholed into token moments, while Career, with a capital C, is the centerpiece around which all else revolves."

It is often said at funerals that "nobody regrets not having spent more time in the office" and that everyone wishes to have spent more time with family and friends. Kids especially grow up so fast, and whenever you concentrate on your job, you miss an important phase of their development. I think it is important to strike a balance. It cannot be true that what you spend a major part of your waking time on, or that which provides your livelihood and a major sense of pride and personal development, would be of secondary importance. All aspects of your body, mind, soul, and spirit need to be in balance. Your life is most rewarding if, like in a Chinese circus, you can balance a lot of plates at the same time. And, yes, from time to time one of those plates will fall. But through practice and perseverance you can learn to balance a lot of things and gracefully pick up again what you may have dropped on the floor.

In the process I hope my children have learned a lot, have seen what enormous and ridiculous differences in opportunities and income there are in the world, have seen how many kids never get a chance to go to a proper school or play with fun toys, and have understood that they have choices to make in life. I hope they have seen what possibilities they can create for themselves and have some understanding that to make money, build a life, and do something meaningful requires significant perseverance, discipline, creativity, and focus. I truly think we have been able to give them a broader range of experiences than most parents. What they do with it is up to them. But I was very satisfied when my son at the age of ten discovered that there were significantly more totem poles in Canada than in the Caribbean, and that there could be a possibility for an export-import business there. I was also happy that when teaching as an intern in an orphanage in Bangalore at seventeen, he learned to appreciate how difficult life is for a teacher who has to deal with forty kids in one classroom.

Ninety percent or more of the companies in the world are family businesses. Yet most family businesses do not survive beyond the first generation, and only 6 percent last to the third generation. They fail for a long list of predictable and preventable reasons. Many family businesses are rife with conflict. There are stories of super-rich parents at the throats of their children, brothers suing sisters, and every other permutation of family conflict imaginable. Family members feel freer to tell each other the truth and keep less distance than strangers who work together do, focusing on the strengths and usually ignoring or compensating for the weaknesses. Happy family businesses resemble each other; unhappy family businesses are unhappy, but each in its own unique way.

From an early age I told my children that it was neither the intention nor the plan for them to become part of the business. It is a choice many entrepreneurs face. Do you build your business as a family business, where you always give priority to family members, or do you build a business with strangers and keep the family members out? Many family businesses at some stage make the decision to no longer let the family run the business, as the business has grown too large to be run without expert managers, domain specialists, or career leaders. In our case, as we depend mostly on knowledge and experience to service clients, I do not think it would make either our children or our colleagues very happy if key positions were handed over to the children of the founders. Luckily, both of my children have developed different interests. I also think it is much more satisfying in almost any situation if the children get their chance to earn their own positions, make their own mistakes, and foster their own talents without being force-fed by their parents. In small family businesses, farms and shops for example, succession within the family may make sense; in larger or more professional companies it may make more sense to create a meritocracy and relegate the family members to the level of shareholders within a family office setup. If someone, whether that person be a relative or a complete outsider, does not have the specific set of demonstrable competencies that probably match a previously identified set of company needs, do not ever give him a job within the company or a seat on the company's board of directors. You are doing neither that family member nor the company a favor.

At a certain moment, I invited one of my best friends to join our company. We had been friends for many years but had pursued different careers until that point. The first year went really well, as it is always a pleasure to work with people you genuinely like. After that, issues started to arise as my friend, in my opinion, assumed a privileged position compared to the other people in the organization. And after a while we had several fallouts and decided it was better to remain good friends than to remain colleagues. And that was a good choice. It is hard to be close friends and colleagues at the same time. Any business requires a certain teamwork with an inevitable formal or informal hierarchy and the trust that the team members are treated equally and committed equally to their tasks. It goes back to the old story about the breakfast of ham and eggs. The chicken is involved, but the pig is committed. In a well-functioning team, you need everyone to be equally committed.

> "As long as you pursue pleasure, you are attached to the sources of pleasure; and as long as you are attached to the sources of pleasure, you cannot escape pain and sorrow. The soul shines in the hearts of all living beings. When you see the soul in others, you forget your own desires and fears, and lose yourself in the service of others. The soul shines equally in people on the farthest island, and in people close at hand."

—Mundaka Upanishad

Chapter 23

What Is Corporate Social Responsibility?

"Capitalism is the astounding belief that the most wickedest of men will do the most wickedest of things for the greatest good of everyone."

—John Maynard Keynes

What is a business for? Does it exist just to make a profit for the shareholders? In the Anglo-Saxon approach, a company's financiers are its owners, and employees are treated as property and accounted for as costs. Although there may have been some sense to that in the early days of industrialization, it does not reflect today's reality. Now a company's assets are increasingly its employees, who contribute their time and talent, rather than the shareholders, who permanently or, in the case of listed companies, temporarily contribute their money.

Those who carry the company's intellectual property within them, who contribute time and talent rather than money, must have some say in the future of what is also *their* company. However, in our superficial, short-term-view environment, only that which is visible gets counted, and accounting systems are many years behind in recognizing what creates value and what does not. They are basically still focused on the age of industrialization, when material assets were the only ones ending up on the balance sheets, employees were instantly replaceable, and assets that were less tangible were to a certain extent accounted for.

The knowledge in the heads of the employees, the ideas and drive of the entrepreneurs, and the good reputation and the name of a brand are intangible; the contributions of a lifesaving drug or the time-saving improvement on the Internet are also intangible. In fact, all these and more: a faster plane, a revolutionary invention, a great infrastructure or distribution network, a great idea, and a cure for AIDS will never be adequately expressed on the balance sheets of companies, and therefore, by definition, remain undervalued and underappreciated.

Over the next ten or twenty years this will change. The ever-further integrating global economy will drive all major production facilities to the places with the lowest cost per unit. China has enough people to be the production center for all large-scale manufactured goods in the world, and cheaper countries like Vietnam and the Philippines are already nipping at its heels. The less-tangible value added in other parts of the world will sooner or later have to be expressed in different ways.

In the knowledge economy, good business is a community with a purpose and is not just a piece of property. The purpose is not just to make a profit but to make a profit in order to do something better. You always need to ask the question: *If it did not exist, would we invent this company?* And the answer needs to be something like, *Only if it does something better or more useful than anyone else.*

Additionally, businesses play a leading role in solving today's social problems by incorporating the best ideas of governments and nonprofit institutions. Community needs are actually opportunities to develop ideas and demonstrate business technologies. Corporate responsibility can lead to new markets as well as solutions to business problems.

In Japan many companies work under a business credo called *kyosei,* which means the "spirit of cooperation," in which individuals and organizations work together for the common good. The implementation of *kyosei* can be divided into five distinct stages, each one building upon the preceding one.

In the first stage, companies work to build both a reliable and stable stream of income and establish a strong market position. In the second stage, managers and employees resolve to work together, recognizing that both groups are vital to the company's success. In the third stage, this sense of cooperation is extended beyond the company to include customers, suppliers, the community, and even competitors. In the fourth stage, the company takes the cooperative spirit beyond national boundaries and addresses some of the global imbalances present in the world. And lastly, in the fifth stage, a stage that companies rarely achieve, a company urges the national government to work toward rectifying global imbalances.

This may sound pretty modern, but amazingly *kyosei* is directly based on guidelines formulated under the name *Shuchu Kiyaku* by Japanese traders and Confucian scholars in the sixteenth century. They recognized that, for international trade to be successful, not only would everyone need to be treated equally despite differences in race, skin color, and culture, but also a win-win situation would need to be created, not only for the traders and producers involved, but also for the larger communities involved.

Again, how do you integrate this concept into your small entrepreneurial enterprise? At Amicorp we created an overview of what we want to do and what we don't want to do. Simply, we decide what kind of clients to accept, and which ones to avoid (of course, aside from what is already regulated by law and supervisory authorities). Just as a car can be used to drive an injured child to the hospital or to run over someone by a drunk driver, and a knife can be used to carve up a loaf of bread or someone's face, in our business, misuse can occur very easily. Of course you cannot hold responsible the car manufacturer for a drunk driver or a knife manufacturer for a stabbing. But in our business, we singled out groups with a significantly higher risk of ending up on the wrong side of the law from what is ethical or feels good. We started by eliminating risk categories of business that, although technically legal, we did not want to be involved in. We decided we did not want to facilitate the international expansion of the arms industry (however legal and mostly government licensed). Nor did we want to get involved with the gaming and gambling industry (although in our business that could be a very significant source of income). Drugs, pornography, and sex-related business also ended up on that same side. We also reject as clients high government officials or politicians so as to avoid ending up in corruption scandals, people from countries subject to UN embargoes or otherwise failed or highly unstable countries (such as, at the time of writing, Afghanistan, Iran, Syria, North Korea, and several central African countries), and countries where our business makes little sense, such as the United States and Japan (unless we obtain written tax advice or a copy of the tax return providing how the tax savings are being reported). We also do not help to structure investments that unnecessarily contribute to pollution or the degeneration of the earth, such as unnecessarily polluting open pit mines, deforestation, or industrial fishing fleets. We, of course, do this to protect our own business and to prevent it from ending up in scandals and legal issues, but we also do it because it does not feel good or right to work on something that is just to the detriment of society at large.

We have a department that evaluates all structures and solutions before implementing them. It is staffed by people separate from the people who discovered the opportunities and who may be in love with their own ideas and the nice people they have met. In the end we fall back on the Latin phrase, *in dubio abstinae*—when in doubt don't. There is plenty of business, so why bother finding it close to the edge of what is possible or legal? I know it is hard to resist the exotic flowers that grow close to the edge of the cliff, but once you have made a few mistakes, you quickly learn it is not worth the hassle and the agony to make certain types of mistakes that could easily be avoided.

A business must be sustainable in almost all economic conditions and in all markets. It must provide meaningful, highly differentiated results to its clients; otherwise, it will not survive for long and will create suffering for its employees, clients, suppliers, and financiers. In the words of Michael Gerber, "A business is an economic entity driving an economic reality, creating an economic certainty for the communities in which it thrives."

The triple balance sheet and standards for ethical business practices have been around since time immemorial. You can read three-thousand-year-old practices in Assyrian and Buddhist scriptures, when money and banking had barely been invented. The Bible has over two thousand entries dedicated to money alone. Verses forbid the investment in products dangerous to the health of the individual or society (such as cigarettes and alcohol). They warn against the use of financial products such as futures and options (thou shalt not sell the fruits that are still growing on the tree), and forbid usury by charging for interest on loans. Scholars often argue that Christian Europe started to make real economic progress compared to the Islamic world when those rules were ignored and moneylenders (first Jews and later Christians) accumulated ever-bigger fortunes that allowed for ever-braver ventures and larger investments. Islamic financing, which is currently making a major comeback in Muslim countries, is nothing more than a revisiting of these ancient ethical rules. Banks in other cultures, such as Triodos Bank in the Netherlands and other ethical mutual funds, follow similar principles.

Amicorp has about fifteen thousand customers, a number that is a fraction of what our larger competitors have. If one believes in economies of scale, a small financial institution providing the same services as larger ones should not be able to survive in the face of much-larger competitors. But, it is easy to overlook the dis-economies of scale. While you can measure and demonstrate the economies of a larger back office or the savings from merging two small trust companies, it is harder to identify the negative impact of colleagues who are competing for their jobs, the incompatible computer systems, or the failure of offices to cooperate with each other. And, while we provide the same corporate secretarial and trustee services, we compete on dimensions where we have a clear advantage over a larger institution: relationship, flexibility, care, independence, and speed of service, to name just a few.

These qualities are in demand, but we are clear that we can supply them only on a relatively small human scale. We have no answering machines, no help desks, and no out-of-office reply. It is important to us to know our customers personally, and we can accommodate only a relatively limited number; hence, we turn away quite a significant percentage of our prospective clients. We insist on a twenty-four-hour turnaround time on all decisions and client communications, and we can do so only because we know each intermediary and most customers personally.

There are fundamentally two ways to grow a business. One way is to do more work, and the other way is to get smarter. In attempting to remain at a human scale, we annually confront the latter challenge with only a gradually growing number of staff and customers.

Independence means different things to different people. One facet of it is our ownership; Amicorp is owned by about fifty of its employees, and we are not just trying to maximize profits. We are trying to optimize quality and minimize risk while making a living in trust services and company management. Customers and staff like the fact that we do not try to push any tax planning or financial products, and we deal only in products and services we fully understand with people we know and trust. We never force our opinion upon our clients. Clients who need investment advice, legal opinions, or tax opinions are referred to trusted specialists in those areas. Values play a prominent part in our company, and we treat customers as we would wish to be treated. We have a Community Foundation, and we stimulate our staff to donate time and efforts to charitable or community efforts. A significant part of our staff participates in these efforts.

I think that employee ownership is a suitable ownership structure for any potentially risky or highly personal service business, including ours. However, at some stage the increasing need for optimal transparency may require us to become a public company, but without sacrificing our values at the altar of money. In our case our approach has stood by us in economic difficulties, as it has kept us operating according to conservative policies and has kept us away from scandals. It has also afforded us the choice to not maximize profits at the expense of other goals.

We are sometimes asked how we hold on to good staff, and the truth is that while some people want to earn lots of money as investment or private bankers, there are plenty of others, often more pleasant characters, motivated to do a good job for a reasonable employer and

to have a private life as well. We must do something right, as many of
our people have worked here for ten or more years, and some are in the
second generation—and that for a company that is only twenty years
old. At all times we try to balance the interests of staff, customers, and
employee-shareholders, and we try to make the existence useful and
socially enjoyable. We do this by remaining human-scale and true to
our philosophy, which is not far from Buddhist economics, and if we
continue to harmonize the interests of profit, people, and planet, it
should work for a long time.

A small business creates a standard against which all businesses are
measured, as either successful or not, to upgrade the possibility for all
small business to thrive beyond the standards that formerly existed,
whether stated or not. When companies become large, their responsibility
for the environment and society grows. Many countries had or have
company towns, where whole communities depend on the economic woes
of one or a few companies. The fates of cities like Detroit, Michigan, and
industrial belts all over Europe, Japan, the United States, and China
are directly related to the ups and down of their key industries. Cities
like New York, Hong Kong, and London live by the vagaries of their
financial industries. In those cases it is obvious that sometimes (at least
temporarily) businesses become too big to fail. In the long run every
business, regardless of its size, needs to have an economic value added,
to adhere to the standard laws underlying economics (as always so clearly
pointed out by Warren Buffett), and to contribute to society.

For a small entrepreneurial company it is a little different but not much.
Of course you cannot count on government aid the way big businesses
do, and, of course, your impact on society is a little smaller than that
of the big industries and companies that come up with breakthrough
innovations. But you still contribute to the lives of the people directly
related to your company, any you need to play a positive role in your
local community.

Our Curaçao office is not far from one of the poorer neighborhoods
on the island. A few years ago we decided to celebrate our fifteenth

anniversary by creating a day-care center. We renovated a building to the latest standards in day care, we hired well-qualified staff, and obtained the best educational methods and materials we could get from both the United States and Europe. And we made it all available to the children of our employees, as well as to the children of poor or single-parent families from the neighborhood. We financed it in part through the generosity clients and suppliers showed by "adopting" kids, which resulted in a feeling that exceeds the typical feel-good factor. We experience less crime in our neighborhood, we are closer to some of our employees and suppliers, and some other companies on the island have followed our example and adopted the concept with projects of their own, with which, of course, we assist wholeheartedly.

Our India office picks up training projects that can benefit from the many employees we have with excellent computer skills, the written-off but still usable hardware we have, and the internship possibilities we can offer to well-educated but inexperienced people in a tough job market.

In Indonesia we contribute to a project developed by an old friend, Charles Jacobs, who has retired to the village of Desa Les. This village is on the poorer northern side of the island. The project seeks to create jobs by making the local waterfall into more of a tourist attraction. We created a website, better pathways, nice signs, and maps, and in the process, we learned a lot about the local culture and habits, and we felt as though we were contributing to something positive in this more or less forgotten part of that beautiful island. Now we are looking into other needs of this community, to see whether we can do more.

Any company, anywhere, can do something. In any neighborhood there is some suffering that can be alleviated; in any industry there is a segment of the market that can benefit from your skills and knowledge, and from the services you provide and the products you make. There is always a charity that needs your product, homeless people that need your leftover food, or people who need internships or trainee positions. When you feel good about yourself, and your employees feel good about themselves, you will radiate that and, in turn, attract more business to your company.

To be a responsible corporate citizen, you have to listen to your heart and do what you are capable of doing. Often, this will repay itself back tenfold, in respect, in appreciation, and ultimately in business. You and your employees, who feel good about themselves, will radiate that and, in turn, attract more business to your company.

> *"If a man is called to be a street sweeper, he should sweep streets, even as Michelangelo painted, or Beethoven composed music, or Shakespeare wrote poetry. He should sweep streets so well that all the hosts of heaven and earth will pause to say, Here lived a great street sweeper who did his job well."*

> **—Martin Luther King Jr.**

Chapter 24

How Does One Create Environmental Consciousness?

"Whatever you do, do not run."

—Botswana Game Park ranger

Should you ever accidentally cross paths with a lion when on foot in the African wilderness, the one thing not to do is run away. You will trigger the lion's hunting instinct, resulting in it outrunning and overpowering you.

That need not automatically be a negative thing. We tend to talk about progress in society in terms of longevity, safety, or comfort, but if we compare the life of zoo animals to those on the African savannahs, we may come to realize that the law of the jungle, freedom, health, and being the best we can be—eat or be eaten—also have their advantages in improving the quality of society.

Every night on the savannah the slowest lions have to run faster than the slowest impala to score their dinner; the slowest impala, in turn, must outrun the fastest lion so as to not become dinner. It is the same in business. Every business needs to prove its reason for being time and again. *Too big to fail is nonsense*; the biggest elephant in the bush and the strongest lion on the plain will one day grow weak, die, and be replaced by a younger version. That is the way the universe is designed and destined to be. The old must constantly make space for the new.

This is just one reality you cannot run away from, but there are other problems as well. Your business, like every business, has an impact on the environment. In the case of logging, mining, or industrial fishing, the impact can be huge. In other cases its direct impact is more modest. Nevertheless, each business has some impact, including yours and mine. That impact needs to be justified by the value the business creates. If it does not add enough value to society as a whole, it ought to be terminated, even though it may be both profitable and a source of joy for you, the shareholders, and the employees.

I believe business should try and pursue a quadruple bottom line of profits, people, planet, and passion. This is not only the ethical choice one needs to make, but the *Economist* has also investigated and proven that, "Companies with their eye on their 'quadruple-bottom-line' outperform their less fastidious peers on the stock market." The resources of the earth are finite; it has a limited amount of natural resources, a limited amount of substitutes, and a limited capacity to deal with waste, greenhouse gases, and destruction.

I have been battling with questions such as: Is it environmentally acceptable to ruin a piece of virgin nature on Mount Ararat, Curaçao, with its beautiful green parakeets and increasingly rare iguanas just so I can construct an office tower that will house a number of people who are simply trying to earn a living? Or, is it acceptable to destroy some rare African *hoogveld* where antelope roam and snakes nest so that an *aloe vera* plantation can be developed and produce drinks that strengthen the autoimmune system and prevent people from dying of AIDS or diabetes? Or, is it acceptable to plan a vineyard on the dry slopes of the Andes so that delicious wine can be enjoyed by people thousands of miles away? I do not know for sure, but to borrow some well-worn words from Fidel Castro, "la historia me absolverá." I hope history will prove me right.

The earth was not created to support the human race or, more specifically, just our generation. The earth is supposed to last forever and should serve the needs of many generations of people as well as other species.

Albert Einstein wrote in 1950, "A human being is part of the whole, called by us 'Universe,' a part limited in time and space. He experiences himself, his thoughts and feelings as something separated from the rest—a kind of optical delusion of his consciousness. This delusion is a kind of prison for us, restricting us to our personal desires and to affection for a few people nearest to us. Our task must be to free ourselves from this prison by widening our circle of compassion to embrace all living creatures and the whole of nature in its beauty."

In 2000, two US presidential candidates proposed to internationalize the Amazon Basin, in return for the reduction of some Brazilian foreign debt. Cristovam Buarque, a Brazilian senator, responded that as a Brazilian he opposes the internationalization of the Amazon region. Even though the Brazilian government has not given it the attention that this natural treasure deserves, it is still Brazilian. But as a humanist, realizing the risk of environmental destruction that threatens the Amazon region, he could imagine the advantages of its internationalization.

Taking this thought further, if the Amazon region, from a humanistic point of view, is to be internationalized, then the oil reserves of the world should be internationalized as well. Oil nowadays is just as important to the well-being of humanity as the Amazon region. Nevertheless, the owners of oil reserves feel it is in their right to increase or decrease oil production and to raise or lower the price. The rich of the world feel they have the right to burn this valuable resource. Similarly, the financial capitals of the wealthy nations should be internationalized. If the Amazon region should not be burned down by the decision of a landowner or a country, we should equally not permit that the financial reserves of the world burn down entire nations according to the whims of bankers and speculators.

Likewise, we should also internationalize the great museums in the world. The Louvre cannot belong just to France, the Hermitage not just to Russia. Each museum in the world is a guardian of the most beautiful works produced by human ingenuity. It cannot be permitted that these cultural possessions, like ownership of the Amazon region, be manipulated or destroyed according to the whims of an owner or a country. A couple of years ago, a Japanese millionaire decided to have a painting of a grand master buried with him in the grave. This painting should have been internationalized.

New York, as the base of the United Nations, should also be internationalized. At least Manhattan should belong to all of humanity. Similarly, Paris, Venice, Rome, London, Rio de Janeiro, Brasília, Recife, and every city with its own beauty and its own history should belong to the world.

If the United States wants to internationalize the Amazon region in exchange for Brazilian debt reduction, then the United Nations should internationalize the nuclear stockpiles of the United States, particularly since they have already demonstrated that they are capable of using these weapons to cause destruction that exceeds that of the fires in the Brazilian forests.

Cristovam Buarque concludes this thought by suggesting that we could also internationalize children and treat all of them, regardless of their birthplace, as an asset to humanity that deserves the care and attention of the entire world. When the world leaders attend to all poor children of the world as possessions of humanity, they will no longer permit these children to work when they should be studying or to die when they should be living.

It is also remarkable that proposals such as internationalizing Brazilian resources have not been heard of anymore since the Brazilian national debt has greatly decreased as a percentage of GNP, while US debt has greatly increased as a percentage of GNP.

In parts of the world where people live closer to nature than in the postindustrial world, the concept of careful stewardship of natural resources is more often engrained in ethics, politics, and the daily way of thinking. I vividly remember when I was a backpacker on a long-distance bus trip somewhere between Cuzco, Peru, and the Bolivian border, the bus made a meal stop at a restaurant along the endless road.

The portion size matched that of the Altiplano Indians, so when my meal was consumed, I wanted to order another one. The lady running the place, clearly not independently wealthy, flatly refused to accept my business. Plenty of food was ready for the additional buses that might or might not pass by her restaurant. Her reasoning was that that I should not want more than my fair share. It was enough for the others; it should also be enough for me. Had I listened more intently and better understood her meaning, instead of grumpily accepting a bruise to the ego, I would perhaps not be overweight today.

Later in this book I describe Bhutan's measuring of National Happiness and their placing an important weight on their environment. Previously mentioned was *Ubuntu*, an African ethic or humanist philosophy focusing on people's allegiances and relations with each other. It is a philosophy that supports the changes that are necessary to create a future that is economically and environmentally sustainable.

Since the transition from the apartheid regime to an equal representation system, South Africa has introduced a lot of new legislation, and especially jurisprudence, that is more based on the black majority's cultural affinities than on the Anglo-Saxon laws, or on traditions of the European Boer, who had been ruling the country before. Judge Colin Lamont expanded on the definition of *Ubuntu* during his ruling on the widely followed hate-speech trial of Julius Malema (Malema was a leader of the youth wing of the ANC and was strongly opposed to the continued presence and economic power of white people in South Africa). According to Judge Lamont, "*Ubuntu* is recognized as being an important source of law within the context of strained or broken relationships amongst individuals or communities and as an aid for providing remedies which contribute toward more mutually acceptable remedies for the parties in such cases."

Ubuntu is a concept that:

- is to be contrasted with vengeance; vengeance only breeds hatred

- dictates that a high value be placed on the life of a human being—any human being

- is inextricably linked to the values of, and places a high premium on, dignity, compassion, humanity, and respect for the humanity of another

- dictates a shift from confrontation to mediation and conciliation

- dictates good attitudes and shared concern

- favors the reestablishment of harmony in the relationship between parties and that such harmony should restore the dignity of the plaintiff without ruining the defendant

- favors restorative rather than retributive justice, and promotes mutual understanding rather than punishment

- operates in a direction favoring reconciliation rather than estrangement of disputants

- works toward sensitizing a disputant or a defendant in litigation to the hurtful impact of his actions to the other party and toward changing such conduct rather than merely punishing the disputant

- favors face-to-face encounters of disputants with a view to facilitating differences being resolved rather than conflict and victory for the most powerful

- favors civility and civilized dialogue premised on mutual tolerance

This is a concept that could benefit the world. In other contexts, such as the business environment and in modern Western politics, *Ubuntu* would make for a less contentious environment and a more harmonious society.

How do you make your small service company more environmentally responsible? There are many little things one can do that in the aggregate will add up. We began by inspiring the people at Amicorp to establish an environmental statement or policy. We use electronic media and technology to cut down our paper use, and we use video or *skype* conferences, instead of physical ones. Also, we limit the number of flights and long-distance trips for *personal* meetings to the occasions when it is *really* necessary to see each other. We introduced a visible and easily accessible *reduce, reuse, and recycle* practice for paper, batteries, metal, plastic, and glass. If we travel, we try to stay in hotels that are more environmentally aware than those that simply install a mundane linen reuse program printed on the only green piece of paper in the hotel. However immaterial the gesture may seem, I refuse the envelope they want to put around my invoice when I check out. Do you have any idea how many people stay in hotels, worldwide, each night? Selecting vegetarian meals, which are often made up of local, seasonal produce, and printing on recycled paper with vegetable-based ink are simple ways you can contribute. We try to organize our office facilities in such a way that energy, lights, and air conditioning are automatically turned off when rooms are not in use. We encourage everyone to come up with additional energy-saving tips and environmentally sound ideas that fit their personal values.

On a larger scale, Barack Obama pledged, "This is the moment when we must come together to save this planet. Let us resolve that we will not leave our children a world where the oceans rise and famine spreads and terrible storms devastate our lands."

Fortunately, there is a growing awareness among people everywhere in the world that we cannot continue to treat the earth as we have in the past. That in itself is good news, but there is no reason for us to wait for others to attack or solve the many problems involved. It is much better to be proactive and, by enthusiastically doing our part, act as an example for the people we work with and our social environment. The little piece we each do in our companies helps.

> *"In my view the successful companies of the future will be those that integrate business and employees' personal values. The best people want to do work that contributes to society with a company whose values they share, where their actions count and their views matter."*

—Jeroen van der Veer

Chapter 25

Why Is Transparency Important?

"We can do what we want, but we cannot want what we want."

—Arthur Schopenhauer

One of the issues many entrepreneurs struggle with at times is how much information to share with others, both inside and outside the organization. We seem to have an inborn fear that information that is shared decreases in value, gets lost, or is ultimately used against us. "Everything you say, can and will be used against you," is often heard in board rooms. The more extreme forms, such as, "The walls have ears" ("Der Feind hört mit"), also resound till this day. It makes me remember a funny story when I had just started out in the trust business. Our office building was being remodeled, and we were forced to hold a client meeting in the room of my then mentor, Pim Ruoff. He explained to our Latin American clients, who were not feeling very comfortable in the noisy and dusty environment, that the trust business is one of full confidentiality—"Everything we discuss remains between these four walls." He had just finished his sentence when one of the walls collapsed, exposing the men at work on the other side of the wall. It was a very clear demonstration, albeit accidental, that confidentiality no longer exists.

But when you come to think of it, a company actually has very little secret information. Of course, you may wish to keep the recipe of your famous apple pie secret or the design of your next year's collection under wraps, but other than that, a company does not have a lot of real secrets.

Salary information needs to be made either completely transparent (as happens in many governments and some large corporations) or kept completely confidential, as incomplete information leads to speculation, and speculation can be damaging to any organization.

Making salary information transparent will help in avoiding discrimination based on race, sex, religion, education, or country of birth within your company. Scientific research has proven that tall, handsome people earn significantly more than less attractive, shorter people. You need to be aware of this and prevent it from happening in your company. In most of Europe and the United States, your life is a lot easier if you are white, and in most of the Caribbean and South Africa it is a lot easier to be black. In Pakistan it is easier to be a Muslim than a Hindu, and in India the other way around. Even in countries highly focused on equality and treating all races equally, such as Singapore, almost all apartment buildings have separate elevators for the residents and for their household staff. As a leader, take note of this. You will not be able to change cultural biases and outright discrimination, but you can at least make sure the differences are transparent, acknowledged, and seen for what they are. Positive empowerment is as wrong as discrimination. The *Black Economic Empowerment* legislation in South Africa, however well intended, is as racist as the apartheid legislation was; the Norwegian quotas on the number of women that a company is obliged to put on their board are as demeaning to the women as they are to the men. Be aware of the differences, acknowledge them, and celebrate them, but make very sure they stay far from your compensation policy, your promotion and succession planning, and your reward values system.

Most corporate information can, and at some stage will, be made public. The increased use of the Internet has greatly reduced the amount of information that is, or can be kept, confidential. One cannot expect information that is shared though e-mail, blogs, or on social network sites to remain confidential. Not only can anyone from inside the organization easily transfer such electronic information out, hackers and governments can without much thought or effort retrieve any e-mail you have written in your life. Literally what your mind expresses electronically becomes ingrained onto silicon and is easily retrievable even many years later.

When the Internet was first popularized around 1995, Amicorp became one of the first companies in Curaçao to have a website. We actually had the second website on the island, beaten only by the Tourist Bureau. We published not only some basic information about the island on the website, but also how our solutions worked and how much we usually charge. Once this leaked out, we got an avalanche of negative comments from the Big 5 tax advisors and competitors around us. If we would make our business transparent, the advisors would lose business, and the competitors would end up in a downward-spiraling price war. Three years later, everyone had websites.

Instead of trying to protect information from falling into the wrong hands, which, of course, is a losing battle, you should make sure only the right type of information is being produced in the first place. Have strict internal ethical codes for the use of the Internet as well as other means of communication, however private. Make sure everyone expresses himself only with proper respect for other human beings and other organizations. No use of profane language, no lies, no misleading information, no embarrassing pictures, and no tasteless jokes. No excuses.

Make sure the quality of your processes and procedures is such that you have nothing to be ashamed of. The public eye can help to keep everyone honest. If you do not want to be ashamed because it leaks out that your products are produced in some Chinese sweatshop, then go over there and check for yourself whether the working conditions are fair or not. Don't rely upon a "don't ask, don't tell" mentality.

Your clients have the right to know how your goods are being produced, and sooner or later they will want to see for themselves, so make sure your factories are model outfits, and you can be proud to show them. Even if you benefit from cheap labor, it can be used in a humane and fair way! If you operate chicken farms, the animals can be raised in organic and animal-friendly ways; or if you operate a busy kitchen, it can be kept clean. When book reviews are posted, book sales go up. Being open and transparent helps you when promoting your products and services. Put as much information as you can in brochures, on your website, on YouTube videos, etc.

If every production facility had a video camera in it, quality would obviously go up. If every restaurant's kitchen were made visible from the dining floor, cleanliness would doubtless be a priority. With full transparency, confidence in your product increases. Employee behavior improves as well because it's hard to torture a chicken, spit in the soup, or mistreat a junior colleague if you know you're being watched and run the risk of being caught.

You might argue that taking better care of your chickens, maintaining the cleanliness of your kitchen, or improving working conditions for your workers results in a cost increase. But the answer to that is a resounding *no*. When consumers get used to transparency, they're also more interested in the quality of what you sell, and are more likely and willing to pay extra. They'll certainly cross the street to buy from an ethical provider. And once people start moving in that direction, the cost of being an unethical provider gets so high that you either change your ways or fade away.

A nice example is the production of coffee. Many years ago coffee workers were singled out as clear examples of exploited workers. A few coffee sellers started to use the fact that they were paying and treating their workers fairly as a marketing tool. Nowadays many coffee brands boast that their coffee beans are handpicked by well-compensated, happy workers, who are always smiling in their spanking clean, traditional costumes, while harvesting only perfect coffee beans.

Once information about ethical and clean producers becomes commonplace, clients will more willingly seek out those producers and will reward the ones who consistently take better care of their clients, their suppliers, and their workers. The entire trade or profession doesn't suffer—merely the careless producers do.

In all cases, sunlight is an antiseptic, and the marketplace rewards those who behave. The entire market grows when the standards are raised. Consumers and those who want their admiration ought to reward those in favor of transparency.

At Amicorp we continuously try to be as transparent as possible toward all parties we deal with. We have regular Friday afternoon sessions, and sometimes off-site weekends with suppliers, intermediaries, and tax advisors in the field. We brainstorm about new solutions for specific tax-planning challenges in specific markets as they evolve. Everyone benefits from such sessions. Not only is information shared, and new solutions created through the dialogue from different points of view, but also emotional bonds are forged between companies and individuals. Information that is shared, multiplies. Ideas that are put on the table become food for thought and often result in further ideas or initiatives.

We often undertake joint marketing and sales efforts, whereby the tax advisor focuses on tax-planning aspects, and we on the aspects related to practical execution. This cooperation works as long as there is mutual trust, based on open sharing of information. That trust is built by travelling together, getting to know each other, working together, and sharing doubts and unfinished thoughts.

We take the same approach toward our clients; we organize round-table meetings, forum discussions, in-house training sessions, and lunch-break informational meetings to share relevant information, exchange new ideas, and present building blocks for novel solutions. Again, it is not only information that is shared this way, as transparency, openness, and sharing are all meant to create mutual trust, which is at the basis of each and every sale. We keep no secrets; we are open about how we charge for our work and how we put together our solutions; we introduce our employees, both front office and back office, to our clients, and we invite our clients to come and see our facilities for themselves.

Internally we always make sure that each client, each intermediary, and each supplier knows a number of different people within the organization, so there are always more channels of communication. The salespeople bring in prospective clients, the compliance department checks their background, and a third team of people, independent from the previous two, decides on whether to accept the prospects as clients. We use a two-signature policy and a four-eyes principle in everything we do. This prevents anyone from making side deals, approving unacceptable transactions, or colluding in other ways with clients. Every employee annually needs to take at least one two-week holiday, during which time other people manage his portfolios, and each employee has an "e-mail buddy," who has unlimited access to his e-mail in-box. We allow no voice mail, or external out-of-office mail messages. The latter measures not only maintain continuity in case someone travels or falls ill, but also lets everyone know that whatever he or she does within the company needs to be in the open and can and will be monitored when the need arises. Clients are always clients of the organization and not of any particular individual within it.

Apart from what we can do ourselves, there is also help we can get from others. For instance, in our business there is an increasing drive for supervision and regulation, as large amounts of money pass hands and money launderers can sometimes sneak through. We have always promoted transparency in our business, invited the need for more supervision and sensible regulation, and disclosed each transaction to the transferring banks involved. We support the need to produce sound and proper paper trails and track records and financial statements, preferably audited. Only slowly did the notion sink in that our business is much better off being fully *transparent* than being *confidential*. One day, not too far into the future, we will be subject to consolidated supervision, just as banks currently are; we may even become listed on a securities exchange. With all of our laundry hanging outside on clotheslines in the sun, all of the neighbors can see whether the sheets are spotless.

> *"If you put good people in bad systems you get bad results. You have to water the flowers you want to grow."*
>
> **—Stephen R. Covey**

Chapter 26

What Is the Need for Good Corporate Governance?

Out of the night that covers me,
Black as the Pit from pole to pole,
I thank whatever gods may be
For my unconquerable soul.

In the fell clutch of circumstance
I have not winced nor cried aloud.
Under the bludgeoning of chance
My head is bloody, but unbowed.

Beyond this place of wrath and tears
Looms but the Horror of the shade,
And yet the menace of the years
Finds, and shall find me, unafraid.

It matters not how strait the gate,
How charged with punishments the scroll,
I am the master of my fate:
I am the captain of my soul.

—William Ernest Henley

As explained earlier, a company is a lifeless legal entity. It is not a *human being*. It has no *feelings*, no *soul*, no *mind*, no *conscience*, no *consciousness*, and no *ethics*. It does have a *body* or *bodies*. When it starts out, the entrepreneur performs all of the functions by himself; he is the manager and the shareholder and has no need for supervision or arbitration. When the company grows, the responsibilities and functions are inevitably divided.

By the time a company becomes large and attracts capital from several different sources, it will have many bodies: the bodies of the people who perform its functions and in its name. Those are the people who subsequently need to give the company their *brains*, their *soul*, their *mind*, their *conscience*, and their *ethics*. In larger companies, the management, monitoring, and governance are usually seen as separate functions to be performed by separate bodies, even if some of the membership of those bodies overlaps. This is the corporate equivalent of the separation of powers. Management is the executive function, responsible for delivering the results; monitoring is the judicial function, responsible for delivering its results according to the laws and customs of the land. Monitoring ensures that standards are met, people are treated fairly, the environment is taken into account, society at large is served, and ethical principles are observed. Governance is the legislative function responsible for overseeing management and monitoring and, most importantly, governing the company's future, for strategy, policy, and direction.

According to the *Harvard Business Review*, "When these three functions are combined in one body, the short-term tends to drive out the long, with month-to-month management and monitoring issues stealing the time and attention needed for governance. The big decisions then go wrong." That is why, when your company grows and attracts outside financing, maybe even has private equity involved, and management becomes to a large extent separated from control and ownership, a board of independent directors separate from the day-to-day management is needed.

Board members primarily focus on four areas:

1. **Strategy.** Long-term strategy and execution are paramount. The mission, the vision, and the corporate goals, as well as a clear plan on how to reach them, is outlined in chapter 8. The board increasingly focuses its attention on balancing stakeholder needs (employees, shareholders, clients, suppliers, (local) community) as part of strategy and execution. The board also has a responsibility to see that sustainability is embedded in the company's strategy, goals, and execution.

2. **Performance Management.** Performance management asks the question, "How are you as the entrepreneur, or now the management, doing against the company's mission and vision, and what additional resources and measures are needed to achieve the goals?"

3. **Talent.** The talent discussion is the cornerstone of all execution and is concerned with leadership and management, including entrepreneur/CEO succession.

4. **Risk Management.** The board enforces a clear and updated risk profile (including the risk appetite of the company) in conformity with the company goals. Risk comes from anything you are doing that you do not adequately understand. The board needs to make sure it fully understands the risks a company takes and to make sure everyone else in the company understands those risks as well.

Many boards of listed companies believe that rewarding managers through stock options is an effective incentive leading to long-term shareholder value. Equity ownership, by definition, aligns managers and shareholders. But effective incentive implies a motivation to really do something, as opposed to a simple desire to see the share price go up. Most senior executives will tell you, however, that movement in the stock price over several years usually has more to do with external factors than with the decisions and actions of management.

Management actions do matter; they matter indirectly, over a long period of time and often in unpredictable ways, making equity ownership a weak motivator. While the alignment provided by equity ownership does motivate managers to seek out the drivers of shareholder value, equity by itself is inherently incapable of providing a sufficiently detailed guide for value creation to managers. And, of course, value consists of many more things than just an increase in stock price. If a company is to contribute a lot more than just value to shareholders, it needs to provide job security to its competent loyal workers, it needs to be careful with the environment, and it needs to be a positive force in society.

To reward the managers based on limited performance indicators is asking them to focus on one aspect at the expense of the other aspects. In addition, there is a limit to how much more a manager can earn in a company compared to his coworkers. In the end *all* contribute to the success of the company (or should not be employed by it) and financial success is the result of the efforts and ideas of the team, not just the managers at the top. Each company should have a moral limit on how much more the managers can earn (in salary or other benefits) compared to the average earnings of its employees. In our company we carefully watch this parameter.

By their nature, the goals and targets of outside shareholders, "At best passive investors, and at times corporate raiders relentlessly searching for value" are short-term and money-based, whereas the mission, vision, and targets of the company are people-based and long-term. In the end, managers are responsible, not to the *institution* they manage, but to the shareholders, employees, and customers. The company cannot function effectively if any of the three groups is dissatisfied. If that happens, shareholders will withdraw capital, employees will withdraw their labor, and customers will simply move to another service provider.

While not everyone agreed with this, Arie de Geus, a union leader in the Netherlands, stood by his convictions that, "In most countries, the law gives the shareholder the power of hiring and firing the people who run the company. These powers were fine in the past, as long as the shareholder had a common purpose with the people who ran the company. But nowadays, in nine out of 10 cases the primary shareholders are managers of other corporate entities, with purposes and goals of their own. Managers are ultimately responsible for protecting and maintaining the institution they manage. Then the directors become the referees that will ensure that the managers are indeed doing their job of protecting the corporation."

I am not convinced that directors can really do this. I tend to agree more with Peter Drucker, who said, "Whenever an institution malfunctions as consistently as boards of directors have in nearly every major fiasco of the last forty or fifty years it is futile to blame men. It is the institution that malfunctions." Put differently: recruit a group of strong-minded people, arrange for them to meet not much more than four to six times a year, have vague or nonexistent performance targets for them, and include in the group a number of outsiders with no knowledge of the industry or the company. Will they function as a team? Highly doubtful. Yet this is how corporate boards are typically formed, and they are expected to provide decisive leadership and deliver corporate performance to exacting governance standards. Going forward, a more realistic format will need to be developed in order to create relevant checks and balances within a company.

John Kenneth Galbraith, a famous British economist, put it this way, "Shareholders, owners, and their alleged directors in any sizable enterprise are fully subordinate to the management. Though the impression of owner authority is offered, it does not, in fact, exist. An accepted fraud. Stockholders are invited each year to the annual meeting, which, indeed, resembles a religious rite. There is ceremonial expression and, with rare exception, no negative response. Infidels who urge action are set aside; the management position is routinely approved. The shareholders who previously suggested some social policy or environmental concern have their proposals printed with supporting argument. These are uniformly rejected by management."

Berkshire Hathaway, one of the most successful investment companies in the world, managed by Warren Buffett, who invests only in industries he can understand and in strategies built on common sense, is considered one of the rare exceptions, and thus a bit eccentric. The annual general meetings of shareholders of that company have become interesting country fairs, with real debate and interaction, and genuine influence by the shareholders. In a speech at Salomon Brothers, Buffett said, "If you lose money for us, we will be forgiving. If you lose reputation for us, we will be ruthless. You make the situation clear by stating your intentions and you back them up in the design of your compensation program. If there is any suggestion of bad behavior, the money goes back to the company. That is the only fair and credible way. Any CEO who won't come in on that basis is somebody you don't want to bet on because he is not willing to bet on himself."

A former president of a Central Bank in Europe, totally misguided, came up with the exact opposite idea, "Being a manager and being a significant shareholder of the same bank at the same time is a conflict of interest." Luckily in some other countries, board members are obliged to have at least some "skin in the game," own at least some shares, so that they take their tasks seriously. Fortunately, most people realize that in order for a company to be successful, its management and its board must be both competent and deeply involved, submitting to shared corporate values, and working in unison in the best interest of the shareholders, employees, and clients. Those interests need to be and remain aligned at all times with a common mission statement and vision. To put it bluntly, when the directors enter a board meeting they need to ask only two questions: One, are we going to fire the CEO today? And two, if not, how can we help? Helping should not be limited to talking. Good governance is all about right behavior. The board will be able to influence the behavior of management and staff only by setting the right example by challenging and stimulating all in the company to give the best of themselves. This can be done only when it is truly hands-on.

"By framing rules you cannot improve corporate governance. You lay down more rules and they get broken more. By contrast in improving your value system you can improve the corporate governance practice."

—B. Muthraman

Chapter 27

What Causes Happiness, and Where Does One Find It?

"If you want others to be happy, practice compassion. If you want to be happy, practice compassion."

The Dalai Lama

We all strive to be happy. Happiness is more important to us than both health and wealth. But happiness, unlike health and wealth, is something we can attain on our own, without the need for outside help. Happiness is basically a choice, one of the many we can make every single day. According to Aleksandr Solzhenitsyn, "A man is happy so long as he chooses to be happy and nothing can stop him."

Genghis Khan, who was responsible for the death of some forty million people, more than Hitler, Mao, and Stalin, stated the following, "The greatest happiness is to vanquish your enemies, to chase them before you, to rob them of their wealth, to see those dear to them bathed in tears, to clasp to your bosom their wives and daughters." A scientific support to this claim is made by mapping Y chromosomes in Asia, showing that one in five hundred is directly related to him.

Luckily, for most people happiness is different. To achieve happiness we need to have a good temper and feel positive feelings, such as peace, joy, love, and serenity. We need to maintain those feelings most of the time (and preferably all of the time). And we need to somehow eliminate negative feelings such as anxiety, anger, fear, greed, and resentment.

196

Initially this will require great effort, as we tend to develop plenty of negative feelings over the course of our life. Where we live and the climate we enjoy also seem to have an impact. According to an Ipsos poll, 53 percent of Indonesians are very happy most of the time. Forty percent of Mexicans and Indians are also very happy, while only 8 percent of Russians and South Koreans are happy most of the time.

Eliminating negative feelings starts with introspection. It means you will need to learn to observe your own sensations, emotions, and thoughts. After a while you will see how they are constantly popping up and receding below the surface. Your life is full of change and transformation. Your thoughts change, as do your emotions.

You will also see that everything in the universe is linked; nothing can exist by itself; everything is interrelated in the united field of interdependence and mutual causation. You will see that you suffer negative feelings and thoughts because you did not understand or realize that we share the same nature as all transient beings. Understanding the true interconnectedness of everything and everyone dissolves anxiety, greed, anger, fear, and other negative feelings and thoughts. It makes you realize that your business will not be successful if your employees, suppliers, clients, shareholders, and society are not all benefiting from it.

What holds us back is our ego. The ego is the perception that we have of ourselves. We tend to identify ourselves with our material possessions, our financial status, or our social role. The ego makes us believe that we are what we have (more stuff makes us more important), that we are what we do (the higher we rank, the more important we are), that we are what others think of us, (the desire for status, a corner office, power), and that we are separate from everyone else, and that we are even separate from what is missing in our lives (that which is outside of us is outside of our control). It is the mental clinging of our ego to the objects or subjects with which we identify that causes us to suffer.

To liberate ourselves from our ego, we need to understand the principles of interdependence and nonself. Interdependence is easy to understand: nothing can exist without the existence of everything else. Just as a leaf cannot exist without the tree, the rain, the land, and the world around it, a company cannot exist without its employees, suppliers, clients, and products or services. Its pencils are made by a company at one side of the world, its paper comes from trees that once grew at the other side of the world, and huge investments in infrastructure and technology had to be made by others to create the oil industry that would provide the fuel to transport the pencils and the paper to your office. Meanwhile all of the people involved would need to eat the food produced by farmers in yet again other parts of the world and to live in houses constructed by others, all financed by banks and organized by civil servants, managers, politicians, consultants, etc.

If the trees were not impermanent but had a nature by themselves, it would be impossible to turn them into your writing paper; oil could not become transportation, and grain could not become bread.

The reality of life is that everything is impermanent; things never stay what they are. There is neither birth nor death, neither creation nor destruction, and neither one nor many. These are just false distinctions created by our mind. The reality is things constantly change. Heraclitus once told us, "The only constant is change." Situations change, our bodies change, our minds change, and all of these things are related to and influence the existence of all other things. Nothing can exist independently of all the rest.

The lesson to be drawn from this is that one cannot become attached to anything or anyone. Not being attached to anything or anyone frees you from suffering. Suffering is derived from the separation from what we love or the union of what we hate. We need to become aware that things and people change constantly, and all are connected with each other and thus develop nonattachment. It is what Buddhists call *Right Seeing*; the first step on the eightfold noble path to Enlightenment.

The second step on that path is *Right Thought:* these are thoughts in which there is neither confusion nor distraction, neither anger nor hate, and neither desire nor lust. To overcome distraction you need to learn to concentrate. To overcome anger, hatred, and all other negative emotions, you will need to contemplate on what causes them in your mind and in the minds of those who have aroused them in you. To overcome desire, think about impermanence, and to overcome lust think about the effects of death. At the same time build positive thoughts: kindness, compassion, shared joy, and nonattachment.

Right Speech, Right Action, and *Right Livelihood* are moral precepts: do unto others as you would have them do unto you. Because doing the opposite creates guilt and suffering in yourself. *Right Effort* is the will to implement the right ways to live your life, and *Right Will*, or Right Mindfulness, consists of focusing your attention on the world around you and interacting with it. This is known as presence in reality, and it teaches us not to obsessively focus on our own inner thoughts (which are not more than that, just thoughts) but to focus on the outer world, the reality, by *Right Concentration.*

We need to learn to observe our thoughts with detachment, to realize they are not the product of our will, but rather grow autonomously in ourselves and are nourished by our fears and attachments. By focusing on the witness within us and looking at our thoughts with detachment, we will be liberated from thoughts, emotions, sensations, will, and consciousness. This is best done by practicing meditation.

So, in other words, by being aware that everything is constantly in a state of change, we can learn nonattachment, and through that we can gain control of our mind. By being in control of our mind, we achieve *presence in reality.* By appreciating the true nature of reality and how everything is related, we can aspire to reach universal love, where through compassion and devotion to other people we aim for the happiness of everyone and do not want anything in return. This for us results in a life filled with peace and joy. Fifteen-year-old Anne Frank wrote a few months before her death in a concentration camp, "Whoever is happy will make others happy too. He who has courage and faith will never perish in misery."

How do we produce thoughts that cause suffering? They are automatically produced by our subconscious (memory) as a manifestation of the tension derived from traumas, fears, losses, failures, and uncertainties that exist in our memory. Thoughts that cause suffering, and create tension, constitute almost the whole of our mental activity, because these thoughts reproduce and perpetuate themselves. By observing our negative thoughts with detachment (by being the *detached witness*), we can neutralize them. One can also replace unwanted negative thoughts by more pleasant thoughts of kindness, love, and compassion.

You need to realize that the thoughts produced by your mind are just products of your body; it is similar to the way your body produces heat and waste. You can manipulate your mind by looking into it and using your senses to become aware that your thoughts are the product of your unconscious mind. By using techniques like *Vipassana* you can quite easily attain mental emptiness and neutralize or eliminate negative thoughts. Meditation or prayer can help further. You will see that the fantasies of your mind are not real. They are generated by your attachment to people, things, and memories, or even by you yourself and, therefore, by your anger, your hate, your fears, your desires. And we accept them as truths. The only things that are real in this concept are the things we see around us, in our here and now; everything else exists only in our mind. You become unhappy, and you suffer because of expectations you create in your mind—because you cling to your ego.

Nonattachment to anything prevents you from suffering. This does not mean you cannot love, you cannot care about other people, or you should be indifferent; it simply means you do not desire to *possess* the other person, material things, wealth, status, power, or whatever else is desirable.

It is what it is, of course, and I surmise, however painful, in the end it is good. All things in life come to an end and morph into something new. If the same feelings would stay forever, we would become numb to them.

A Spanish saying goes, "*El amor es como una ola, cuando llega te besa, te abraza, y con facilidad te abandona.*" Love is like a wave, when it comes it lifts you high, shakes you, maybe even scares you a bit, leaves you out of breath, and then it easily leaves you. Sooner or later another wave will come, perhaps stronger or not, but the sea always leaves you hoping for another, and perhaps better, wave.

Love seems to always make one suffer. When else do we laugh alone if not when in love? But I think this is also where nonattachment comes in handy. Awareness of the impermanence of each and every thing allows you to develop nonattachment. The people and the things in our lives are not eternal. Everyone we meet will also exit our life; we cannot command their presence. If we want to be loved by someone, this reflects a need of our own, a need for the presence, love, and dedication of the other person. We need to realize this and learn to be free to enjoy the people we love when they are there and to enjoy something else when they are there no longer. We can do the same with material attachments and even, after some practice, with vices, cravings, addictions, and desires for anything that is not there, by appreciating and enjoying what is, in the moment we are living in.

Once you attain nonattachment, you will no longer want anything in return for what you do and what you share. Your aim will become the happiness of all. Then you are in contact with the universe, and basically you become the whole universe. According to Gautama Buddha, "Understanding and love are the same, without understanding there can be no love." Understanding leads to compassion, because we know about our friends', families', and colleagues' past, life, and problems. We become interested in their past, their interests and wishes, and there we identify with them. The compassion we feel for others, in fact, is the compassion we feel for ourselves. The more we are able to include everyone, the happier we will feel and the more meaningful our lives become. True love is to love others, preferably all others, without the need to be loved in return by any others. True love does not expect anything in return. For example, a mother does not need anything from a child. It is unconditional love.

So, why is all this Buddhist theory in a book about business? An old Tibetan saying goes, "There is only one sure thing to keep a person from breaking out of jail. And that is if the person never realizes that they're in jail in the first place." If you want to change your mind-set and be happy, you must first realize you are unhappy, and that you yourself do the things that prevent you from being happy. If you are unaware of how the mind works, of what your role in the universe is, of how you can make the universe do whatever you need it to do to achieve your goals, you will never achieve your goals. You may not be able to detach yourself from suffering, and you may not become happy.

Not many people, companies, or countries put happiness as a core goal. The United States has the *pursuit of happiness* embedded in its Constitution. In practice, I think, the pursuit of money and power in the short run seem to be more important. Bhutan, on the other hand, is the only country that measures its progress as a nation not by an increase of Gross National Product per person, but by Gross National Happiness per person. The areas considered by the government of Bhutan as crucial for reflecting the values of Gross National Happiness are: psychological well-being, health, time use, education, culture, good governance, ecology, community vitality, and living standards. The government of Bhutan promotes happiness as a national policy, and it takes it very seriously. This has great impact on government policies. Instead of promoting mass tourism, which would benefit the general economy, it keeps the influx of tourists low by imposing high visa fees and keeps the impact on the local culture and infrastructure to a minimum. One indication of how willing the government is to take tough measures that it believes will maximize overall happiness is a ban on the sale of tobacco. Bhutanese may bring into the country small quantities of cigarettes or tobacco from India for their own consumption but not for resale, and they must carry the import-tax receipt with them anytime they smoke in public.

My home country, Singapore, where for example, you cannot buy chewing gum, so as to keep the streets clean and shiny, and China, a country often reproached for its lack of a functioning democracy, are two other countries that are taking steps in the same direction of government policies toward happiness and well-being. In 2011 the UN General Assembly passed, without dissent, a Bhutanese-initiated resolution inviting member states to develop additional measures to better capture the goal of happiness. In France and to a lesser extent in the Nordic and Germanic countries, progress in *well-being* is more and more preferred over progress in *wealth*. In Italy, and in much of Latin America, *La Dolce Vita* provides a cheerful outlook on life regardless of the country's economic status. They clearly understand that your outlook on life determines how happy you feel. Swami Vivekananda phrases it the other way around, "We would be happy to do the millions of things that we are not able to do. This will is there, but we are not able to fulfill our desires. Thus we feel a desire, but we are unable to realize that desire; we undergo a reaction we call suffering. What is the cause of desire? I am, only me. As a result, I myself am the cause of all the suffering that I have known."

In our company, Amicorp, we are happiest if everything works smoothly, if our employees are happy with the way things are organized, if our products and services are innovative and competitive, if our clients enjoy the service they are receiving from our team, if our suppliers feel we give them fair terms, and if our competitors know we do not speak badly of them and feel we compete fairly and openly. The more we are able to give every party what he deserves, the better the company does. When we hire people who do not understand this, the machine immediately starts to sputter, as clients, suppliers, bankers, and society at large react to whatever we do. Positive actions beget positive reactions; negative actions create negative reactions. In the words of Je Rimpoche, "Whatever you want from life, you must do for someone else first. If you do something for someone else, everything else will work out." The Tibetan teacher to the first Dalai Lama, Chandra Kirti, commented that if you do so, "The odds of success in all things are 100 percent."

Where can you find yourself? At home, your true self lies beyond your ego. Your brain cannot show you how to get there; your heart has already been there. And your soul has never left it. And on your way there, do not forget to have fun and enjoy yourself. In the words of Priscilla Lotman, "Life is short, break the rules, forgive quickly, kiss slowly, love truly, laugh uncontrollably."

> *"Attend to your own inner health and happiness. Happiness radiates like the fragrance of a flower and draws all good things toward you. Allow your love to nourish yourself as well as others. Do not strain after the needs of life. It is sufficient to be quietly alert and aware of them. In this way life proceeds more naturally and effortlessly. Life is here to Enjoy."*
>
> **—Maharishi Mahesh Yogi**

Chapter 28

How about Love, Desire, and Sex in the Workplace?

"She discovered with great delight that one does not love one's children just because they are one's children but because of the friendship formed while raising them."

—Gabriel García Márquez

Life happens one moment at a time. And we can only live it as it comes along. We need to use every day as best as we can, since the number of days we have is limited. Friedrich Nietzsche once explained that we have a public life, a private life, and a secret life. Work is very much part of our public life, but it cannot be lived in complete separation. You cannot go to your workplace leaving part of whom and what you are at home. You cannot separate your public from your private life. You cannot have one personality and set of emotions at work and a different personality and set of emotions at home.

All the talk about a *work/life* balance and trying to separate the two is basically missing the point. Work is an essential part of life, and life is an essential part of work. You have to be alive to go to work (at least in my world), and you have to enjoy and learn from what you do (at least most of the time), otherwise you are in the wrong work environment. Work is such an important part of not only where you *spend your time*, but also where you *live your life* that it makes no sense to be there unless you are fully present. You cannot be watching the clock every day and waiting for it to strike five before you start living your life. If you think like the cynical characters in the Dilbert cartoons, you are wasting a very important part of your life.

To live, to love, to learn, and to leave a legacy all play their role every day while you are at work, whether you are the leader, a manager, or have a supporting role. Of course, we all put on a mask and play a role while we are at work. We have lessons to teach, examples to set, goals to achieve, and tasks to accomplish. We have the corporate mission and vision to work on and the values to live by. But we also have our own personal goals, our own personal values, and our own personal desires that we bring to work each day.

We also bring to work our personal desire to love and be loved. I think that the desire to love and be loved is one of the key drivers of why people seek each other's company in a workplace. The desire to love and be loved has been known for at least the past three thousand years. The *Bridadaranyaka Upanishad* notes, "The Cosmic Being created the world because by himself he knew no joy. He wanted to be two." We always need the interaction with others around us to enjoy what we do, to celebrate our successes, to share our sorrows, and to mourn our losses.

In the time we were cavemen this was easy. There was a perfect work/ life balance as everyone in the tribe contributed to the hunting and the gathering in accordance with his or her abilities, and in return received respect, love, a social life, and a fair share of the fruits of their labor Muhammad Yunus said, "All human beings are entrepreneurs. When we were in the caves we were all self-employed … finding our food, feeding ourselves, socializing. That's where human history began … As civilization came we suppressed it. We became laborers because they stamped us, 'You are labor.' We forgot we are entrepreneurs."

When we moved to subsistence farming and small workshops, this did not really change. In most of the world, shopkeepers still live in or above the shop, farmer families share all the tasks, and many small *mom-and-pop* enterprises provide at the same time an income, a social life, and emotional satisfaction to the members of the family that participate in them.

The ever-growing part of the world that emerged into the industrial or even postindustrial world created industrial farming, large factories, impersonal offices, cubicle seating, traffic jams, networking, bio-breaks, silo thinking, work-related stress, and office politics. For those of us who live in the Western world, it is often hard to realize that the world we have created in the last one hundred to 150 years is one that denies to a large extent our origins, who we are and what we are as human beings. We have come to think that an impersonal way of dealing with each other, based on *organograms*, flowcharts, key performance indicators (KPIs), and endless review meetings, is an acceptable way of organizing human behavior.

I do not think it is. Human behavior is structured largely around the two basic drivers of love and fear. Most modern organizations have the *fear* factor pretty well under control but not necessary the *love* factor. Organograms and KPIs build fear in people: fear of being unable to leave the box one is in, fear of not making the target, fear of breaking a rule, fear of being stuck and incapable of bringing out the best in oneself.

The better organized a company (the more rules, corporate governance, and stricter defined roles and goals), the more fear is created.

If, on the other hand, a company focuses on explaining its mission and its vision on how to work toward that mission, fear will diminish. If a company explains its values as the broad bandwidth within which to operate and stimulates its employees to be creative, to make mistakes, to step outside the borders, and to find their own voice, then its employees will no longer fear. And if a company offers ways to achieve the goals and the mission, to work together based on skills and personal preferences, and be complimentary rather than structuring itself based on hierarchy and organograms, an organization will flourish because its employees will flourish.

People have to love where they work, with whom they work, and what they do in order to make that place a success. Where there is no love, nothing is created, and nothing has the possibility to grow.

John Lennon, albeit it in a slightly different context, explains it as follows, "There are two basic motivating forces: fear and love. When we are afraid, we pull back from life. When we are in love, we open to all that life has to offer with passion, excitement, and acceptance. We need to learn to love ourselves first, in all our glory and our imperfections. If we cannot love ourselves, we cannot fully open to our ability to love others or our potential to create. Evolution and all hopes for a better world rest in the fearlessness and open-hearted vision of people who embrace life."

What makes people love their work? What makes people anticipate with joy the start of a new workday? In previous chapters we saw it was things like enjoying the work at hand, feeling part of making the world a better place, servicing clients, working on useful projects or products, and the ability to increase one's skills, knowledge, and experience. Being appreciated and feeling part of a team is also a necessity, just as the more basic need to earn money and be able to sustain a family is as well.

I have always been amazed by how easy it has been for military leaders of all times and all ideologies to lead their soldiers into battle and make them overcome their very realistic fear of death in order to achieve often uninspiring goals, such as taking a particular hill. When those soldiers are asked why they did it, very few refer to the underlying ideology of the strategic battle they were waging or the ideals their army was fighting for, but rather all of them refer to the love and camaraderie they felt for their colleagues, the respect they had for their direct leader, and the pride they have in the success of a small team within the larger army. The love they had for their comrades was substantially stronger than the fear to lose their lives.

As an entrepreneur you want your employees to "go through fire" to achieve the goals of the company; you want them to risk their lives for the benefit of the team. Of course you cannot instill the camaraderie that is needed for that with cadaver discipline, endless exhausting marches, shared hardship, and enemy fire. The relationship a military commander has with his men, and the reasons why they are working together, is a different one than the one a corporate leader or entrepreneur has with his men.

You must at least earn the respect of your people, but better still is to earn their love. In *Anna Karenina*, Leo Tolstoy wrote, "Respect was invented to cover the empty place where love should be." Respect can be earned by being a subject matter specialist, a hard-working individual, and/or a values-based person who does the right thing. But, in order to do the right thing, something more is needed.

Love is a difficult subject to speak about in a business environment, as it quickly gets confused with desire and sex. Conventional wisdom says that love belongs in the private life. Love in the public life is a threat to the love in the private life, and desires in the workplace should not even leave the realm of the "secret life."

Nevertheless one's desires are at the basis of any achievement. The act of seeking by itself is already a source of joy. The *Mahabharata* describes it as, "He who does not desire pleasure will not seek to enrich himself. Without desires, neither does a man desire to fulfill his duty. He who is without desire is envious of nothing. This is why desire is the most important thing. There has never been, is not, and will never be anything that seems superior to what we desire. Desire is the essence of all action, on which all notions of duty and wealth are based. Just as cream is the essence of milk, so pleasure is the essence of duty, the source of wealth."

People need to constantly enjoy what they are doing. They need the appreciation of their colleagues, the pat on the back by their supervisors, the envy of their competitors, and the feeling of achievement generated by a team when goals are achieved, companies are built, and the world is changed for the better.

If a number of people love what they are doing, love working together, and love the experience while they are doing it, there is nothing they can't achieve; there is nothing beyond their reach.

In a small entrepreneurial company, it is a lot easier than in a corporate behemoth to create an environment in which people love what they do, love what they are working toward, and love who they are working with. Having missed out on the years of the "flower power," Osho, and Woodstock, I have nevertheless remembered the words of the Beatles when searching for a solution to difficult issues.

> *There's nothing you can do that can't be done.*
> *All you need is love, all you need is love.*
>
> ## —John Lennon and Paul McCartney

As an entrepreneur, or as a leader, you will have to bring out that love in your people. You will have to create an environment in which people love what they do and do what they love and love the people they work with. This is not an easy task and cannot be achieved by simply organizing an annual Christmas dinner and dance or even a weekly happy hour. People will basically need to work happily together for forty or more hours each week, and that should not be because they have a beer in front of them.

This is not something you can enforce, put into a manual, or even empower people to do. Carl Jung said in 1912 in his writings *On the Psychology of the Unconscious*, "Where love rules, there is no will power, and where power predominates, love is lacking." Love can only be given, not taken. Respect can only be earned, not enforced. You will need to spend a lot of time and effort on nurturing these qualities.

So far this chapter has addressed the need for love in an almost abstract manner. But in the end, "love for the company" as a separate third party needs to be seen as enjoying your collective consciousness, like a neural net, working in harmony. Otherwise a company is not more than a bunch of corporate documents to a lawyer, a set of financial statements to an accountant, a team of people for a manager, or a number of assets for an investor. Our roles within the company can be seen as *karma*, good or bad, in an environment providing meaning, purpose, and joy, and leaving the *karmaphala* (fruits of our actions) at the disposal of the collective.

In a workplace people spend eight or more hours a day together. They see each other in their good moments and bad moments, in moments of despair and great success, in mourning and in celebration. Enduring friendships are formed in such environments; close bonds are welded. Colleagues socialize outside work, enjoy sports and hobbies together, and so build friendships. Friendships are inevitable as people share interests and spend time together. All of the most powerful moments in life— those moments we feel we really have lived—are moments when we felt loved or were in love. As Leo Tolstoy wrote, "Seize the moments of happiness, love and be loved! That is the only reality in the world, all else is folly. It is the one thing we are interested in here."

Love is ultimately the attachment between human beings. People enjoy being together, working together, laughing together, and achieving things together. And in a fair number of cases there is also a sexual attraction, as, by definition, people start loving the ones they rub shoulders with. The Dalai Lama solved the temptation when he stated, "Sometimes in my dreams there are women … When such dreams happen, immediately I remember, 'I am a monk.' … It is very important to analyze 'What is the real benefit of sexual desire?' The appearance of a beautiful face or a beautiful body—as many scriptures describe—no matter how beautiful, they essentially decompose into a skeleton. When we penetrate to its human flesh and bones, there is no beauty, is there? A couple in a sexual experience is happy for that moment. Then very soon trouble begins."

When attraction exists in the workplace between people who enjoy each other's company, sexual desires often arise.

Many people start relationships in the workplace, get married, and live happily ever after. Others have affairs with colleagues and even have sex

211

in the workplace. Lots of statistics are available on the subject, and in all cases, many more men than women seem to be involved (strangely enough, but that is how statistics work). In our company we have quite a number of couples who met at work. We also have a number of people who ultimately left the company because a relationship they built at work did not work out. Matters of the heart are often the reason why people request a transfer, are unhappy in their work, or achieve unusually successful things.

In a corporate environment, the notion that *sex* is on the minds of its employees is usually ignored, denied, belittled, or referred to the human resources department. But attraction between individuals is natural; uncontrolled urges that cross a limit are what need to be corrected. As an entrepreneur, you need to define that limit in some manner that is easy to interpret so the violation will become easy to catch. A safety net is needed, keeping in mind how scandals tarnish the image of the collective.

Awareness of one's sexuality is different. The pursuit of becoming aware of one's sexuality in the workplace ... now that's something else, and may create lots of difficulties. In a societal mix driven by diversity, the balance of awareness gets shaken and sometimes stirred.

Most men think about sex often. Studies suggest that it is over half the time they are awake. I have checked this with friends and colleagues, and almost all agree. It means that men have thoughts about sex when they pass by the receptionist entering the office, the coffee lady when getting their coffee, when in meetings with clients, suppliers, or superiors, and when alone working on whatever the daily task is. Women apparently *think* a lot less about sex and *speak* a lot more about it, but then again they are much better at multitasking than men.

The great majority of these thoughts and feelings never lead to conscious action. They are neither expressed nor lead to any action. But they are there all of the time, and they determine why some people work well together and others avoid each other. They answer the question as to why some people get promoted beyond their level of competence or why people work harder on the tasks of some colleagues than on the tasks of others. Just as James Bond can get anything he wants done by Ms. Jane Moneypenny, every company has its Bonds and Moneypennys. There is nothing against this attraction, as it is part of normal human behavior, and it makes life more enjoyable and more rewarding even if, or perhaps especially if, it's never consummated. Consciously or unconsciously, suppressed or not, sexual attraction or repulsion is constantly at play in collaboration, or in what appears to be team effort.

In total contradiction to this, company policies are mostly written in such a way that love, desire, and sex are completely ignored. Differences between the sexes are no longer allowed, and men and women are treated scrupulously as equals. In the Nordic countries this goes as far as allowing men pregnancy/parental leave. And a few countries, such as France and Norway, are now forcing listed companies to have a quota of women on their boards and committees. This, of course, undermines the very essence of treating people equally while celebrating their differences. The humanoid civilization has degraded to a certain extent because pure job descriptions are breached (hunter, gatherer). Today, the gatherer can hunt. The hunter can do some gathering. The evolution of society has progressed much faster than the evolution of our mind or body. In an attempt to provide inclusion, we missed the forest for the trees and speak in terms of quota. In my workplace I want people to be rewarded for what they achieve, to be in specific roles because of what they are as a person and because of what their strengths are, and to have their sex remain as just one of the many qualities they happen to possess.

Most entrepreneurial companies do not need such artificial quotas, as the average outfit (mom and pop) usually has a fair representation of the sexes on its board anyway. Nowadays every manager is afraid of being accused of sexual harassment and avoids even the most innocent of hugs or moments with a person of the opposite (or third) sex alone behind closed doors. The personal zone has shrunk so much that it's easy to cause offense even with what used to be a harmless question.

I think it makes more sense to celebrate the differences between the sexes than to ignore them. Respecting each other's needs and sensitivities rather than denying or regulating them, and benefitting from each other's natural strengths rather than creating unnatural divisions of responsibilities makes for a harmonious workplace.

The work environment needs to become less sexist and more aware of the strengths associated with each gender. There is no denying that men generally are better at going straight for their goals, and women generally are more detail oriented, more cautious, and more caring. A booth at an exhibition does attract more visitors if, in addition to brochures and giveaways, there are attractive presenters. A company will give a better first impression if the receptionist has a pleasant phone voice. A company get-together is more fun if one does not need to worry about correctly choosing each and every word or slapping only the colleagues of the same sex on their backs.

Sexual differences within the work environment are mostly ignored or strictly ritualized; the moment contact with the outside world is established, and the immediate threat to the private world is diminished, sex is back en vogue. Almost any product in the world is routinely promoted by scantily clad ladies, in attractive postures, trying to sell a feeling rather than a product. The Pirelli calendar adorns every garage workshop. There are many more billboards promoting underwear than car parts or business books.

In the Hindu tradition men's physical strength and power, as well as a piece of their soul, have their source in *viriya*, a word meaning both sexual energy and diligence, life force, the essence of maleness. Viriya can either move downward in sexual intercourse, where it is emitted physically as semen, or it can move upward, through the spinal cord, by *kundalini*, directly into the brain, in its more subtle form known as *ojas*. Hindus consider the downward movement a debilitating waste of vitality and energy, and the upward movement by the observance of *brahmacharya* (a form of abstinence) as a source of creativity, longevity, will power, and inspiration. The sexual energy present in any coed work environment can be spilled or directed by the right combination of interaction, thought, discipline, and practice into enhanced inspiration and creative energy.

As an entrepreneur you will need to set the tone. Create an environment in which love, trust, and freedom blossom, and men and women work together in a natural and caring manner. At the same time, have a strong set of values that prevent abuse and excess. And with the words of the Dalai Lama in mind, "Do not ever screw the crew." Or to quote one of Mohandas Gandhi's favorite passages from the wordier Bhagavad Gita:

> *"If one ponders on objects of the senses there springs attraction; from attraction grows desire. Desire flames to fierce passion, passion breeds recklessness; then the memory—all betrayed—lets noble purpose go, and saps the mind, till purpose, mind and man are all undone."*

Chapter 29

Can Your Business Become an Addiction?

"To him she seemed so beautiful, so seductive, so different from ordinary people, that he could not understand why no one was as disturbed as he by the clicking of her heels on the paving stones, why no one else's heart was wild with the breeze stirred by the sighs of her veils, why everyone did not go mad with the movements of her braid, the flight of her hands, the gold of her laughter. He had not missed a single one of her gestures, not one of the indications of her character, but he did not dare approach her for fear of destroying the spell."

—Gabriel García Márquez

Being an entrepreneur brings rewards on many different levels, but it also has its seductions and pitfalls. It is all too easy to lose sight of what is valuable in the relentless search for value. Being distracted by net worth in your search for self-worth can ultimately yield your worthlessness.

Once your small business becomes successful, and you are on a roll as an entrepreneur, it is only natural to want to make your business grow. By itself there is nothing wrong with that. Growing a good idea or multiplying a good service or product one hundred times over is good for your business, employees, and clients, as well as for society.

But there are several places where you can easily go off track. As John Lennon said, "Part of me suspects that I'm a loser and the other part of me thinks I'm God Almighty." One common pitfall is to become addicted to your success. Once you are successful in one location, one business, or one product, you may be tempted to think you are invincible in the business world.

Do you know why businesses fail? The number one reason a business fails is because it runs out of cash. While there may be different contributing factors for this, one of the popular ones is a result of rapid expansion. Your being able to create a success out of one idea, product, or service does not mean you automatically can multiply it. When a company grows, different skills and specialties will be needed. You will certainly not possess all of them.

This has also happened to me—in fact a few times in my life. I was tempted to bite off more than I could chew. Hoping all of the different pieces of the puzzle would eventually fall into place left me having to make some very painful adjustments.

Another common pitfall is becoming obsessed with money, status, and power. In business, earning money is a way to keep score, a measure of financial success, but money has value only when it is used. It is tempting to use the money you earn on superfluous signs of wealth, such as lavish parties, expensive clothing, or numerous cars. But that is not adding much value (other than of course to the businesses providing these services and products). The value comes out of the money when the money is used productively to grow a business, create jobs, or help people, the environment, and society.

Successful people often have an urge to surround themselves with status symbols. It builds on their narcissistic nature, and it confirms their top dog position in the company as well as in the larger society. Depending on the size of the company, this may start with a larger office chair and slightly bigger cubicle space and go all the way up to first-class travel, a corporate jet, and a trophy wife.

You may think that there is nothing against these status symbols, provided the profit and loss account of the company and the cashflow can support them, and the shareholders endorse this fruitless use of their money. The problem is that these status symbols poison the mind.

217

They make people think they are more important, more intelligent, and better leaders than others, and they become blinded by their success, stop listening to the people around them, and start believing they can reach beyond the sky.

A while ago I read about the rise and fall of AHOLD, a Dutch supermarket conglomerate. The company grew, like most companies do, from humble beginnings. It began as a small neighborhood grocery shop until it became a multinational supermarket chain. When it completed one hundred years in existence it obtained the "Royal Supplier" status, which is something highly regarded in the Netherlands. It built a huge office tower to house top management far away from the day-to-day supplier and shopping hustle and bustle, and became involved in complicated financial engineering, as well as purely financial mergers and acquisitions. At the time of the opening of the swanky new office tower, a small statue of an elderly lady with two shopping bags was revealed. It bore the text, *Lest we forget for whom we work*. Less than a year later the company nearly went under, because that is exactly what they did. They *forgot* they were still a supermarket.

In our company we make an effort to keep all visible signs of status symbols as limited as possible. There is no business class flying or overly lavish parties. We have no supersized offices or any good-looking-but-little-producing secretaries. We, of course, are hoping that in doing so we keep everyone with their feet on the ground and working as a team.

Mergers and acquisitions make a lot of sense for small companies that want to add locations; increase market share; purchase knowledge, new products, or new technology; or increase their supplier and client base. Mergers between large corporations hardly ever generate synergies and seldom create additional value for the investors. Megamergers are for megalomaniacs. They are basically just penis enlargers for the top management of the acquiring company and a way to earn a huge bonus or an increase of their stock options for the top management of the company to be acquired. Mergers and acquisitions can easily become an addiction, releasing adrenalin and creating a feeling of success, or speed, on which the company, or at least its top management, thrives. Bankruptcy by narcissism is an oft-recurring event. Herb Kelleher, the former president of Southwest Airlines said, "Think small and act small, and we'll get bigger. Think big and act big, and we'll get smaller." We, as a company, saw this in practice when for our tenth-year anniversary in 2003 we visited Southwest Airlines and studied efficiency and flexibility.

Southwest Airlines did an impressive job keeping everyone with both feet on the ground. They have no strict separations in job descriptions. Everyone helps out making the planes leave in time, loading the luggage, keeping the place clean, and servicing the customers. I particularly liked their "family wall," where employees are encouraged to put pictures of their family life and things that interest them. They integrate their personal lives with what they do at work. They mix all of what they do with a good amount of humor, and a lot of the employees we met clearly enjoyed their job for reasons way beyond their compensation package. Just for the fun of it, they let us do the exercise of evacuating a smoke-filled plane as quickly as possible. My team was certainly incapable of vacating the plane within two minutes.

When I was a kid, I was collecting and exchanging stamps, like so many kids did in those days. One day I was tempted by one of my friends to exchange a series of rare, and probably quite valuable, colonial era Dutch East Indian stamps. The lackluster stamps had belonged to a recently departed great-uncle of mine. In exchange for these stamps, I was to acquire a series of large, triangular, colorful stamps from Paraguay. I didn't even know where that country was on a map. When my mother found out, she explained to me in very clear language that I had let the bright colors and unique shape cloud my judgment. I was wrong in letting myself be fooled by the color and shapes of the stamps instead of their intrinsic and emotional value. Of course at that moment it was too late to turn back the clock on the exchange. I remember the story, however, and whenever I am about to close a transaction, I try and think for a moment whether I am tempted by the shape, the color, and the smell of the transaction, or the business logic and the intrinsic value of the transaction. I have to admit that on many occasions there is at least a hint of falling in love with the transaction involved, especially when I myself come up with the original idea.

Once we acquired the business of some "friends." These business associates we had worked with on an ongoing basis for several years. Being gentlemen, and working on the basis of one's word as one's bond, we did not take the usual precautions of doing a thorough and independent due diligence. After a while it turned out the financial information we had been presented had been skillfully falsified, and the company we bought (with borrowed money) was not nearly generating the business and money we had originally thought. When the bank financing the operation was informed that the company had a fabricated set of books, the financing umbrella was swiftly closed. We ended up losing our friends, a lot of business, and many clients and employees who left the sinking ship. We had to sell off two of the best pieces of our business to repay the money we lost on this stupid mistake, and it took a few years to emotionally recover.

Of course the mistake was mine. I had been fooled by the shape and color of the stamps, and we had failed to check out their intrinsic value.

A third way to get off track is as a result of the halo effect created around leaders in companies. In many cultures, especially the more paternalistic ones such as France, Asia, and much of Latin America, leaders get few push-backs from their colleagues/employees. As Sudhir Kakar says about the Indian business culture, "An Indian has a heightened dependence on external authority figures. An Indian tends to search for authority figures he can idealize, whose perfection and omnipotence he can then adopt as his own. Thus the automatic reference for superiors is a nearly universal psycho-social fact. And when it comes to leadership in the larger social institutions of business and government in India, charisma plays an unusually significant role." The business cultures of many European and US companies are not much better.

You will need to be constantly aware of these traps. They will lure you off track and drive your energy in the wrong direction; they will make you waste time and money on the things that do not matter. You will have to search deep within yourself in order to find out what does matter.

Your success as an entrepreneur will give you the unique opportunity to use money, power, influence, networks, knowledge, and experience in ways that can change the world. It can best be summed up deep in the chapters of one of my favorite books, *The Secret Letters of the Monk Who Sold His Ferrari*:

> *"There are no extra people alive today. Every single one of us is here for a reason, a special purpose, a mission. Yes, build a beautiful life for yourself and those you love. Yes, be happy and have a lot of fun. And yes, become successful, on your own terms, rather than those suggested to you by society. But above all else, be significant. Make your life matter, be of use. And be of service to as many people as possible. This is how each of us can shift from the realm of the ordinary into the height of the extra ordinary. And walk among the best who have ever lived."*

> **—Robin Sharma**

Chapter 30

What Does Religion Have to Do with It?

> "In the monotheistic traditions of Christianity, Judaism and Islam there is only one God and one life. In the Hindu tradition there are many gods and many lives. In Buddhist and Taoist tradition there are no Gods, but also many lives. Ultimately you want to achieve enlightenment, a state of no more suffering and an end to an endless procession of lives, deaths, rebirths of the wheel of life."
>
> **—Dalai Lama**

We have seen in an earlier chapter that Albert Einstein discovered that matter is pure, condensed energy, and that matter and energy are made of something totally ethereal, which in physics is called *information*, or more precisely, *mind*. Our minds built the universe. Biblical theology (Proverbs 8:12, 22) actually agrees and says God's "wisdom" built the universe. The difference between science and religion is that the unfettered use of human logic does not lead by itself to a just and moral society. The biological basis of our moral judgments teaches us that the human genome in our amino acids is programmed for survival and seeking pleasure and not for moral thoughts and actions.

The mathematician Sir James Jeans stated the accepted reality about our universe as, "The Universe is more a great thought than a great machine." Whether it is the big bang theory, which states that out of the light all matter was created, or the Bible, which says that from the creation of heavens and earth all matter was created, both agree that all matter was created; every physical object in the universe was built, including all life on earth and our human bodies.

Borrowing the much older words of the Sufi Farid Al-Din 'Attar, "The heart is the dwelling place of that which is the Essence of the Universe. Within the very heart and soul is the very Essence of God. Like the saints, make a journey into yourself; like the lovers of God cast one glance within. As a lover now, in contemplation of the Beloved be unveiled within and behold the Essence. Form is a veil to you and your heart is a veil. When the veil vanishes, you will become all light."

Statistically it is absolutely unrealistic to assume that the fabrication of the universe and the development of the diverse life forms on earth have evolved in a random way. In the groundbreaking words of George Wald, which won him a Nobel Prize, "It has occurred to me that the questions of the origin of consciousness in humans and of life from non-living matter, are related. This is with the assumption that 'mind,' rather than emerging as a late outgrowth in the evolution of life, has existed always as the matrix, the source and condition of physical reality—the stuff of which physical reality is composed is mind-stuff. It is 'mind' that has composed a physical Universe that breeds life and so eventually evolves creatures that know and create: science-, art-, and technology-making animals. In them the Universe begins to know itself."

In one mix of protons, neutrons, and electrons, you get a grain of sand. In another mix, the same protons, neutrons, and electrons produce a brain that can record facts, produce emotions, feel love, and integrate those facts, emotions, and experiences. They are the same protons, neutrons, and electrons, even though one mix seems passive and the other is dynamically alive. Mind, therefore, must be embedded in even the smallest of particles. The combination of the individual pieces of mind present in each and every particle makes up the collective mind of the being that is formed.

Freeman Dyson states that sentience and awareness emerge at very basic levels, "Atoms are weird stuff, behaving like active agents rather than inert substances. It appears that mind as manifested by the capacity to make choices is to some extent inherent in every atom." Mind, as information or wisdom, is present in every atom. Mind is ubiquitous in our universe, just as wisdom is the basis of all existence.

Any plant or animal expresses in physical form the ethereal energy from which it is made. And that elemental energy is none other than the manifestation of the wisdom from which it is built. I compare it with the old *Lego blocks* we played with as children. The same blocks make a house one day, a fire truck the next, and a horse or a cowboy on the third. Like the Lego blocks, the "pieces of mind" embedded in the building blocks move from function to function.

I find it remarkable that it took science so many years and so many Nobel Prize winners to come to roughly the same conclusions the main traditions of wisdom reached thousands of years ago. Dust to dust, ashes to ashes. While the mind, captured in those dust particles, moves on in the winds of time, from transient being to inert materials to another transient being, it builds up ever-greater experience and awareness.

Mind can function as a synonym for spirit, soul, or self; scientific works, in particular, often consider *mind* as a synonym for *soul*. Most major religions or belief systems teach that only humans have souls, while others, mostly older animistic systems, teach that all living things, and even inanimate objects such as rivers, have souls. More and more this latter view is being accepted as closest to the scientific truth.

Immanuel Kant identified that the soul as the *I* in the strictest sense and that the existence of inner experience can neither be proved nor disproved. "We cannot prove the immateriality of the soul, but rather only so much: that all properties and actions of the soul cannot be cognized from materiality." It is from the *I*, or soul, that Kant proposed transcendental rationalization but cautioned that such rationalization can determine the limits of knowledge only if it is to remain practical.

Buddhism does not deny the existence of immaterial entities, and it makes a distinction between bodily states and mental states, but it denies the existence of a permanent entity that remains constant behind the changing corporeal and incorporeal components of a living being. Just as the body changes from moment to moment, so thoughts come and go. And there is no permanent, underlying mind that experiences these thoughts; rather, conscious mental states simply arise and perish with no "thinker" or "silent witness" behind them. When the body dies, the incorporeal mental processes continue and are reborn in a new body. Because the mental processes are constantly changing, the being that is reborn is neither entirely different from, nor exactly the same as, the being that died. However, the new being is continuous with the being that died—in the same way that the *you* of this moment is continuous with the *you* of a moment before or when you were a child, despite the fact that you are constantly changing.

Carl Jung said, "All ages before ours believed in Gods in some form or other. Only an unparalleled impoverishment in symbolism could enable us to discover the gods as psychic factors, which is to say, as archetypes of the unconscious. No doubt this discovery is hardly credible yet."

The great majority of people in the world believe in, to some extent, one God or another. For thousands of years or so there have been arguments, wars, inquisitions, trials, immolations, excommunications, and so forth, all related to the existence of and the correct way to envision God.

Just as it is highly unlikely, and not possible to construct scientifically hard proof that the universe and everything in it is the result of pure coincidence, it is not possible to come up with hard proof that the universe was created by a God (and if created by a God, which one of the many that are revered by different religions). Behind every theory, every religion, there is a "leap of faith" somewhere. No religion has convincingly solved all the puzzles of the universe.

If God or Gods exist, there remain plenty of unsolved mysteries. To just name a few, why do some people destroy in the name of *their* God, convinced they are righteous, while harming others who believe in *their* God, who preaches something totally different? Why, if God is omnipresent, can we not see him or most of the time, even sense his presence? If everything is already predestined, are we then here just to play out what has already been decided? And, if God is all merciful and all loving and omnipotent, then why is so much of the world suffering and in turmoil? Why are there so many tears and fears? What is their purpose? If God is omnipotent, shouldn't he be able to make the universe a harmonious place, full of love and mercy and justice? If God is a fair and impartial judge, he should reward the just and punish the wicked. Nevertheless, bad things happen to good people. Does God perhaps see things we do not? Or, is reincarnation true and these good folks are just currently reaping what they have sown in some past not-so-good life? Maybe there is order and justice in the world; maybe it is being run by an all-knowing, all-powerful, all-loving, and intelligent existence, but who really knows? I definitely do not.

Gautama Buddha dealt with all this as follows, "Enlightenment is a way of saying that all things are seen in their intrinsic empty nature, their Suchness, their ungraspable wonder. Names or words are merely incidental, but that state which sees no division, no duality, is enlightenment. Perfect wisdom can't be learned or distinguished or thought about or found through the senses. This is because nothing in this world can be finally explained, it can only be experienced, and thus all things are just as they are. Perfect wisdom can never be experienced apart from all things. To see the Suchness of things, which is their empty calm being, is to see them just as they are."

Maharishi Mahesh Yogi phrases it slightly differently, "Once the mind gets to the transcendence, it knows 'itself.' It's not the mind that knows Being; Being knows 'itself.' As long as there is some activity, we say mind; when activity subsides, it's pure awareness. It is not knowing; it is Knowingness. Being is known on the level of Knowingness, not the level of thinking."

And Lao Tzu in the Tao Te Ching said, "A mind free of thought, merged within itself, beholds the essence of Tao. A mind filled with thought, identified with its own perceptions, beholds the mere forms of this world." I think that maybe we are just not advanced enough yet to understand the bigger scheme at work, and our theories, wisdom, and traditions are not detailed enough yet to explain the reality behind what we experience.

I can sympathize with John Lennon, who once said, "I believe in God, but not as one thing, not as an old man in the sky. I believe that what people call God is something in all of us. I believe that what Jesus and Mohammed and Buddha and all the rest said was right. It's just that the translations have gone wrong."

The will of "God" has been misused over the centuries by any and all for purposes that have nothing to do with religion. Quotes from the Bible, the Koran, and the Vedanta have all been taken out of context to justify almost any vile action undertaken by man. Bishop Desmond Tutu illustrated it painfully as, "When the missionaries came to Africa they had the Bible and we had the land. They said, 'Let us pray.' We closed our eyes. When we opened them we had the Bible and they had the land."

Most people in the world have a religion. The "rules" to human beings vary from one religious tradition to another, but all provide a moral compass or a number of *key performance indicators* we need to adhere to in order to achieve a meaningful and moral life:

- The Ten Commandments (Thou shalt not kill, steal, commit adultery, etc.)

- Do not kill any living thing (Buddhism)

- Bonuses and merit can be earned by being or doing "good"

- Be involved in regular prayer, contemplation, meditation; communicate with yourself and with God

- Undertake a meaningful pilgrimage (Islam)

- Be involved in charity; share a significant part of what you
  have and what you earn

Religion creates a moral framework to man's life that nature by itself does not impose. For many atheists, such an imposed, and not always completely rational, framework is unacceptable. Karl Marx said that religion is opium for the people. It's a system created by man to enslave fellow man into obedience, subservience, and an ordered society. Although in essence he may not be far away from the truth, one hundred years of communist systems in the world has demonstrated that humankind needs more than pure rationality to keep itself within morally acceptable boundaries.

How is all this relevant for us setting up and running, let us say, a coffee shop? It is easy, of course, if you see yourself as God Almighty. Then, consequently, you would be the coffee, you would be the shop, and you would be the brewing process and the enjoyment of the coffee-drinking process. And it would be easy to make the shop a success.

As a religious person you can pray and ask your God for insight, help, and strength to make the coffee shop a success. And if you sincerely believe, your faith will give you both the wisdom to understand what is needed to make the coffee shop function, and the power and strength to do whatever it takes to make it a success.

As an agnostic person you can, as demonstrated above, also feel in control of the universe. By putting your mind to making the shop a success, you will slowly but surely align everything around you in such a way that the shop will have to become a success. In the end, for me, it's not all that different. The focused mind will ultimately create the result; there is no doubt about it. Everyone is able to point at events in his life where the outcome of the situation was highly uncertain, but after intense focused attention on the issue, the situation turned out for the better; it moved toward the desired outcome. This is not coincidence or heavenly interference; this is the result of focused attention and of converting mind into matter.

Mao Zedong wrote about it as follows, "As a modern man I am decidedly undecided. Firmly rational when everything goes according to plan, master of my own destiny. When everything goes wrong, I pray, and I must confess there have been too many cases where chains of unlikely lucky events turned the situation around after intense prayer to fully attribute the outcome to coincidence."

I remember several similar situations on my own long march to success. I have prayed more than once, especially in the fledgling years of Amicorp, for a specific deal to go through or for a series of events to happen in order to make our company survive a particularly rough patch. And I have often been surprised at how unexplainably all the bits fell in place in just the nick of time.

Barack Obama, although a regular churchgoer and clearly a proponent of the enlightenment tradition, is trying to reconcile opposing traditions in his country. He asks the secularists not to dismiss religion as inherently irrational, and the believers not to think that they alone should define the nation's morality. You should do the same in your company.

During your life you will meet with people from many different religions. They will bring their religions to work and to business, just as they bring their culture, their caste, their race, their skin color, their sexual interests, and their personal preferences to work. You had better make sure you understand at least the basics of the different belief traditions you work with. That counts not only for your employees, but also for your customers and your suppliers. Otherwise you will not understand why your coffee shop in a Muslim neighborhood will not sell products unless its offerings are *"halal"* and during Ramadan season only after the sun has set. That may be the most obvious of examples, but you will need to understand as well why the Indians will never say no to a direct question, why the Chinese and Japanese do not want to lose face, and why a Latin American macho or a person of Pashtun ancestry is quickly offended, especially if you seem to be gazing roughly in the direction of his wife.

In our company, we are trying to accept and respect all wisdom traditions. Although our IT department is mainly staffed by Muslims, a Ganesh statue stands over the server room. My new office in Singapore was designed in consultation with a Feng Shui master, and there is a painting of Koi fish in the water behind my desk.

Whatever your own beliefs, respecting the belief traditions of all the people you are working with (employees, clients, and suppliers) is extremely important. Belief traditions have survived for many centuries, not only because they favored those in control of the system, but also because they provide hope, order, consolation, and explanation for the many aspects of life that we still do not understand.

> *"A religion that takes no account of practical affairs and does not help to solve them is no religion."*
>
> **—Mohandas Gandhi**

Chapter 31

Where Will It End?

We shall not cease from exploration
And the end of all our exploring
Will be to arrive where we started
And know the place for the first time.

—Thomas Stearns Eliot

All good things, as well as all bad things, eventually come to an end. That includes your active life as an entrepreneur. You may be in poor health or getting old, you may perhaps even be bored; maybe you are eager to move on to greener pastures and enjoy your well-earned rest. Whatever. At some stage you have to separate from your business.

People who are not entrepreneurs themselves do not always understand why this is difficult. I have heard the question a thousand times, *"You should have enough money, why don't you sell the business and retire?"* Or, *"Why don't you let others run the business and enjoy life?"* People who ask the questions don't understand that, for an entrepreneur, running a business is more fun than playing Sudoku or chasing a little white ball over the well-manicured grass or partying. For me, doing business is my way of enjoying life—of getting the most out of my life. The activities I take part in during my *free* time are also more fun as they combine with or contrast to my *work*. If I were doing the *fun* things all the time, they would be much less fun; just as I don't indulge in more than three or four meals a day or enjoy sex or strawberries *all* the time.

231

Running a business *part time* is not an option in most cases. There is only so much you can delegate, and in order to keep the business outstanding, and standing out from the crowd, you will most likely have to give it 100 percent. Your neighbor is also working hard and is not stupid either. If you are no longer striving for excellence, you will very soon be forgotten.

Entrepreneurs who want to leave their business often take several years to come to that decision, and they need counseling, false starts, and often a *wake-up call* in order to come to a decision. A heart attack may be the most extreme of wake-up calls but, sadly, is a very common one. Realizing you are getting old, losing interest, or losing your touch is hard. It is almost like, for older people, the decision to give up your own house and freedom and move into a home for the elderly.

Once you plan to leave, you are faced with a number of choices as to what to do with your company.

The key choices you have are:

- close it down

- leave it to your children, colleagues, or friends

- sell and merge it with the business of a competitor

- sell it to a purely financial investor, such as a venture capitalist or private equity investor

None of these choices is particularly easy.

Closing down may be a good alternative if what you are running is a mom-and-pop activity that has little franchise value by itself. You sell out your stock, you sell the furniture, cash in your receivables, terminate the lease, and you are done. In such cases none of the *goodwill* will translate into cash for you. Your life's work will disappear without a trace.

Leaving the business to your children has always been and still is a very common approach with small farmers and shopkeepers, as well as a few large corporations. If your company is bigger, leaving it to your children is a viable alternative only if your kids truly are the best prepared and the most suitable people to continue running the business. If the sole purpose of putting your children in charge of a significant business is to keep control over the family silver, it is better to organize something at the shareholder level, such as a family office, a service we routinely offer to wealthy families in emerging-market countries, and introduce some control mechanisms while attracting professional management. Leaving your business to your children, of course, has the attraction of combining your need to live for your children with the opportunity to see your work live on in the lives of future family generations.

You can have some of the same experience if you transfer the ownership of your company to your close business associates and friends. These are people who have also contributed significantly to your business, may have been there *almost* as long as you, and may be as capable if not more so than you are. You may have to concede on the financial side of the transaction to get a deal financed, but that may be compensated on the emotional side by knowing that your life's work continues, and the goodwill built is being preserved.

Selling to a competitor is emotionally much more challenging. Your company will disappear; a different name will appear on *your* building; your colleagues will switch allegiances; your clients and suppliers will work with a competitor that originally may have been a friend or a friendly "enemy" of your business. On the other hand, it may provide you with a clean break from your past, better prospects for your employees and clients in the long run, and it may give you a nice sum of cash you can use to enjoy life or start something new.

Selling to a financial engineering company or private-equity firm is an additional alternative. For the entrepreneur this is often a more painful alternative. In exchange for money, usually more than in the other alternatives, you sell the soul of your company to the devil. The purpose of a private-equity company generally is to extract "value" by rationalizing the business processes, rightsizing the workforce, increasing the pricing, squeezing suppliers and clients, and leveraging the business. And after all the value has been squeezed out, the remaining structure is sold again or discarded for scrap. You have to be pretty pressed for money or have little heart for your business to prefer this route. And if you have read the rest of this book, you know it is a recipe for disaster for any quality company that has the intention of being there for the long run, to serve more purposes than earning short-term maximum returns for its shareholders.

The alternatives that are *truly* feasible for separation from your company are limited. But the structure of the transaction is, of course, largely determined by you. There is no need to have all kinds of experts and advisors tell you, the entrepreneur, how to separate yourself from the company you've created. In the worst case scenario you can decide to die in harness and leave those left behind with the task of sorting out the mess you created.

Once you have made the decision and you have sold your company in one way or another and you have left the day-to-day management, you are faced with what to do with all the newfound money and free time. Do you really think playing bridge or golf will be as much fun as running a business? How often can you cruise around the Caribbean or babysit your grandchildren? Maybe you want to take on another meaningful task—perhaps something smaller and less time consuming than the previous one. Maybe something with a totally different focus; an entirely different challenge is what you need. Maybe something such as teaching or coaching, or community or charity work, will strike your fancy.

To a certain extent you will continue to employ the skills you have acquired over your lifetime, and to a certain extent you will start over. Giving up the status, power, and the recognition you had when you were running your company, however big or small it may have been, may take some getting used to. You may be getting older, but you are also wiser. The reality that you may not live to see trees mature is no reason to not plant them. As you get older, it may become more urgent to plant them today. Your children and grandchildren will be grateful to you for that. Opportunities missed, adventures not taken, and dreams not pursued, in the end will hurt much more than projects that failed.

Do not underestimate how narcissistic you may have become in the process of setting up and growing your own company. You fall in love with your own accomplishments, you get addicted to success, and you express your power and pride in the monuments you build to yourself. Your happiness as a successful entrepreneur was to a large extent related to the pride and joy you got from running your business. When that business is gone, you will need a replacement, another source of pride and joy.

Near to the wine project that my INSEAD friends and I have undertaken in Valle de Uco, Mendoza, Argentina, is another wonderful winery, *Salentein*, owned by a former car dealer from the Netherlands. The man started in his late sixties to produce a beautiful wine. The huge vineyard, with its cavernous cathedral-like winery, triggered the development in the whole valley. The man was in a family rivalry with his brother, who had built another great winery, *Bernardus*, in the Napa Valley. My initial reaction was, how narcissistic can one be, to build such a mausoleum to one's ego? Why go through all that at this stage in your life? To prove what?

One of my friends politely pointed out to me that I had built a titanium-clad office building in the shape of Noah's ark, on top of Mount Ararat, in Curaçao. That one hurt. Nevertheless, I continued leveling another part of Mount Ararat, to erect a lighthouse-shaped tower right next to it, which, once finished, will be able to be seen from half the island. I guess olive trees on the slopes and some pigeons are going to be next.

Peggy Noonan said, "In a way the world is a great liar. It shows you it worships and admires money, but at the end of the day it doesn't. It says it adores fame and celebrity, but it doesn't, not really. The world admires, and wants to hold on to, and not lose, goodness. It admires virtue. At the end it gives its greatest tributes to generosity, honesty, courage, mercy, talents well used, talents that, brought into the world, make it better. That is what it really admires. That is what we talk about in eulogies, because that is what's important. We don't say, 'The thing about Joe was he was rich.' We say, if we can, 'The thing about Joe was he took care of people.'"

Selling your business and going on to the next phase is just that, a next phase. The things you are here to do, the ones that really matter, do not change once you have money in the bank and have nothing more to do. You always have more to do; your life's goals will not be achieved until your last breath has expired.

> *Do not go gentle into that goodnight,*
> *Old age should burn and rave at close of day;*
> *Rage, rage against the dying of the light.*

—Dylan Thomas

Chapter 32

How Much Money Is Enough?

"The wealthy man is the man who is much, not the one who has much."

Karl Marx

In a book about business there has to be a chapter about money. As they say, "There are only two groups of people who think a lot about money, the rich and the poor," and so money takes up a disproportionate amount of time in the minds of many of us.

Most people who aspire to operate their own business one day, but never really do, see starting and running a business as a way to become rich quickly—a prospect they consider attractive but unattainable. And yet, most of the inspiring and successful entrepreneurs I meet, who actually did start and build a successful business, hardly ever talk about money. It is not an important goal in life. Money is just a by-product of bigger and more important goals to be achieved.

There are many simple "secret recipes" to becoming rich. I like the one of Nassim Nicholas Taleb, "The fastest way to become rich is to socialize with the poor; the fastest way to become poor is to socialize with the rich." There are several reasons for this. Firstly, there are more poor people than rich people, so if you find a solution that works for poor people, your potential market is many times greater than if you provide a service for a rich person. Secondly, catering to the rich is many time more expensive than catering to the poor. It requires fancier office space, more expensive dinners, and a higher paid staff, *and* it's a smaller and more personal market to cater to. Thirdly, but most importantly, associating with rich people makes you aspire to their lifestyle; it causes you to spend more money, thus forcing you to make more money. The most successful businesspeople are the ones who cater to the masses, just as the more successful statesmen cater to the poor—Nelson Mandela, Mohandas Gandhi, Jesus Christ to name a few. So catering to the poor may create a big power base, although it does not explain how to do it.

In the Bible (Matthew 25:14–30) the process of getting rich is explained in the following simple story, "For it is just like a man about to go on a journey, who called his own slaves and entrusted his possessions to them. To one he gave five talents, to another, two, and to another, one, each according to his own ability; and he went on his journey. Immediately the one who had received the five talents went and traded with them, and gained five more talents. In the same manner the one who had received the two talents gained two more. But he who received the one talent went away and dug a hole in the ground and hid his master's money. Now after a long time the master of those slaves came back and settled accounts with them....

"But his master answered and said to he who received one talent, 'You ... ought to have put my money in the bank, and on my arrival I would have received my money back with interest. Therefore take away the talent from him, and give it to the one who has the ten talents.' For to everyone who has, more shall be given, and he will have an abundance; but from the one who does not have, even what he does have shall be taken away. Throw out the worthless slave into the outer darkness; in that place there will be weeping and gnashing of teeth."

Harsh as this lesson may be, it comes pretty close to current economic reality—*the rich get richer*. Having money helps make more money, and it requires initiative, insight, and risk in order to increase your assets. Money also helps you acquire things such as power, status, affection, and sometimes even love. It is an important motivating factor, although clearly subject to the second Law of Gossen (it requires ever-greater quantities to achieve a similar burst in motivation); money temporarily satisfies the ego, and is a way to "keep score." Even billionaires secretly look at the *Fortune 500* lists to see how they are doing compared to their competitors. But the quantity of money is usually not a goal by itself. The amount of money you accumulate carries no weight as to how much you are worth, how and why others value you, or how happy you are.

China, traditionally a country of hard-working people, got into serious difficulties, including mass starvation, when, among other things, money was taken away as a motivator after the Communist victory culminating in the Cultural Revolution in the 1960s. The situation really improved only when Deng Xiaoping in the early 1980s declared, "To get rich is glorious." He sparked a huge turnaround in Chinese society that led to thirty years of double-digit growth; China became the second-largest economy in the world, and the standards of living of the great majority of Chinese people were uplifted significantly. Yet, even if all manufacturing jobs in the West were transferred to China, it would continue to have a significant number of underemployed people as well as poverty-stricken people in parts of the country.

If you are really focused, there are many ways to make lots of money with relatively limited effort. But that has little to do with doing business. Sound and sustainable business is never just about making a lot of money, as I hope this book makes clear.

Once you have money, you will see for yourself that it makes you neither more nor less happy. Of course you need enough money to lead a decent life, but for that you really do not need that much. If you have little money, lower your needs and wants to suit your income; if you have more, use what you have to benefit yourself and others. Be aware that the most harmful addictions in your life are: a fixed income, food, and drugs. The higher your income, the more difficult it is to buy your freedom, become an entrepreneur, or leave the rat race altogether and focus on more meaningful things in life than money. The more overweight you are the closer you are to a heart attack, and the more alcohol or drugs you use the more difficult it becomes to see beyond your illusions.

I once backpacked for about a year overland to India, Nepal, and Indonesia. I also backpacked for about a year all over Latin America. In both cases, everything I needed was in that back pack, and over the months it would get lighter rather than heavier. If you have to carry your stuff around every day, you think about what you really need, and, believe me, it is amazingly little. A few changes of clothes, a couple of good books, and a toothbrush go a long way. Similarly, as the months progressed, I would spend less money every week, instead of more.

Later, my family and I moved a few times internationally, and every time a container full of stuff followed us to the new location. Upon unpacking, we realized that all the stuff that had been traveling for months was not really essential to our lives, and so we threw away many of the things in the container. Accumulating more stuff means you need to take care of more stuff. Accumulating less stuff means you have fewer worries.

You can have a big house or a small house, but a small house is guaranteed to give you fewer headaches than a big one. You do not need to buy a big yacht to enjoy a day on the water. You can find friends with boats, charter a boat from time to time, or enjoy the water from the shore.

What you are worth is not determined by how much money you have in the bank, or how well invested you are in the stock market. It is determined by your values and by how much value you add to your environment. If you give away a significant part of what you have earned yourself, you will feel more valuable, and your value to society will increase. You will notice that the more you give, the more you will receive. Your good actions will attract positive energy, and good things will come your way in ever greater abundance. And giving something is not always just about money—it is also about your advice, your ideas, your experience, your friendship, your smile, and your love.

The more you give from the heart, the more you will get back. A client who is very happy will send significantly more referrals than one who is only somewhat happy. People who remember you as a giving person will speak positively about you and think positively about you, and more and more good things will come your way. This is, of course, not a one-time deal. It works when you are *always* a giving person and when you treat everyone you meet well, not when you calculate whether it is worth your time, smile, friendship, etc.

Your success depends on how thoughtful and sincere you are in helping other people reach *their* goals in life. These cannot be just a few people, nor simply the people you like personally, but rather all people around you—your friends and family, of course, but also your employees, your clients, and your suppliers, and even your competitors and the people you may not necessarily like very much. Your positive approach and your positive actions will multiply, just as any negative action or negative thoughts will also multiply.

Be authentic. Be who you really are. Do not pretend to be different from what and who you are. What is inside you will always come out somehow. People who are not authentic will in the end be exposed, and they will not feel really happy until what they think, what they say, and what they do are in synch.

I know there is no need for greed. According to the Talmud, "Who is rich? The one who appreciates what he has." Whenever I feel that I am getting carried away by the lure of material goods, I compare the value of something I don't really need, to the value of something that has real value, to get to the intrinsic or *real* value of money.

For example, I express the value of a new car by how many orphans the cost of that car would feed, clothe, and educate in India. The cost of a $40,000 car can equate to providing for one hundred Indian orphans for a year.

A $10,000 bonus to an already well-paid person in Western Europe or the United States translates to ten or more full-time jobs for eager and intelligent young people in many emerging-market countries. It makes you balance your thoughts on who is more deserving. The additional cost of just one business-class ticket over an economy-class ticket pays for several lifesaving operations in Indonesia. And flying economy delivers you to your destination at the same time as business class.

There is no virtue in accumulating money and then not using it productively. It needs to be meaningfully invested or wisely spent. Accumulating money just for the sake of accumulating more and more of it serves no purpose. According to J. Paul Getty, "Money is like manure. You have to spread it around, or it will start to stink."

Be open. If you are open to receive from others, you can give effectively. Be grateful for everything that comes your way. Being wealthy brings responsibility with it. The old sayings that *Noblesse Oblige,* and *To whom much is given, much is expected,* are still valid today. Wealth is not just to be accumulated, just as energy is not to be stored; it is to be used for the betterment of your life and that of others.

Warren Buffett, one of the richest people on earth, famously said, "Wall Street is the only place where people who have accumulated wealth go in limousines to be advised on what to invest their money in by twenty-something year olds who ride the subway to work every day and have not a penny to invest." He decided to leave his children only a "modest" sum of money (I think it was something like $10 million each) and give the rest of his billions to charity (mostly to the Bill and Melinda Gates Foundation, a foundation that among other things is working on eradicating polio). His rationale is that the greatest pleasure he had in life was making investments and building his company. He did not want to deny his children the pleasure and the satisfaction of building something meaningful for themselves.

While there is no need to wait to distribute your money until after you have died, I think it's a pretty good example to follow. I know my kids may not agree with Warren Buffett's statement now, but I am pretty sure they will once they have built up their own lives.

> *"Then Jesus said to them, 'I tell you the truth, it is hard for a rich man to enter the Kingdom of Heaven. Again I tell you, it is easier for a camel to go through the eye of a needle than for a rich man to enter the Kingdom of God.'"*
>
> **—Bible, Matthew: 20:23**

Chapter 33

Is Death the End in Mind?

"When we go before him, God will ask, 'Where are your wounds?' And we will say, 'I have no wounds.' And God will ask, 'Was there nothing worth fighting for?'"

—Reverend Allan Boesak

When I was a kid, I always asked my father to tell stories about the war (the Second World War), as stories about that time seemed to have more intensity than stories about good times. One day he told me about how in the final winter of the war (September 1944 to March 1945) in the area between Arnhem and Nijmegen in the Netherlands, he was a member of a resistance group trying to disrupt the German war effort by attacking food transports. At this point in the war, the Germans were scraping their last reserves together. Food transports were poorly guarded by badly trained and weakly motivated conscripts who were too old, too young, or too handicapped to fight at the front lines. Of course, these soldiers were no match for the well-armed, well-motivated young resistance fighters who had lived all their lives on the land they were fighting for. On several occasions my father's unit ended up surprising a convoy, and as they could not take prisoners between the fluctuating front lines, ended up executing the soldiers who tried to surrender in battle.

After the war my father was offered a medal for his valiant contributions, but he would not accept it, as he considered the fighting he had done to be nothing more than his duty, but he also failed to see the moral superiority of it even though he was fighting against a clearly criminal regime. For the rest of his life he remained haunted by memories of the faces of the sometimes very young people they executed at that last stage of the war.

Living in the same village his entire life, my father was a simple farmer who was involved in all possible social activities. He was a coffin bearer for the church as well as the registrar for the Frisian stud cattle register in the village. At the time of his funeral a great many people showed up. They all appreciated his kindness, his moral stances, and his contributions to the people in the village.

I always think about his story when I am making difficult decisions, such as letting employees go or making major investments. No economic decision or action benefiting a small group of stakeholders of the company justifies major disadvantages to the other stakeholders. Even the employee who does not fit, the client who does not pay, or the supplier who does not deliver quality deserves respect and deserves to be treated as a human being. However you react to someone today will come back to you in one form or another a different day. Making a profit, obtaining a commercial gain, or beating a competitor never justifies crossing the line into what is ethically or morally wrong. Doing so will make you feel miserable inside.

My father developed a serious heart condition in his early fifties; he had been a heavy smoker most of his life. This forced him to give up farming and sell the farm to pay the hospital bills. Not having proper health insurance, he ended up in a menial job at the local government, which to him was a major blow to his ego, though he never complained about it.

At the time I was studying a mere one hundred kilometers away from my home. One rainy November day my father unexpectedly visited me in the middle of the week—something he had never done before. It was a melancholic conversation. We spoke for quite a while about his moments of pride as well as his regrets in life. He shared with me the things he had wanted to do but never actually got to do. He confided he had always wanted to visit England, a country he had never been to, and which over the years of German occupation had produced an almost magical lure to him. I had never known of this hidden wish before. My father was a man who did not need much for himself. The thought crossed my mind to offer for us to go there together immediately, but exams were looming, so I did not propose the idea. The thought stayed with me, however, and I devised a concrete plan later that evening to invite him for a joint trip to England as soon as my exams were done. Two days later he died of another heart attack, never making it to England.

I still regret not having made the offer during his visit or over the phone after I had thought about it later that day. Since that day, however, I live with much more of a sense of urgency. What is here today will be gone tomorrow. There are not endless quantities of time to complete our plans and follow our dreams. Every day, once gone, will be gone forever, and that will bring us one day closer to inevitable death. I now look at myself in the mirror and habitually ask myself whether I have made the most of the day, the month, or the year. I consciously sort between the needful, the unnecessary, and the more valuable activities in life. I also distinguish between the people who bring me pleasure or joy, and the ones who burden or bore me, consciously letting go of the ones who are full of negativity, anger, or boredom. I keep a bucket list of things to do in life and regularly check whether I am making progress. Once the Grim Reaper comes for me, I want to be able to think back on a life that is full of achievements, experiences, friends and family, joyful moments, beauty, meaning, and love. In the historic words of Boris Yeltsin, "A man must live like a great brilliant flame and burn as brightly as he can. In the end he burns out. But this is far better than a mean little flame."

You need not mourn, but you should welcome the inevitability of death, as death helps us to see beyond the materialistic level of life. It inspires us to be grateful for and generous with whatever we have while we are here on earth. Death makes it easier for us to let go of ego and false pride and inspires us to be courageous, creating meaningful relationships and true meaning in the process. It allows us to better appreciate the value and uniqueness of each moment. The unexamined life, as Plato acknowledged over two thousand years ago, is not worth living.

Thinking of death holds a key to immortality, because it urges us to discover and identify with our deeper self—the part of us which can never really die. And it forces us to think about what we live for. Many people do not think about that until late in life, and others have their "end in mind" from the very beginning. Ernesto "Che" Guevara once said, "We cannot be sure of having something to live for unless we are willing to die for it." The thing we live for—the ideals, the ideas, the good works—is one thing, and perhaps the most important thing. The people we live for, our loved ones, are another thing altogether.

We will see the people we love most, our parents, grandparents, partner(s), friends, and other people all die. Fate may have us even see one or more of our children die. As human beings we attach ourselves to them; we may even feel ourselves inseparable from them. This connection comes from our being mammals that are incapable of surviving the first few years of our lives without constant care, feeding, and protection by others. In the Asian belief, man strives to sever any deeply emotional attachment to other transient beings, in order to avoid the pain and suffering related to inevitable loss. In the Christian-Judaic traditions, on the other hand, man consoles himself at the thought of seeing his loved ones in the afterlife.

What does this all have to do with being an entrepreneur and trying to grow a successful business? A lot. When building a company you can easily become obsessed with making more money or building a bigger business. You may start thinking you are invincible; you may even get lured into benefiting yourselves or your company at the expense of others. You may forget where you come from, who you are, and why you are in this world. *Memento Mori.*

There are many stories in Taoism and in Buddhism about people who spend their whole lives looking for the *Valley of the Flowers*, constantly searching for something outside their reach—yet to be found and yet to be enjoyed. At the end of their lives, they look back, and only then do they realize that the journey they have made was what was important, not the destination. We already live in paradise, we are gardeners in the Garden of Eden (Genesis 2:15); we just need to open our eyes and minds and learn to recognize it as such. We must enjoy the moment and relish the ride.

Whatever our mission and vision for our business, what is important is what we do today with our business, how we treat clients and employees today, how we fit our business today into society and the environment, and how we make money today in a manner that we can enjoy and be proud of later. The Dalai Lama advised, "Plan like you will live forever, but live and enjoy as if this is your last day on earth."

Who judges us in the end? The only relevant judge is our own judgment— not God's judgment or the judgment of society, our family, colleagues, or people around us. However great our need for affirmation, we ourselves determine whether we are successful in life or not, whether we have followed an honorable path or not, whether we have truthfully followed the dictates of the heart, and whether we have done what we could, shared enough love, and enjoyed the process. Frank Sinatra immortalized the song "My Way," which has become an epitaph for many, including me. He sang, "For what is a man, what has he got? If not himself, then he has naught. To say the things he truly feels and not the words of one who kneels. The record shows I took the blows and did it my way! Yes, it was my way."

A few years ago, my brother had a serious car accident; he lost a leg, and till this day remains largely paralyzed. He was between life and death for many days and had many operations and tremendous pain afterwards. The event thoroughly changed his life and his relationship with his wife and children. He is now much more aware of what is important in life and is enjoying his life more, even though he lives with severe disabilities.

Many years ago I also went through a very traumatic experience and nearly lost my life. When I walked away from it, the world somehow looked different. The trees seemed greener, the air much fresher, the birds sang louder, and the sun shone much brighter. Having seen my whole life flash by in seconds, I intuitively understood what I had been doing wrong until then and thus changed my priorities. Realizing that my life can be gone in a second and having been close to the end of it taught me to be much more appreciative of what I have and the ones I love. If I now think back to that afternoon, I feel the strength to deal with difficult decisions, and I appreciate all of the great things in my life. I don't think a life-changing event is necessary to reach that point of appreciation, as it is something we all have within us, but it certainly did make a difference in my life.

Fidel Castro, former president of Cuba, said many years ago, "I think that a man should not live beyond the age when he begins to deteriorate, when the flame that lighted the brightest moment of his life has weakened."

Our death will come soon enough. Be ashamed to die before contributing something meaningful to society. We must have our affairs in order and our children set on their own path in life. We can bid our loved ones farewell, and our worldly possessions can be left in a will. Our achievements in life can inspire others to continue our work. According to John Lennon, "Dying is like changing cars. The vehicle is replaced but the ride continues."

"Death is not extinguishing the light; it is putting out the lamp because the dawn has come."

—Rabindranath Tagore

Chapter 34

Is This It?

"You wayfarer in the Universe who go through life like a meteor, make sure your fall into the void is not in vain. Do not go straight from nothing to nothing but give a meaning to your fleeting presence in this fleeting reality, cultivating the most sublime of achievements, and the highest goal of Consciousness, which makes Matter great: love through non-attachment. A Buddha is inside you: make him grow until you become another of his incarnations. In the eternal flow from nothing to nothing make sure that between one nothing and the other Consciousness and Love take their place in the evolution of this Universe."

—Giulio Cesare Giacobbe

From time to time, in all of us, the question comes up whether there is life after death. Many people are convinced that after they die they will go to heaven and bask in the presence of God's spirit all day; others believe that if they live and die courageously, they will be rewarded with the physical company of many virgins; and still others believe that a turn of the wheel of *Samsara* will bring them to the next life, acknowledging the karma they built up in this life as well as benefiting from the knowledge they have attained in their past lives, until hopefully one day they have learned enough to escape the endless succession of reincarnations through enlightenment. Agnostic people generally believe they die, their body gets disposed of, and that is the end of that.

Business rarely, if ever, figures in thoughts about the afterlife. I am not familiar with any religion that suggests you might be running a bigger business or be a more successful entrepreneur in your afterlife. Nobody is rewarded in the afterlife with more employees, a better business, or even more money. The thousands of investigations into near-death experiences never record people seeing the bright lights of industrial complexes, the peace and quiet of laboratories and libraries, the alluring sounds of city traffic, or the welcoming voices of their bankers and auditors. So, for all practical purposes, business in the afterlife seems to not exist.

Hindus, Buddhists, and many faithful of other religions believe in previous lives—in the regressions or memories of the many people who recall previous lives. It often becomes clear what profession they, or their spirit, had in a previous life. People vividly remember they were laborers, warriors, craftsmen, etc. Entrepreneurship has existed since our forefathers were cave dwellers, yet nobody remembers running a listed company; nobody remembers his previous lives' business plans, mission statement, or financial statements. Previous lives are peopled with loved ones, relatives, rivals, and demons—not customers, employees, bankers, and accountants.

So what does this mean? Simply put, business clearly does not dominate the memories of previous lives or the prospects of life after your death.

Not too long ago I was involved in negotiations concerning the acquisition of a smaller-sized company in India. We were having dinner with the owners of the takeover candidate, and the discussions had reached a dead end. The owners, two Hindu businessmen in their forties, clearly had serious doubts about letting go of their baby, and money and sweet talk were not going to change that. The discussion drifted toward previous lives. It was an interesting discussion, as members of various religions as well as down-to-earth agnostic people were gathered at the table. The ones who had notions of previous lives shared them with the others, and somewhere a connection that to that point we had not been able to make in our current lives was made on the level of a previous one. Three weeks later a deal was closed.

How you look at the possibility of future lives has a clear impact on how you act in this life. If you believe that attachment to material goods as well as to close personal relationships stands in your way to enlightenment, it will be hard to build a successful commercial business. If you believe you will have many spins of the wheel of life to go, you may not be as driven to make as much out of this life as you can. Completely "living in the now" may seem to stand in the way of sound long-term business planning. With this, I am kind of sitting on the fence. As much as I am willing to believe in continuous consciousness in one form or another after this life, I am too much a rationalist to be 100 percent convinced. I believe in making the best out of this life in the meantime. Live boldly and courageously. Enjoy life. Create value. Make someone happy. Share what you have. A day not lived to the fullest is a day that is wasted. We are all certain to die, but around me I see so many who I am not certain are even alive.

Upon our death, the unified field of all energy will recycle our molecules, at a more rapid speed than it does while we are alive. Some of our molecules will end up in other people around us; other molecules will end up in the earth and in what lies or grows in it. Ashes to ashes, dust to dust. And that way we will make space for those who come after us, to enjoy and have their best go at the opportunities life offers. In the process, your spirit seemingly disappears, and cannot (yet) be scientifically traced.

However, we certainly and visibly live on in what we leave behind. The memories of the people who remember us can be measured as energy waves. Our children have our physical and mental traits and some of our characteristics and habits. Our works, savings, and sayings may survive us. And yes, the businesses we create as good entrepreneurs should survive us as well, provided they were indeed good businesses.

Your spirit lives on in your children as well as in the company you leave behind. The mission, vision, and values of a company do not change just because you are no longer there. They are carried forward and morphed into something new by those who come after you. This can give great satisfaction, as leaving a legacy is important for many people and often is an important driver for narcissistic people, who very often become entrepreneurs.

I wrote this book in part to capture the spirit and the values of the company I helped to build so it can be understood and improved upon by others after I am gone. I want my children to be proud of what I leave behind, just as I am proud of what my dad left behind. Thank goodness my forefathers were not pirates, colonialists, criminals, or porn stars. I would undoubtedly feel a lot less proud of them.

There is also great responsibility attached to a company surviving the initial dreams, efforts, and values of its founders. The earth is struggling with mountains of toxic waste created by companies that do not care about the future. Millions of people in the past few years have lost their homes as greedy salespeople, incentivized and motivated by commissions, sold them on mortgages they could not afford. Countless people in the majority of the countries around the world are toiling in misery as the social, economic, and political systems of these countries allow for near- or below-survival level wages, and for nepotism, corruption, and the accumulation of wealth and power by few at the expense of many.

As an entrepreneur you may not be able to solve all of the world's problems, even though people such as Bill Gates, in his attempt to eradicate polio, and many others make impressive contributions. But you can certainly try and be an example in your direct environment. If all entrepreneurs do the same, the effect on the world will be pervasive.

All companies need to take some responsibility and do what they can. Pay honest wages to all employees (neither too little to those at the bottom of the pyramid, nor too much to those at the top), treat all stakeholders as equal fellow human beings, and do not work just for the one-sided benefit of the shareholders or the employees. Appreciate your resources and take care of the earth, air, and water. Do not produce mindless and useless products or products that contribute to greed, corruption, bad habits, misery, poverty, disease, and discrimination. Sell healthy drinks instead of bottled sugar water and wholesome food instead of junk. Participate in tax planning compliant with the laws of all countries involved instead of tax evasion. Give sound financial advice instead of complicated derivatives with high front-load fees, or build houses made of natural and earth-friendly materials instead of plastics and asbestos.

We are what we leave behind. Our intentions, good or bad, and our spirits will live on. Our forefathers did not leave us the earth and all of its resources for us to squander. We have borrowed it from the generations who come after us. It is important that we treat it responsibly and add value to it. I am trying to do my bit; I expect you will do yours.

I intended to end this last chapter with Bob Marley's "One World" (as it was in the beginning, so it will be in the end), but ultimately decided to share with you the well-known 1932 poem by Mary Frye. She wrote this when she could not go to pay her respect to a good friend who had died far away.

"Do not stand at my grave and weep,
I am not there; I do not sleep.
I am a thousand winds that blow,
I am the diamond glints on snow,
I am the sun on ripened grain,
I am the gentle autumn rain.
When you awaken in the morning's hush
I am the swift uplifting rush,
of quiet birds in circling flight.
I am the soft star-shine at night.
Do not stand at my grave and cry,
I am not there; I did not die."

—Mary Frye

"Don't let it be forgot, that once there was a spot, for one brief shining moment, that was known as Camelot." I hum this tune as I read back over the thoughts I wrote down in this book; I realize that at times my fantasies got the better of me. There have been times when I did not act consistently with my own beliefs and values. At times I am afraid to speak up or afraid that I'll upset someone. I do not always take full responsibility and accept the moral choices I make. I sometimes get angry although I know it never solves anything and in Asia it makes you lose face. Enlightenment does not seem to lie around the corner for me. I can promise myself only to do better today and tomorrow—to be the best I can be.

Nevertheless, it has been an honor and great fun to write this book. It helped me in piecing together different parts of my thoughts and ideas, in ironing out inconsistencies, and in commending to paper what little I have learned over the course of this lifetime.

If, in addition to my own redemption, I can with this scripture reach only one person who will say that some of my ideas have helped him deal with his business issues, deal with his inner "demons," or get closer to solving the puzzle of life, it will have a value beyond myself. If you enjoyed reading this book, pass it on to someone else, and point out those messages you think will be valuable to that person. We can all use guidance on our lifelong quest to the Valley of the Flowers while busy hacking our paths through the Garden of Eden.

I welcome your questions, your comments, and your constructive criticism at t.knipping@amicorp.com.

Toine Knipping is a born entrepreneur. From an early age he has been involved in starting up and managing businesses. In 1992 he and a colleague started their own company, called Amicorp. Since that time Amicorp has grown to be a multijurisdictional financial-services group with about forty offices in twenty-seven countries and seven hundred employees.

Toine is a focused, determined, and driven person with a big heart, a brilliant mind (that never stops working), and a great sense of humor. He is also a natural leader and a visionary. He is very demanding and will settle for nothing less than the *best* quality in everything he does. You will often hear him say "whatever it takes," which is a motto he really lives by. He truly enjoys what he does, and that is why it does not feel like work to him and also why he is so successful. For Toine it is not about the money; it is about the challenge, the journey, and the satisfaction. He once said, "Money is just numbers on a piece of paper unless you do something meaningful with it." And by meaningful he usually means something that will positively impact the lives of others.

Toine also participates in running an aloe vera plantation in Curaçao that was in trouble, and he helped to nurture it back to life, later expanding it into a much larger project in South Africa producing skin products, health drinks, and products that strengthen the autoimmune system. With fellow students from INSEAD, he is building a vineyard and producing a wine from scratch in Mendoza, Argentina.

Toine has always enjoyed travel and working with and trying to understand different cultures. He is a philanthropist and supports several nonprofit organizations and projects.

Toine lives in Singapore and South Africa with his wife, Paula, and has two children.

References

Albion, M. 2006. *True to Yourself: Leading a Values-Based Business.* San Francisco: Berrett-Koehler.

Aldrich, S. P. 1996. *Men Read Newspapers, Not Minds, and Other Things I Wish I'd Known When I First Married.* Colorado Springs, CO: Tyndale House.

Aubrey, B. 2011. *Managing Your Aspirations: Developing Personal Enterprise in the Global Workplace.* Singapore: McGraw Hill.

Axelrod, A. 2010. *Gandhi, CEO: 14 Principles to Guide & Inspire Modern Leaders.* New York: Sterling.

Baer, J., and Maslund, A. 2011. *The Now Revolution: 7 Shifts to Make Your Business Faster, Smarter and More Social.* Hoboken, NJ: John Wiley & Sons.

Baggini, J. 2004. *What's It All About? Philosophy & the Meaning of Life.* London: Oxford University Press.

Baghai, M., and Quigley, J. 2011. *As One: Individual Action Collective Power.* London: Penguin Books.

Baldock, J. 2009. *The Tibetan Book of the Dead.* London: Acturus.

Ball, P. 2006. *The Power of Creative Dreaming: Unlock the Strength of Your Subconscious.* London: Arcturus.

Beahm, G. 2011. *I, Steve.* Chicago: B2 Books.

Bergeth, R. L. 1994. *12 Secrets to Cashing Out: How to Sell Your Company for the Most Profit.* Englewood Cliffs, NJ: Prentice Hall.

Blanchard, K., and Ridge, G. 2009. *Helping People Win at Work.* Upper Saddle River, NJ: FT Press.

Bloomfield, S. 2005. *Venture Capital Funding: A Practical Guide to Raising Finance.* London: Kogan Page.

Branson, R. 2006. *Screw It, Let's Do It.* London: Virgin Books.

Buffett, P. 2010. *Life Is What You Make It: Find Your Own Path to Fullfillment.* New York: Three Rivers Press.

Burg, B., and Mann, J. D. 2007. *The Go-Giver: A Little Story about a Powerful Business Idea.* New York: Penguin Group.

Burton, R. 2006. *The Kama Sutra of Vatsyayana.* New York: Dover Publications.

Carter, C. 2010. *Science and the Near-Death Experience: How Consciousness Survices Death.* Rochester, VT: Inner Traditions.

Charan, R., Drotter, S., and Noel, J. 2001. *The Leadership Pipeline: How to Build the Leadership Powered Company.* San Francisco: Jossey-Bass.

Cholle, F. P. 2012. *The Intuitive Compass: Why the Best Decisions Balance Reason and Instinct.* San Francisco: Jossey-Bass.

Chopra, D. 2003. *Synchrodestiny: Harnessing the Infinite Power of Coincidence to Create Miracles.* Reading, UK: Harmony Books.

Chopra, D. 2009. *Why is God Laughing? The Path to Joy and Spiritual Optimism.* London: Rider.

Chopra, D. 2011. *The 7 Spiritual Laws of Superheroes.* Chatham, UK: Random House.

Coelho, P. 1988. *The Alchemist.* London: Harper Collins.

Coelho, P. 1994. *By the River Piedra I Sat Down and Wept: A Novel of Forgiveness.* San Francisco: HarperCollins.

Coelho, P. 1999. *Veronika Decides to Die.* London: HarperCollins.

Coelho, P. 2003. *Warrior of the Light: Short Notes on Accepting Failure, Embracing Life, and Rising to Your Destiny.* London: HarperCollins.

Coleman, D. 1995. *Emotional Intelligence: Why It Can Matter More Than IQ.* New York: Random House.

Collins, J. 2001. *Good to Great: Why Some Companies Make the Leap ... and Others Don't.* New York: HarperCollins.

Collins, J. 2001. *Good to Great: Why Some Companies Make the Leap ... and Others Don't.* London: Random House Business Books.

Collins, J. 2009. *How the Mighty Fall, and Why Some Companies Never Give In.* New York: HarperCollins.

Collins, J. C., and Porras, J. I. 1994. *Built to Last: Successful Habits of Visionary Companies.* New York: HarperCollins.

Colvin, G. 2008. *Talent Is Overrated.* London: Nicholas Brealey.

Cooper, D. 2000. *A Little Light on the Spiritual Laws.* Findhorn, UK: Findhorn Press.

Covey, S. R. 1989. *The 7 Habits of Highly Effective People: Poweful Lessons in Personal Change.* New York: Simon & Schuster.

Covey, S. R. 1989. *The 7 Habits of Highly Effective People: Powerful Lessons in Personal Change.* New York: Free Press.

Covey, S. R. 1990. *Principle Centered Leadership.* New York: Fireside.

Covey, S. R. 2006. *The Speed of Trust: the One Thing that Changes Everything.* New York: Simon and Schuster.

Crosbie, A. 2004. *Don't Leave It to the Children: Starting Building and Sustaining a Family Business.* Mumbai, India: Corpus Collossum Learning.

Daniels, A. C. 2000. *Bringing Out the Best in People: How to Apply the Astonishing Power of Positive Reinforcement.* New York: McGraw Hill.

Das, G. 2009. *The Difficulty of Being Good: On the Subtle Art of Dharma.* New Delhi: Penguin.

Das, R. 2010. *Be Love Now: The Path of the Heart.* New York: HarperCollins.

Dauphinais, W. G. 1998. *Straight from the CEO.* New York: Fireside.

Debroy, B. 2011. *The Mahabharata.* New Delhi: Penguin Books.

Draho, J. 2004. *The IPO Decision: Why and How Companies Go Public.* Cheltenham, UK: Edward Elgar.

Dreher, D. 2000. *The Tao of Innner Peace.* London: Penguin Books.

Dyer, W. W. 2004. *The Power of Intention: Learning to Co-Create Your World Your Way.* Carlsbad, CA: Hay House.

Dyer, W. W. 2008. *Living the Wisdom of the TAO: The Complete Tao Te Ching and Affirmations.* Carlsbad, CA: Hay House.

Dyer, W. W. 2009. *Excuses Begone: How to Change Lifelong, Self-Defeating Thinking Habits.* Carlsbad, CA: Hay House.

Fenner, P. 2007. *Radiant Mind: Awakening Unconditioned Awareness.* Boulder, CO: Sounds True.

Flaherty, J. E. 1999. *Peter Drucker: How the World's Formost Management Thinker Crafted the Essentials of Business Success.* San Francisco: Jossey Bass.

Friedman, T. L. 2007. *The World Is Flat: A Brief History of the 21st Century.* New York: Picador, USA.

Gadiesh, O., and MacArthur, H. 2008. *Lessons from Private Equity Any Company Can Use.* Harvard, MA: Harvard Business Press.

Gallo, C. 2010. *The Presentation Skills of Steve Jobs: How to Be Insanely Great in Front of Any Audience.* New York: McGraw Hill.

Gardner, H. 2008. *5 Minds for the Future.* Harvard, MA: Harvard Business Press.

Gerber, M. E. 2010. *The Most Succesful Small Business in the World: the Ten Principles.* Hoboken, NJ: John Wiley & Sons.

Gerber, M. E. 2010. *The Most Succesful Small Business in the World.* Hoboken, NJ: John Wiley & Sons.

Gladwell, M. 2000. *The Tipping Point: How Little Things Can Make a Big Difference.* Boston: Little Brown.

Gladwell, M. 2005. *Blink: The Power of Thinking Without Thinking.* New York: Back Bay Books.

Gladwell, M. 2008. *Outliers: The Story of Success.* London: Penguin Books.

Glassman, S. A. 2010. *It's About More Than the Money: Investment Wisdom for Building a Better Life.* Upper Saddle River, NJ: Pearson Education.

Godin, S. 2007. *The Dip: The Extraordinary Benefits of Knowing When to Quit (and When to Stick).* London: Piatkus Books.

Godin, S. 2008. *Tribes: We Need **You** to Lead Us.* New York: Penguin.

Godin, S. 2010. *Linchpin: Are You Indispensable?* London: Penguin.

Hagstrom, R. G. 1994. *The Warren Buffett Way: Investment Strategies of the World's Greatest Investor.* New York: John Wiley and Sons.

Haidt, J. 2006. *The Happiness Hypothesis: Finding Modern Truth in Ancient Wisdom.* Cambridge, MA: Perseus Books.

Hamm, S. 2007. *Bangalore Tiger: How Indian Tech Upstart Wipro Is Rewriting the Rules of Global Competition.* New Delhi: Tata McGraw.

Harvard Business Review. 2003. Harvard Business Review on Corporate Responsibility.

Heppell, M. 2004. *How to Be Brilliant.* Harlow, UK: Pearson Education.

Hiam, A. 2003. *Motivational Management: Inspiring Your People for Maximum Performance.* New York: American Management Association.

Hsieh, T. 2010. *Delivering Happiness: A Path to Profits, Passion and Purpose.* New York: Business Plus.

Jansen Kraemer Jr, H. M. 2011. *From Values to Action: The Four Principles of Value-Based Leadership.* San Francisco: Jossey-Bass.

Jung, C. G. 1978. *Psychology and the East.* London: Princeton University Press.

Kabat-Zinn, J. 1994. *Wherever You Go, There You Are: Mindfullness Meditation for Everyday Life.* Chatham, UK: Piatkus Books.

Kakar, S. 2009. *Mad and Divine: Spirit and Psyche in the Modern World.* New Delhi: Penguin Press.

Kakar, S. 2010. *The Crimson Throne.* New Delhi: Penguin Books.

Kakar, S. 2011. *The Essential Sudhir Kakar.* New Delhi: Oxford University Press.

Kaye, B., & Jordan-Evans, S. 1999. *Love 'em or Lose 'em.* San Fransisco: Berrett-Koehler.

Kets de Vries, M. F. 2007. *Coach and Couch: The Psychology of Making Better Leaders.* Houndsmills, UK: Palgrave MacMillan.

Kets de Vries, M. F. 2009. *Sex, Money, Happiness, and Death: The Quest for Authenticity.* London: Palgrave Macmillan.

Kets de Vries, M. F. 2011. *Reflections on Groups and Organizations.* Chichester, UK: John Wiley & Sons.

Kets de Vries, M. F., Carlock, R.S., Florent-Treacy, E. 2007. *Family Business on the Couch: A Psychological Perspective.* Chichester, UK: John Wiley & Sons.

Kiechel, W. I. 2010. *The Lords of Strategy: The Secret Intellectual History of the New Corporate World.* Boston: Harvard Business Press.

Kihn, M. 2005. *House of Lies: How Management Consultants Steal Your Watch and Then Tell You the Time.* New York: Warner Business Books.

Kim, K. R. 2011. *Essence of Good Management.* New Delhi: Times Group Books.

Kim, W. C., & Mauborgne, R. 2005. *Blue Ocean Strategy: How to Create Uncontested Market Space and Make the Competition Irrelevant.* Boston, MA: Harvard Business School Publishing.

Kinslow, F. J. 2010. *The Secret of Quantum Living.* New York City: Lucid Sea.

Kiyosaki, R., and Kiyosaki, E. 2008. *Rich Brother, Rich Sister.* Johannesburg, South Africa: Jonathan Ball.

Kleeburg, R. P. 2005. *Initial Public Offering.* Mason, OH: Thomson Higher Education.

Krogerus, M., and Tschaeppeler, R. 2011. *The Decision Book: Fifty Models for Strategic Thinking.* London: Profile Books.

Kundtz, D. 2009. *Awakened Mind: One-Minute Wake Up Calls to a Bold and Mindful Life.* San Francisco: Conari Press.

Lama, D. 2009. *The Art of Happiness: A Handbook for Living.* New York: Riverhead Books.

Lama, T. D. 2009. *Becoming Enlightened.* London: Random House.

Lipton, B. H. 2005. *The Biology of Belief: Unleashing the Power of Consciousness, Matter & Miracles.* USA: Hay House.

Logan, D., and King, J. 2008. *Tribal Leadership: Leveraging Natural Groups to Build a Thriving Organization.* New York: Harper Business.

Long, J., and Perry, P. 2010. *Evidence of the Afterlife: The Science of Near-Death Experiences.* New York: Harper One.

Luce, E. 2007. *In Spite of the Gods: The Strange Rise of Modern India.* New York: Doubleday.

Mackay, A. 2007. *Recruiting, Retaining and Releasing People: Managing Redeployment, Return, Retirement and Redundancy.* Burlington, MA: Elsevier.

Magid, B. 2008. *Ending the Pursuit of Happiness: A Zen Guide.* Sommerville, MA: Wisdom Publications.

Mandela, N. 2010. *In gesprek met mijzelf.* Antwerp, Belgium: Uitgeverij Unieboek.

Marriott, J., and Brown, K. A. 1997. *Marriott's Way: The Spirit to Serve.* New York: HarperCollins.

Maxwell, J. C. 2003. *There Is No Such Thing as "Business Ethics."* New York: Center street.

McTaggart, L. 2007. *The Intention Experiment.* New York: Free Press.

McTaggart, L. 2008. *The Field: The Quest for the Secret Force of the Universe.* New York: HarperCollins.

McTaggart, L. 2011. *The Bond: Connecting through the Space between Us.* New York: Simon & Shuster.

Megre, V. 1996. *Anastasia.* Kahului, HI: Ringing Cedars Press.

Melaver, M. 2009. *Living above the Store: Building a Business that Creates Value, Inspires Change and Restores Land and Community.* White River Junction, VT: Chelsea Green.

Millman, D. 2000. *Living on Purpose: Straight Answers to Life's Tough Questions.* Novato, CA: New World Library.

Millman, D. 2006. *Wisdom of the Peaceful Warrior: A Companion to the Book that Changes Lives.* Tiburon, CA: New World Library.

Moritz, A. 2009. *Hear the Whispers, Live Your Dream.* USA: Enerchi Wellness Press.

Moss, P. 2010. *Chinese Proverbs: Ancient Wisdom for the 21st Century.* Hong Hong, HK: Form Asia Books.

Murphy, B. J. 2010. *The Intelligent Entrepreneur: How Three Harvard Business School Graduats Learned the 10 Rules of Successful Entrepreneurship.* New York: Henry Holt.

Nhat Hannh, T. 2007. *The Art of Power.* New York: HarperCollins.

Norbeerg-Hodge, H. 2009. *Ancient Futures: Lessons from Ladakh for a Globalizing World.* San Francisco: Sierra Club Books.

Obama, B. 1995. *Dreams from My Father.* New York: Three Rivers Press.

Ofman, D., and Verpaalen, G. 2006. *You Just Wouldn't Believe It.* Utrecht, Netherlands: Servire.

Osho. 2001. *Zen: The Path of Paradox.* New York: St. Martin's Griffin.

Owen, J. 2005. *How to Lead.* Harlow, UK: Pearson Education.

Peirce, P. 1997. *The Intuitive Way.* New York: Simon & Shuster.

Peirce, P. 2009. *Frequency: The Power of Personal Vibration.* New York: Simon & Schuster.

Pinault, L. 2001. *Consulting Demons: Inside the Unscrupulous World of Global Corporate Consulting.* New York: Harper Business.

Pirsig, R. M. 1974. *Zen and the Art of Motorcycle Maintenance: An Inquiry into Values.* New York: Wolliam Morrow.

Ponlop, D. 2011. *Rebel Buddha.* Boston: Shambhala.

Rhyne, E. 2009. *Microfinace for Bankers and Investors: Understanding the Opportunities and Challenges of the Market at the Bottom of the Pyramid.* New York: McGraw Hill.

Rothschild, B. 2000. *The Body Remembers: The Psychophysiology of Trauma and Trauma Treatment.* Los Angeles: W. W. Norton.

Ruiz, D. M. 1997. *The Four Agreements: A Toltec Wisdom Book.* San Rafael, CA: Amber-Allen.

Ruiz, D. M. 2004. *The Voice of Knowledge: A Practical Guide to Inner Peace.* San Rafael, CA: Amber-Allen.

Sawyer, R. D. 1994. *Sun Tzu's, Art of War.* Boulder, CO: Westview Press.

Schroeder, G. L. 2009. *God According to God: A Scientist Discovers We've Been Wrong about God All Along.* New York: HarperCollins.

Sharma, R. 2011. *The Secret Letters of the Monk who Sold His Ferrari.* London: Harper Collins.

Shenson, H. L. 1990. *How to Select and Manage Consultants: A Guide to Getting What You Pay For.* San Diego: University Associates.

Singh, K. 2011. *On Women, Sex, Love and Lust.* New Delhi: Hay House India.

Slywotzky, A. 2002. *The Art of Profitability.* New York: Warner Books.

Smith, H. W. 2000. *What Matters Most: The Power of Living Your Values.* New York: Simon & Schuster.

Stengel, R. 2010. *Mandela's Way: Lessons on Life.* London: Random House.

Sutton, R. I. 2007. *The No Asshole Rule: Building a Civilized Workplace and Surviving One that Isn't.* New York: Business Plus.

Tart, C. 2009. *The End of Materialism: How Evidence of the Paranormal Is Bringing Science and Spirit Together.* Oakland, CA: New Harbinger.

Thakkar, H. 1996. *Theory of Karma.* Ahmedabad, India: Hemant M. Shah.

Tiggelaar, B. 2007. *Can Do: How to Achieve Real Personal Change and Growth.* London: Marshall Cavendish.

Tolle, E. 1999. *The Power of Now: A Guide to Spiritual Enlightenment.* London: Hodder & Stoughton.

Tolle, E. 2005. *A New Earth: Create a Better Life.* London: Penguin.

Tolle, E. 2006. *A New Earth: Awakening to Your Life's Purpose.* New York: Penguin.

Tutu, D. 2011. *God Is not a Christian.* Chatham, UK: Random House.

Vitale, J. 2007. *Zero Limits.* Hoboken, NJ: John Wiley & Sons.

Waldo Trine, R. 1918. *The Higher Powers of Mind and Spirit.* London: G. Bell & Sons.

Welch, J., and Welch, S. 2005. *Winning.* New York: HarperCollins.

Whitmont, E. C. 1982. *Return of the Goddess.* New York: Continuum.

Wilber, K. 1991. *Grace and Grit: Spirituality and Healing in the Life and Death of Treya Killam Wilber.* Boston: Shambhala.

Wileman, A. 2008. *Driving Down Cost: How to Manage and Cut Costs Intelligently.* London: Nicholas Brealey.

Yogi, M. M. 1977. *De wetenschap van het Zijn en de Kunst van het Leven.* Den Haag, Netherlands: Pantha Rhei.

Yunus, M. 2010. *Building Social Business: The New Kind of Capitalism that Serves Humanity's Most Pressing Needs.* Philadelphia: PublicAffairs.